DE OF THE STREET

# CODE OF THE STREET

## DECENCY, VIOLENCE, AND THE MORAL LIFE OF THE INNER CITY

Elijah Anderson

W. W. NORTON & COMPANY    NEW YORK / LONDON

Copyright © 1999 by Elijah Anderson

For information about permission to reproduce selections from this book,
write to Permissions, W. W. Norton & Company, Inc.,
500 Fifth Avenue, New York, NY 10110.

The text of this book is composed in Janson
with the display set in Deviant Universe
Composition by Binghamton Valley Composition
Manufacturing by The Maple-Vail Book Manufacturing Group
Book design by JAM Design

Library of Congress Cataloging-in-Publication Data

Anderson, Elijah.
Code of the street : decency, violence, and the moral life of the
inner city / Elijah Anderson.
p.   cm.
Includes bibliographical references and index.
**ISBN 0-393-04023-2**
1. Afro-Americans—Pennsylvania—Philadelphia—Social conditions.
2. Afro-Americans—Pennsylvania—Philadelphia—Social life and
customs.   3. Inner cities—Pennsylvania—Philadelphia.
4. Philadelphia (Pa.)—Social conditions.   5. Philadelphia (Pa.)—
Social life and customs.   I. Title.
F158.9.N4A52   1999
303.3'3'0896073074811—dc21                                    98-36800
                                                                  CIP

W. W. Norton & Company, Inc., 500 Fifth Avenue, New York, N.Y. 10110
http://www.wwnorton.com

W.W. Norton & Company Ltd., 10 Coptic Street, London WC1A 1PU

1 2 3 4 5 6 7 8 9 0

*This book is dedicated to the cherished memory of:*

| | |
|---|---|
| Samuel | Charlotte |
| Roosevelt | James T. |
| Ed Lee | Arlene |
| Perry | Jesse L. |
| Robert | Augusta |
| Leonard | Shang |
| L. C., Sr. | Jerlene |
| Leighton, Sr. | J.B. |
| James T. | Philip |
| David | Bernice |
| Freddie | Annette |

*And with profound and ardent hope for the lives and dreams of:*

| | |
|---|---|
| Sydney | Ruby |
| Muffin | Robert Earl, Jr. |
| Michael Torrance | Joe, Jr. |
| Benjamin | Nuabe |
| Timothy | Stacy |
| Michael | Camille |
| Taura | Caitlin |
| Luke | Syreeta |
| Shemika | Fiona |
| Jada | Jeremy |
| Delisa | Tamika |
| Jamila | Terry |
| Carla | Wilson (Junebug), Jr. |
| Billy | Jesse, Jr. |
| Terriam | Hashid |
| Gabriele | James T., Jr. |
| Kendrick | Roderick |
| Mariah | Melanie |
| Malik | Anjanette |
| Anita | Joel |
| Christopher | Robert T. |

# Contents

# Preface

**T**HE present work grows out of the ethnographic work I did for my previous book, *Streetwise: Race, Class, and Change in an Urban Community* (1990). There I took up the issue of how two urban communities—one black and impoverished, the other racially mixed and middle to upper middle class—coexisted in the same general area and negotiated the public spaces. Here I take up more directly the theme of interpersonal violence, particularly between and among inner-city youths. While youth violence has become a problem of national scope, involving young people of various classes and races, in this book I am concerned with why it is that so many inner-city young people are inclined to commit aggression and violence toward one another. I hope that lessons derived from this work may offer insights into the problem of youth violence more generally. The question of violence has led me to focus on the nature of public life in the inner-city ghetto, specifically its public social organization. And to address this question, I conducted field research over the past four years not only in inner-city ghetto areas but also in some of the well-to-do areas of Philadelphia.

In some of the most economically depressed and drug- and crime-ridden pockets of the city, the rules of civil law have been severely weakened, and in their stead a "code of the street" often holds sway. At the heart of this code is a set of prescriptions and proscriptions, or informal rules, of behavior organized around a desperate search for respect that governs public social relations, especially violence, among so many residents, particularly young men and women. Possession of respect—and the credible threat of vengeance—is highly valued for shielding the ordinary person from the interpersonal violence of the street. In this social context of persistent poverty and deprivation, alienation from broader society's institutions, notably that of criminal justice, is widespread. The code of the street emerges where the influence of the police ends and personal responsibility for one's safety is felt to begin, resulting in a kind of "people's law," based on "street justice." This code involves a quite primitive form of social exchange that holds would-be perpetrators accountable by promising an "eye for an eye," or a certain "payback" for transgressions. In service to this ethic, repeated displays of "nerve" and "heart" build or reinforce a credible reputation for vengeance that works to deter aggression and disrespect, which are sources of great anxiety on the inner-city street.

In delineating these intricate issues, the book details not only a sociology of interpersonal public behavior with implications for understanding violence and teen pregnancy but also the changing roles of the inner-city grandmother and the "decent daddy," the interplay of decent and street families of the neighborhood, and the tragedy of the drug culture. The story of John Turner brings many of these themes together. And the "conversion of a role model" concludes the book by further illustrating the intricacies of the code and its impact on everyday life.

In approaching the goal of painting an ethnographic picture of these phenomena,[1] I engaged in participant-observation, including direct observation, and conducted in-depth interviews. Impressionistic materials were drawn from various social settings around the city, from some of the wealthiest to some of the most economically depressed, including carryouts, "stop and go" establishments, Laundromats, taverns, playgrounds, public schools, the Center City indoor mall known as the Gallery, jails, and public street corners. In these settings I encountered a wide variety of people—adolescent boys and young women (some incarcerated, some not), older men, teenage mothers, grandmothers, and male and female schoolteachers, black and white, drug dealers, and common criminals. To protect the privacy and confidentiality of my subjects, names and certain details have been disguised.

My primary aim in this work is to render ethnographically the social and cultural dynamics of the interpersonal violence that is currently undermining the quality of life of too many urban neighborhoods. In this effort I address such questions as the following: How do the people of the setting perceive their situation? What assumptions do they bring to their decision making? What behavioral patterns result from these actions? What are the social implications and consequences of these behaviors? This book therefore offers an ethnographic representation of the code of the street, and its relationship to violence in a trying socioeconomic context in which family-sustaining jobs have become ever more scarce, public assistance has increasingly disappeared, racial discrimination is a fact of daily life, wider institutions have less legitimacy, legal codes are often ignored or not trusted, and frustration has been powerfully building for many residents.

A further aim of the ethnographer's work is that it be as objective as possible. This is not easy or simple, since it requires researchers to try to set aside their own values and assumptions about what is and is not morally acceptable—in other words, to jettison the prism through which they typically view a given situation. By definition one's own assumptions are so basic to one's perceptions that seeing their influence may be difficult, if not impossible. Ethnographic researchers, however, have been trained to look for and to recognize underlying assumptions, their own and those of their subjects, and to try to override the former and uncover the latter.[2] In the text that follows, I have done my best to do so.

Earlier versions of some parts of this book have been published in the *Atlantic Monthly*, the *Public Interest*, and the *Annals of the American Academy of Political and Social Science*; in *W. E. B. DuBois, Race, and the City*, edited by Michael B. Katz and Thomas J. Sugrue; in *America's Working Poor*, edited by Thomas R. Swartz and Kathleen M. Weigert; in *The Urban Underclass*, edited by Christopher Jencks and Paul Peterson; and in *Violence and Childhood in the Inner City*, edited by Joan McCord. I would like to express my gratitude to the Harry Frank Guggenheim Foundation for financial support for initial work on violence and the inner-city street code.

Last but not least, I would like to take this opportunity to thank the following colleagues and friends who over the years have helped in all sorts of ways—by discussing portions of this work with me, rendering research assistance, providing editorial advice, or simply giving moral support: William Pryor, Alison Anderson, Harold Bershady, James Short, Victor Lidz, Acel Moore, Robert Washington, Tukufu Zuberi, the late Marvin Wolfgang, Reverend William Gipson, Renee Fox, William J. Wilson, William Labov, Herman Wrice, Nancy Bauer, Mori Insinger, Tom Gavin, Eric Cheyfitz, Cara Crosby, Karen Kauffman, Ronald Mincy, Howard S. Becker, Jack Katz, Gerald Jaynes, Joel Wallman, Robert Alsbrooks, Joan McCord, James Kurth, C. B. Kimmins, Richard Greene, Reverend Fletcher Bryant, Christine Szczepanowski, Hilary Hinzmann, Gerald D. Suttles, and Andrew Roney. I am very appreciative of the careful attention given this work by the editorial staff at W. W. Norton, particularly Starling Lawrence, Patricia Chui, Nancy Palmquist, and Otto Sonntag. As always, I am indebted to Nancy Anderson for her steadfast support through the years, without which this work would have resulted in a lesser product. Thanks also to my wonderful teenage children, Caitlin and Luke, with whom I have discussed many of these issues. And I would like to express my gratitude to my informants who shared with me intimate details of their lives and who, for reasons of confidentiality, must remain anonymous.

# CODE OF THE STREET

# Down Germantown Avenue

**G**ERMANTOWN Avenue is a major Philadelphia artery that dates back to colonial days. Eight and a half miles long and running mostly southeast, it links the northwest suburbs with the heart of inner-city Philadelphia. It traverses a varied social terrain as well. Germantown Avenue provides an excellent cross section of the social ecology of a major American city. Along this artery live the well-to-do, the middle classes, the working poor, and the very poor—the diverse segments of urban society. The story of Germantown Avenue can therefore serve in many respects as a metaphor for the whole city. This book, which is about the "code of the street," begins with an introduction to the world of the streets by way of a tour down Germantown Avenue.

One of the most salient features of urban life in the minds of many people today is the relative prevalence of violence. Our tour down Germantown Avenue will focus both on the role of violence in the social organization of the communities through which the avenue passes and on how violence is revealed in the interactions of people up and down the street. The avenue, we will see, is a natural continuum characterized largely by a code of civility at one end and a code of conduct regulated by the threat of violence—the code of the street—at the other.[1] But the people living along this continuum make their own claims on civility and the street as well.

We begin at the top of the hill that gives Chestnut Hill its name. Chestnut Hill is the first neighborhood within the city of Philadelphia as you come into town from the northwest. Often called the "suburb in the city," it is a predominantly residential community consisting mostly of affluent and educated white people, but it is increasingly becoming racially and ethnically mixed. The houses are mostly large, single buildings, surrounded by lawns and trees. The business and shopping district along Germantown Avenue draws shoppers from all over the city. At the very top of the hill is the large Borders bookstore. Across the street is the regional-rail train station, with the local library in close proximity. Moving southeast down the avenue, you pass a variety of mostly small, upscale businesses: gourmet food shops, a camera shop, an optician's, a sporting goods store, a bank, jewelry stores, and clothing boutiques. Many of the buildings are old or built to look old and are made of fieldstone with slanted slate roofs, giving the area a quaint appearance. You see many different kinds of people—old and young, black and white, affluent, middle class, and working class. Women push babies in carriages. Couples stroll hand in hand. Everyone is polite and seems relaxed. When people pass one another on the sidewalk, they may make eye contact. People stand about nonchalantly on the sidewalk, sometimes with their backs to the street. You don't get the feeling that there is any hostility or that people are on guard against the possibility of being compromised or insulted or robbed. A pleasant ambiance prevails—an air of civility.

At this end of Germantown Avenue, the community appears to be racially integrated in its public relationships, perhaps self-consciously so. You see integrated play groups among small children on the playgrounds. At the bank, there is relaxed interaction between a black teller and a white client. There are biracial groups of friends. At the Boston Market restaurant, blacks and whites eat together or simply sit side by side. A black man drives by in a Range Rover; two well-dressed black women pull up in a black Lexus. In their clothing and cars, the people who make up the black middle class choose styles and colors that are noticeably expensive: they are *interesting difference w/ est racial middle class.*

expressive in laying claim to middle-class status. The white middle-class people are likely to be driving older cars or wearing worn clothes.

In the upscale stores here, there is not usually apparent a great concern for security. During the day the plate-glass windows have appealing displays; some shops even have unguarded merchandise out on the sidewalk.

Once in a while, however, a violent incident does occur in Chestnut Hill. A holdup occurred at the bank in the middle of the day not long ago, ending in a shoot-out on the sidewalk. The perpetrators were black, and two black men recently robbed and shot up a tavern on the avenue. Such incidents give the residents here the simplistic yet persistent view that blacks commit crime and white people do not. That does not mean that the white people here think that the black people they ordinarily see on the streets are bound to rob them: many of these people are too sophisticated to believe that all blacks are inclined to criminality. But the fact that black people robbed the bank and that blacks commit a large number of crimes in the area does give a peculiar edge to race relations, and the racial reality of street crime affects the relations between blacks and whites. Because everybody knows that the simplistic view does exist, even middle-class blacks have to work consciously against that stereotype—although the whites do as well. Both groups know the reality that crime is likely to be perpetrated by young black males. The distinctions of wealth—and the fact that black people are generally disenfranchised and white people are not—operate in the back of the minds of people here.

A black male walking into the stores, especially a jewelry store, can see this phenomenon. The sales personnel pay particular attention to people until they feel they have passed inspection, and black males are almost always given extra scrutiny. Most blacks in Chestnut Hill are middle class or even wealthy, although others come into the neighborhood as dayworkers. Yet many are disturbed by the inability of some whites to make distinctions—particularly between people who are out to commit crime and those who are not.

The knowledge that there are poor blacks farther down the avenue leads people "here" to be on guard against people from "there." Security guards tend to follow young black males around stores looking for the emblems and signs that they are from "there" and not from "here." And at night, stores do have exterior security devices, although these devices are designed to appear decorative.

These factors can, but most often do not, compromise civility between the races in Chestnut Hill; in fact, people get along. This is evident at the "Farmer's Market" just off the avenue. The market caters to the residents of the local community but at the same time draws shoppers from miles away. It is open from Thursday through Saturday. On Saturdays it is especially vibrant, and the general ambience is friendly. Here is a flower shop, there a vegetable grocer, a butcher, a coffee retailer, a Middle Eastern foods store, and an Asian woman selling fresh fish. Because the clientele is affluent, the quality of the foods and service is high. The shoppers are mainly well-to-do white women, occasionally accompanied by a disheveled husband wearing worn tennis shoes and a moth-eaten sweater. On Saturday mornings the place becomes something of social scene, buzzing with activity. Younger and older couples shop, laugh, and talk. Residents from a wide radius come here to shop, but also to bump into friends and neighbors. A set of tables and chairs—conveniently located next to the coffee bar—allows people to take a break from their shopping and to socialize with friends; here children occasionally sit and wait for their parents. Street violence is the farthest thing from anyone's mind. In this market you can observe the racial diversity of the local community. Contrary to the negative stereotype of American race and ethnic relations, people here are quite civil and respectful to one another. There is no racial tension here; comity and good will are dominant themes. And it is safe to say that almost everyone here is law-abiding. Although most of the people are white, virtually every ethnic group is represented, including Jewish, Italian, Iranian, Irish, Amish—and a few middle-class black people are always present as well. The black people who come here are always middle class and are treated well, if not subtly patronized. Generally, blacks like it here. On close inspection, however, one notes that few shops employ black people; a black face behind the counter is rare. While this reality may bother some, most black shoppers make nothing of it. It is just something mentally noted and politely accepted, serving as a background understanding that prevents some from feeling completely welcome here.

Around the corner, on the avenue again, the Chestnut Hill Grill provides an outdoor restaurant, and it is not unusual to see blacks and whites, or a certain diversity of people, eating and drinking here, at times in a common party. Such scenes strongly belie the widely held image of great tensions in race relations. At this end of the avenue, race and ethnicity are played down, and social harmony is a rather common theme.

Down the hill, beyond Boston Market, is Cresheim Valley Road, a neighborhood boundary. On the other side, we are in Mount Airy, a different social milieu. Here there are more black homeowners interspersed among white ones, and there is more black street traffic on Germantown Avenue. Mount Airy itself is a much more integrated neighborhood than Chestnut Hill, and the black people who live here are mostly middle class. A perfunctory look at this part of Germantown Avenue might give the impression that this is a predominantly black neighborhood, mainly because there is so much black street traffic. Here the shops and stores along the avenue tend to be used by blacks much more than by whites. But many businesses, including an upscale restaurant, a dance studio, and a barbecue grill, have a racially and economically mixed clientele. Generally, though, white and middle-class black adults from here tend to use the stores in Chestnut Hill, finding that they offer goods and services more consistent with their tastes. As a result, the shops in Mount Airy tend to have a greater black presence. And on the annual Mount Airy Day fair, Germantown Avenue is full of people reflecting its racially mixed character and harmony. But farther down the avenue this scene changes rather abruptly.

A sign that we are in a different social setting is that exterior bars begin to appear on the store windows and riot gates show up on the doors—at first on businesses such as the state-run liquor store. Pizza parlors, karate shops, takeout stores that sell beer, and storefront organizations such as neighborhood health care centers appear—establishments not present in Chestnut Hill. There are discount stores of various sorts, black barbershops, and other businesses that cater both to the black middle class and to employed working-class and poorer blacks. Many of the black middle-class youths use the street as a place to gather and talk with their friends, and they adopt the clothing styles of the poorer people farther down the avenue. So people who are not familiar with black people are sometimes unable to distinguish between who is law-abiding and who is not. The resulting confusion appears to be a standing problem for the police and local store owners, and it may lead to a sense of defensiveness among middle-class residents who fear being violated or robbed. But promising protection on the street, it is a confusion that many youths seem not to mind and at times work to encourage.

Continuing down the avenue, we pass the Mount Airy playground, with its basketball court, which in mild weather is always a buzzing place. Evenings and weekends it is full of young black men playing pickup games; occasionally adolescent girls serve as spectators. There is a real social mix here, with kids from middle-class, working-class, and poor black families all coming together in this spot. For young men the basic urban uniform of sneakers and baggy jeans is much in evidence—and that gives pause to other people, particularly whites (who tend to avoid the avenue's public spaces). In many ways, however, the atmosphere is easygoing. The place isn't crime ridden or necessarily feared by most blacks, but it betrays a certain edge compared with similar but less racially complex settings farther up the avenue. Here it is prudent to be wary—not everyone on the street recognizes and respects the rule of law, the law that is encoded in the criminal statutes and enforced by the police.

Yet next to the playground is a branch of the Free Library, one of the best in the city, which caters mainly to the literate people of Mount Airy, black and white. Indeed, the social and racial mix of the community is sometimes more visible in the library than on the street itself. Along this part of Germantown Avenue, Mount Airy boasts many beautiful old buildings. But the piano repair shops, sandwich stores, and other businesses located in them tend to have exterior bars and riot gates, a sign that militates against the notion of civility as the dominant theme of the place. A competing definition of affairs emerges, and that is the prevalence of crime, the perpetrators of which are most often concerned not with legality but with feasibility. Ten years ago fewer bars were on the windows and the buildings were better maintained. Today more relatively alienated black poor people are occupying the public space. There are still whites among the storekeepers and managers of various establishments, but whites often have been displaced in the outdoor public spaces by poorer blacks. Moreover, the farther down the avenue you go, the less well maintained the buildings are. Even when they are painted, for example, the painting tends to have been done haphazardly, without great regard for architectural detail.

In this section a prominent billboard warns that those who commit insurance fraud go to jail. (No such signs appear in Chestnut Hill.) There is graffiti—or evidence that it has recently been removed. More dilapidated buildings appear, looking as though they receive no maintenance. Yet among them are historic buildings, some of which are cared for in ways that suggest that people appreciate their historic status. One of them is the house where the Battle of Germantown was fought during the Revolutionary War. Another was a stop on the underground railroad.

As Mount Airy gives way to Germantown, check-cashing agencies and beeper stores as well as more small takeout stores appear, selling beer, cheesesteaks, and other snack food. More of the windows are boarded up, and riot gates and exterior bars become the norm, evoking in the user of the street a certain wariness.

On the avenue Germantown gives the appearance of a segregated, black, working-class neighborhood. But this is deceptive. Many whites, including middle-class whites along with middle-class blacks, do live here, but they tend to avoid the business district. Or the stores simply do not attract them. On Germantown Avenue, discount stores of all sorts appear—supermarkets, furniture stores, and clothing stores—and of the people you pass now, many more are part of the "street element." Here people watch their backs and are more careful how they present themselves. It isn't that they are worried every moment that somebody might violate them, but people are more aware of others who are sharing the space with them, some of whom may be looking for an easy target to rob or just intimidate.

Germantown High School, once a model of racially integrated, quality education, is now almost all black and a shadow of its former academic self. Many of the students are now impoverished and associated with the street element, and even most of those who aren't have a need to show themselves as being capable of dealing with the street. In fact, the hallways of the school are in many ways an extension of the street. Across the street from the high school is a store selling beer, and young people often hang out there.

Continuing down the avenue, we pass blocks of small businesses: taverns, Chinese takeout places, barbershops and hair salons, Laundromats, storefront churches, pawnshops. Groups of young people loiter on street corners. We also begin to see empty lots and boarded-up buildings, some of them obviously quite grand at one time. A charred McDonald's sign rises above a weed-covered lot. A police car is parked at the corner, its occupants keeping a watchful eye on the street activity. After a time, the officers begin to drive slowly down the street.

Just before Chelten Avenue, a major artery that intersects Germantown Avenue, comes Vernon Park. The park has an informal caretaker who is trying to keep it maintained despite the meager municipal resources and the carelessness and even vandalism of some of the people who like to gather there. A mural has been painted on the side of an adjacent building. Flowers have been planted. On warm days, couples "making time" sit about on the benches, on the steps of statues, and on the hoods of cars parked along the park's edge. But even during the day, in public, men drink alcoholic beverages out of paper sacks, and at night the park becomes a dangerous place where drug dealing and other shadowy businesses are conducted. This is a "staging area," so-called because the activities that occur here set the stage for other activities, which may be played out either on the spot in front of the people who have congregated here or else in less conspicuous locations. A verbal altercation in Vernon Park may be settled with a fight, with or without gunplay, down a side street. People "profile" here, "representing" the image of themselves by which they would like to be known: who they are and how they stand in relation to whom.

The streets around the park buzz with activity, legal and illegal.

A certain flagrant disregard for the law is visible.[2] A teenage boy walks by with an open bottle of beer in his hand, taking a swig whenever he pleases.

A young man in his twenties crosses the street after taking care of some business with another young man, gets into his new black BMW automobile, and sidles up next to his girlfriend, who has been waiting there for him. He is dressed in a crisp white T-shirt with "Hilfiger" emblazoned across the back of it, black satin shorts with bright red stripes on the sides, and expensive white sneakers. He makes a striking figure as he slides into his vehicle, and others take note. He moves with aplomb, well aware that he is where he wants to be and, for that moment at least, where some others want to be as well. And his presentation of self announces that he can take care of himself should someone choose to tangle with him.

Here in Germantown public, an area diverse in class and race, there is generally less respect for the codes of civil behavior that underlie life in Chestnut Hill. The people of Germantown are overwhelmingly committed to civil behavior, behavior based on trust and the rule of law, yet there is a sense that violence is just below the surface in some pockets of the community. That fact necessitates a careful way of moving, of acting, of getting up and down the streets. While it may not always be necessary to throw down the gauntlet, so to speak, and be ready to punch someone out, it is important, as people here say, to "know what time it is"—not by the clock but by reading people, places, and situations. And it is important to grasp the public signals of what is yet to come, but then to show one's capability of dealing with these situations. It is this form of regulation of social interaction in public that, as we will see in this volume, makes up the code of the street. People understand that you are not always tested, but you have to be ready for the test when it comes. Mr. Don Moses, an old head of the black community, described the code this way: "Keep your eyes and ears open at all times. Walk two steps forward and look back. Watch your back. Prepare yourself verbally and physically. Even if you have a cane, carry something. The older people do carry something, guns in sheaths. They can't physically fight no more, so they carry a gun."

People here feel they must watch their backs, because anything can happen here, and if the police are called, they may not arrive in time. Robberies and gunfire have been known to occur in broad daylight. People experience danger here, but they also relax and go about their business. In general, there is an edge to public life at Chelten and Germantown Avenues that you don't find in Chestnut Hill.

Two blocks away is a middle-class residential area. Yet Chelten Avenue itself is lined with discount chain stores and fast-food restaurants, which, in contrast to those in Chestnut Hill or Mount Airy, dominate some neighborhood blocks. Also located here are a police station, a state employment agency, and a welfare office; like the chain stores, they represent connections with the wider society of government and large-scale businesses. On Tuesday mornings food-stamp lines snake around Greene Street at Chelten. There are also individual "little people" here, running small, sometimes fly-by-night businesses. These enterprises coexist, serving people who barely have enough to survive, and this lack of resources encourages a dog-eat-dog mentality along Chelten Avenue. Yet there is a great deal of other activity, too. Especially on warm summer days and nights, a carnival atmosphere sometimes reigns. And the fact that this area is diverse both racially and socially works to offset somewhat the feeling of social isolation among the poor black residents of Germantown.

Occasionally, residents of Chestnut Hill drive this far down Germantown Avenue, and seeing what this neighborhood looks like certainly has an impact on their consciousness. Not venturing to look below the surface, they take in the sea of black faces, the noise, the seeming disorder, and the poverty. When reading about urban violence, they associate it with places like this. In fact, this neighborhood is not as violent as they assume. To be sure, hustlers, prostitutes, and drug dealers are in evidence, but they coexist with—and are indeed outnumbered by—working people in legitimate jobs who are trying to avoid trouble.

As you move beyond Chelten Avenue, you pass through quieter stretches that reflect the residential nature of the surrounding streets; such residential streets alternate with concentrated business strips. Many of the businesses are skin, hair, and nail salons. A common aspiration of the poorer girls in these neighborhoods is to go to beauty school and become cosmetologists.

You pass by the old town square of Germantown, which is surrounded by old, historically certified houses. Such houses appear sporadically for a long way down the avenue. Some are badly in need of repair. Just beyond the square is Germantown Friends School, a private school founded 150 years ago on what was then the outskirts of town but which is now surrounded by the city.

Farther down, more and more boarded-up buildings appear, along with even more empty lots. In fact, certain areas give the impression of no-man's-lands, with empty dirt or overgrown lots, a few isolated buildings here and there, few cars on the street, and almost no people on the sidewalks. You pass billboards advertising "forties" (forty-ounce beer), cigarettes, and other kinds of liquor. Churches are a prominent feature of the cityscape as a whole. Along this part of Germantown Avenue, some of the churches are very large and well known, with a rich history and architecturally resembling those in Chestnut Hill and Mount Airy, but others are store-front churches that tend to come and go with the founding pastor.

People move up and down the street at all times of the day. In the middle of the morning, groups of young men can be seen standing on corners, eyeing the street traffic. Morning is generally the safest time of day. As evening approaches, the possibility of violence increases, and after nightfall the code of the street holds sway all along the lower section of the avenue. Under that rule the toughest, the biggest, and the boldest individual prevails. Down farther, a school is in recess. Kids are crowding into a makeshift eatery, where someone is barbecuing hot dogs and ribs and selling them. At play small children hone their physical skills, standing down adversaries, punching each other lightly, playfully sizing each other up. This sort of ritual play-fighting, playing at the code, is commonplace.

As we continue down the street, collision-repair shops appear— former gas stations surrounded by many abandoned cars in various states of disrepair and degradation—and then music stores and a nightclub. Now Germantown Avenue reaches Broad Street, Philadelphia's major north–south artery, nearly at the intersection of Broad and Erie Avenue, which runs east–west. The triangle formed by these streets is one of the centers of the North Philadelphia ghetto. In contrast to residents farther up the avenue, people here are often extremely poor. Unlike Germantown proper, where a fair number of working-class, along with many middle-class people reside, here there is concentrated ghetto poverty. This area of the city is in the depths of the inner city—the so-called hyperghetto— and people here are very much socially isolated from mainstream America.[3]

Just beyond Broad Street is another business strip with the same sorts of establishments we saw farther up the avenue—stores selling clothing, sneakers, furniture, and electronics. Many offer layaway plans. In addition, there are businesses that cater mostly to the criminal class, such as pawnshops and beeper stores. Pawnshops are, in a sense, banks for thieves; they are places where stolen goods can be traded for cash, few questions asked. Check-cashing exchanges, which continue to be a common sight, also ask few questions, but they charge exorbitant fees for cashing a check. As in Chestnut Hill, merchandise is often displayed on the sidewalk, but here it is under the watchful eye of unsmiling security guards. The noise level here is also much louder. Cars drive by with their stereo systems blaring. Farther down, young people walk down the street or gather on someone's stoop with their boom boxes vibrating, the bass turned way up. On adjacent streets, open-air drug deals occur, prostitutes ply their trade, and boys shoot craps, while small children play in trash-strewn abandoned lots. This is the face of persistent urban poverty.

It is also another staging area, where people stand around, "looking things over," as they say. Here, phrases like "watch your back" take on literal meaning. Friends bond and reassure one another, saying, "I got your back," for there are always people in the vicinity looking for opportunities to violate others or simply to get away with something. For the most part, public decency gets little respect. A man opens his car door despite approaching traffic, seeming to dare someone to hit him. Farther down the block a woman simply stops her car in the middle of the street, waiting for her man to emerge from a barbershop. She waits for about ten minutes, holding up traffic. No one complains, no one honks a car horn; people simply go around her, for they know that to complain is to risk an altercation, or at least heated words. They prefer not to incur this woman's wrath, which could escalate into warfare. In Chestnut Hill, where civility is generally the order of the day, people might "call" others on such behavior, but here it is the general level of violence that tends to keep irritation in check—except among those who are "crazy." In this way, the code of the street provides an element of social organization and actually lessens the probability of random violence. When the woman's man arrives, he simply steps around to the passenger side and, without showing any concern for others, gets into the car. The pair drive off, apparently believing it to be their right to do what they just did.

At Tioga Street, Temple University Hospital, whose emergency room sees gunshot and stabbing victims just about every night, the code of the street is very much in evidence. In the morning and early afternoon, the surrounding neighborhood is peaceful enough, but in the evening the danger level rises. Especially on weekends, tensions spill over, drug deals go bad, fights materialize seemingly out of nowhere, and the emergency room becomes a hub of activity. Sometimes the victims bypass the hospital: by the time they are found, there is no place to take them but the morgue. Nearby is a liquor store and a deli selling cold beer. People buy liquor there and drink it on the street, adding to the volatility of the street scene.

On a back street, amid crumbling houses and abandoned stolen automobiles whose carcasses are constantly picked at by some impoverished residents for spare parts, children "rip and run," playing double Dutch (jump-rope games) and stickball. At the corner store young children pass in and out. Mostly they buy cigarettes (for parents or other adults), candy, Slim Jims, potato chips, bread, and soda.

The summer streets are populated by these children and sometimes their mothers, grandmothers, older sisters, and female cousins. It is mostly a very poor neighborhood of women and small children, who make up extremely important kinship networks that work to sustain their members; at times, others are enlisted as fictive kin for needed help. These residents, if they are employed, work as dishwashers, mechanics, and domestics, as well as in other menial jobs.

Some working poor people survive by living with kin and thus sharing household duties and close family life—joys as well as troubles. A large number of the women are on welfare, and many are very apprehensive about "welfare reform." Eligible men seem a scarce presence in their lives.

When present at all, men appear most often in the roles of nephew, cousin, father, uncle, boyfriend, and son, but seldom as husband. A few older men are retired and sit on the stoops, laughing and talking with their friends. Some will extend themselves, helping women in need of support, at times driving them on errands for a negotiated fee, for sexual favors, or in simple friendship.

In a crisis—say, when young women with children become strung out on crack and other drugs to the point of being unable to function as mothers—a friend or relative may help out, but in some of the most desperate situations, the oldest children may take over, procuring and preparing food and performing other household duties. At other times, a grandmother assumes a crack addict's household chores and steps in to raise her daughter's children. In the neighborhood, stories circulate about this or that crack-addicted young mother who is abusing her children in favor of the pipe. Everyone knows someone or knows about someone with a drug habit whose life has been impacted in some way by drugs.

While most residents struggle with poverty, there are some solidly working-class nuclear families living here, at times with a man still employed by a local factory, but this situation is rare. Often those working-class residents who could, have left the area, routed by crime, incivility, and persistent poverty.

Small groups of seven- and eight-year-old street kids hang out on the corners or in the local alleys; they watch the traffic go by, observing the recurring drug sales, although many pretend not to see. Street lore says that local drug dealers employ some of them as lookouts for crack houses or to signal dealers when a new shipment of drugs has arrived at a pickup point.

On summer days residents lean out of their windows to catch a breeze or sit on stoops to watch the traffic go by. There is much street life here, involving young men, young women, old people, middle-aged people. To walk the streets is to observe many pregnant young women, walking or standing around with one or two children. Their youthful faces belie their distended bellies, but they carry on.

The streets are noisy and very much alive with sociability—yells, screams, loud laughter and talk, car screeches, rap music, and honking horns. A car pulls up and honks its horn for a passenger. People are basically courteous, not wanting to provoke others. There are smiles and a certain level of camaraderie. Everybody knows everybody here, and as best they can, some people try to watch out for others.

But many have their hands full watching out for themselves. Like aluminum siding at an earlier time, decorative iron bars have become a status symbol in the neighborhood, and residents acquire them for downstairs windows and doors to be used for protection against thieves and "zombies" (crack addicts). These residents show real concern about any stranger who seems at all questionable.

Now and again a young boy appears, dressed in an expensive athletic suit and white sneakers (usually new; some boys have four or five pair). On certain street corners or down certain alleys, small groups of boys pass the time in the middle of the day. They profile or represent, striking stylized poses, almost always dressed in expensive clothes that belie their unemployed status. They lead others to the easy conclusion that they "clock" (work) in the drug trade. A common view on the streets among the corner men is that the families of some of these boys "know about" their involvements, because they "get some of the money" for help with household expenses. Corner men talk of parents' tacit acceptance and willing ignorance of their youngster's drug dealing, although the parents may express their worry about the boy, about the random gunshots that sometimes come from a passing automobile, about the occasional drug wars that sometimes start up spontaneously, and about the possibility of their son's arrest by the police. They worry often about the police, not just because of the prospect of incarceration but because the family in some cases has come to rely on the drug money.

In the impoverished inner-city neighborhood, the drug trade is everywhere, and it becomes ever more difficult to separate the drug culture from the experience of poverty. The neighborhood is sprinkled with crack dens located in abandoned buildings or in someone's home. On corner after corner, young men peddle drugs the way a newsboy peddles papers. To those who pass their brief inspection, they say, "Psst, psst! I got the news. I got the news. 'Caine, blow. Beam me up, Scotty." These are code words easily understood by those in the know. At times they sell drugs to passing motorists, who stop in broad daylight and hold up traffic during the transaction; yet the police seem indifferent to the dealing or they sometimes abuse the very residents they are supposed to protect. When customers drive up, small children will occasionally be sitting in the backseat, which seems to faze neither the dealers nor the customer. Some of these young men carry beepers, which they use in conjunction with the telephone to make their sales; in fact, as pressure has been placed on the local crack houses and on the open-air street sales, the beeper and telephone have become more important. For other young people the beeper has become a status symbol, emblematic of the possession of money, daring, coolness, and drugs.

Almost any denizen of these streets has come to accept the area as a tough place, a neighborhood where the strongest survive and where people who are not careful and streetwise can become ensnared in the games of those who could hurt them. When the boys admire another's property, they may simply try to take it; this includes that person's sneakers, jacket, hat, and other personal items. In this sense, the public spaces develop an air of incivility about them, particularly at night, and as a consequence many feel that the younger people are uncivilized. But the viewpoints of the young are to be distinguished from those of the older people, who sometimes proudly claim that they were *raised* under a different system with different opportunities and different abilities to realize them, while offering that kids today "just grow up." The older people try to live out their values of decency and law-abidingness; and even though these continue to be important values in the neighborhood, the young generally do not seem as committed to them as the older residents.

As we continue down the avenue, more and more gaps in the rows of houses appear; these gaps represent places where buildings have burned down, have been torn down, or have simply collapsed.

Others are shells; their windows and large parts of their walls are gone, leaving beams exposed. Still others are boarded up, perhaps eventually to collapse, perhaps to be rebuilt. Indeed, signs of regeneration are visible among those of destruction. Here and there a house is well maintained, even freshly painted. Some of the exposed outer walls of standing structures have colorful, upbeat murals painted on them, often with religious themes. We pass a large building, a car repair shop, gaily decorated with graffiti art, including a freshly painted "memorial" for a young victim of street violence. Farther down, we pass a hotel that rents rooms by the hour.

We continue to see signs of the avenue's past life—large churches built by European immigrants at the turn of the century, an old cemetery, an occasional historic building. The many open areas—empty lots, little overgrown parks—underline the winding character of this old highway as it cuts through the grid street pattern that was formally laid out well after Germantown Avenue became an established thoroughfare.

Another business district appears, with the usual stores catering to the very poor. Two policemen pass by on foot patrol. This is another staging area. The concentration of people drawn by the businesses increases the chance that violence will erupt. A lot of people are out, not just women and children but a conspicuous number of young men as well, even though it is still morning.

We enter an area where there seem to be more empty lots and houses you can see right through than solidly standing buildings. Some of the lots are a heap of rubble. Others are overgrown with weeds or littered with abandoned cars. The idea of a war zone springs to mind. Indeed, gunshot marks are evident on some of the buildings. The black ghetto here gives way to the Hispanic ghetto. The faces are different, but the behavior is the same. Yet in the midst of this desolation stands a newly built gated community in the Spanish style. Just beyond it, we reach Norris Street; at this intersection three of the four corners are large empty lots. But we also pass an open area that has been transformed into a community garden. Now, in late spring, vegetables in the early stages of growth are visible.

We are now just north of Philadelphia's downtown. This used to be a bustling commercial area, where factories produced everything from beer to lace and where the goods were stored in huge warehouses before being shipped out, either by rail, traces of which are still manifest, or through the nearby port on the Delaware River. Here and there some of these behemoths remain standing, although one by one they are falling victim to arson.

Finally we reach the other end of Germantown Avenue in the midst of a leveled area about a block from the river and overshadowed by the elevated interstate highway that now allows motorists to drive over North Philadelphia rather than through it—thereby ignoring its street life, its inhabitants, and its problems.

## THE CODE OF THE STREET

Of all the problems besetting the poor inner-city black community, none is more pressing than that of interpersonal violence and aggression. This phenomenon wreaks havoc daily on the lives of community residents and increasingly spills over into downtown and residential middle-class areas. Muggings, burglaries, carjackings, and drug-related shootings, all of which may leave their victims or innocent bystanders dead, are now common enough to concern all urban and many suburban residents.

The inclination to violence springs from the circumstances of life among the ghetto poor—the lack of jobs that pay a living wage, limited basic public services (police response in emergencies, building maintenance, trash pickup, lighting, and other services that middle-class neighborhoods take for granted), the stigma of race, the fallout from rampant drug use and drug trafficking, and the resulting alienation and absence of hope for the future. Simply living in such an environment places young people at special risk of falling victim to aggressive behavior. Although there are often forces in the community that can counteract the negative influences—by far the most powerful is a strong, loving, "decent" (as inner-city residents put it) family that is committed to middle-class values—the despair is pervasive enough to have spawned an oppositional culture, that of "the street," whose norms are often consciously opposed to those of main-stream society. These two orientations—decent and street—organize the community socially, and the way they coexist and interact has important consequences for its residents, particularly for children growing up in the inner city. Above all, this environment means that even youngsters whose home lives reflect mainstream values—and most of the homes in the community do—must be able to handle themselves in a street-oriented environment.

This is because the street culture has evolved a "code of the street," which amounts to a set of informal rules governing interpersonal public behavior, particularly violence.[4] The rules prescribe both proper comportment and the proper way to respond if challenged. They regulate the use of violence and so supply a rationale allowing those who are inclined to aggression to precipitate violent encounters in an approved way. The rules have been established and are enforced mainly by the street-oriented; but on the streets the distinction between street and decent is often irrelevant. Everybody knows that if the rules are violated, there are penalties. Knowledge of the code is thus largely defensive, and it is literally necessary for operating in public. Therefore, though families with a decency orientation are usually opposed to the values of the code, they often reluctantly encourage their children's familiarity with it in order to enable them to negotiate the inner-city environment.

At the heart of the code is the issue of respect—loosely defined as being treated "right" or being granted one's "props" (or proper due) or the deference one deserves. However, in the troublesome public environment of the inner city, as people increasingly feel buffeted by forces beyond their control, what one deserves in the way of respect becomes ever more problematic and uncertain. This situation in turn further opens up the issue of respect to sometimes intense interpersonal negotiation, at times resulting in altercations. In the street culture, especially among young people, respect is viewed as almost an external entity, one that is hard-won but easily lost—and so must constantly be guarded. The rules of the code in fact provide a framework for negotiating respect. With the right amount of respect, individuals can avoid being bothered in public. This security is important, for if they *are* bothered, not only may they face physical danger, but they will have been disgraced or "dissed" (disrespected). Many of the forms dissing can take may seem petty to middle-class people (maintaining eye contact for too long, for example), but to those invested in the street code, these actions, a virtual slap in the face, become serious indications of the other person's intentions. Consequently, such people become very sensitive to advances and slights, which could well serve as a warning of imminent physical attack or confrontation.

The hard reality of the world of the street can be traced to the profound sense of alienation from mainstream society and its institutions felt by many poor inner-city black people, particularly the young. The code of the street is actually a cultural adaptation to a profound lack of faith in the police and the judicial system—and in others who would champion one's personal security. The police, for instance, are most often viewed as representing the dominant white society and as not caring to protect inner-city residents. When called, they may not respond, which is one reason many residents feel they must be prepared to take extraordinary measures to defend themselves and their loved ones against those who are inclined to aggression. Lack of police accountability has in fact been incorporated into the local status system: the person who is believed capable of "taking care of himself" is accorded a certain deference and regard, which translates into a sense of physical and psychological control. The code of the street thus emerges where the influence of the police ends and where personal responsibility for one's safety is felt to begin. Exacerbated by the proliferation of drugs and easy access to guns, this volatile situation results in the ability of the street-oriented minority (or those who effectively "go for bad") to dominate the public spaces.

# ONE

# Decent and Street Families

ALMOST everyone residing in poor inner-city neighborhoods is struggling financially and therefore feels a certain distance from the rest of America, but there are degrees of alienation, captured by the terms "decent" and "street" or "ghetto," suggesting social types. The decent family and the street family in a real sense represent two poles of value orientation, two contrasting conceptual categories.[1] The labels "decent" and "street," which the residents themselves use, amount to evaluative judgments that confer status on local residents. The labeling is often the result of a social contest among individuals and families of the neighborhood. Individuals of either orientation may coexist in the same extended family. Moreover, decent residents may judge themselves to be so while judging others to be of the street, and street individuals often present themselves as decent, while drawing distinctions between themselves and still other people. There is also quite a bit of circumstantial behavior—that is, one person may at different times exhibit both decent and street orientations, depending on the circumstances. Although these designations result from much social jockeying, there do exist concrete features that define each conceptual category, forming a social typology.

The resulting labels are used by residents of inner-city communities to characterize themselves and one another, and understanding them is part of understanding life in the inner-city neighborhood. Most residents are decent or are trying to be. The same family is likely to have members who are strongly oriented toward decency and civility, whereas other members are oriented toward the street—and to all that it implies. There is also a great deal of "code-switching": a person may behave according to either set of rules, depending on the situation. Decent people, especially young people, often put a premium on the ability to code-switch. They share many of the middle-class values of the wider white society but know that the open display of such values carries little weight on the street: it doesn't provide the emblems that say, "I can take care of myself." Hence such people develop a repertoire of behaviors that do provide that security. Those strongly associated with the street, who have less exposure to the wider society, may have difficulty code-switching; imbued with the code of the street, they either don't know the rules for decent behavior or may see little value in displaying such knowledge.

At the extreme of the street-oriented group are those who make up the criminal element. People in this class are profound casualties of the social and economic system, and they tend to embrace the street code wholeheartedly. They tend to lack not only a decent education—though some are highly intelligent—but also an outlook that would allow them to see far beyond their immediate circumstances. Rather, many pride themselves on living the "thug life," actively defying not simply the wider social conventions but the law itself. They sometimes model themselves after successful local drug dealers and rap artists like Tupac Shakur and Snoop Doggy Dogg, and they take heart from professional athletes who confront the system and stand up for themselves. In their view, policemen, public officials, and corporate heads are unworthy of respect and hold little moral authority. Highly alienated and embittered, they exude generalized contempt for the wider scheme of things and for a system they are sure has nothing but contempt for them.

Members of this group are among the most desperate and most alienated people of the inner city. For them, people and situations are best approached both as objects of exploitation and as challenges possibly "having a trick to them," and in most situations their goal is to avoid being "caught up in the trick bag." Theirs is a cynical outlook, and trust of others is severely lacking, even trust of those they are close to. Consistently, they tend to approach all persons and situations as part of life's obstacles, as things to subdue or to "get over." To get over, individuals develop an effective "hustle" or "game plan," setting themselves up in a position to prevail by being "slick" and outsmarting others. In line with this, one must always be wary of one's counterparts, to assume that they are involved with you only for what they can get out of the situation.

Correspondingly, life in public often features an intense competition for scarce social goods in which "winners" totally dominate "losers" and in which losing can be a fate worse than death. So one must be on one's guard constantly. One is not always able to trust others fully, in part because so much is at stake socially, but also because everyone else is understood to be so deprived. In these circumstances, violence is quite prevalent—in families, in schools, and in the streets—becoming a way of public life that is effectively governed by the code of the street.

Decent and street families deal with the code of the street in various ways. An understanding of the dynamics of these families is thus critical to an understanding of the dynamics of the code. It is important to understand here that the family one emerges from is distinct from the "family" one finds in the streets. For street-oriented people especially, the family outside competes with blood relatives for an individual's loyalties and commitments. Nevertheless, blood relatives always come first. The folklore of the street says, in effect, that if I will fight and "take up for" my friend, then you know what I will do for my own brother, cousin, nephew, aunt, sister, or mother—and vice versa. Blood is thicker than mud.

## DECENT FAMILIES

In decent families there is almost always a real concern with and a certain amount of hope for the future. Such attitudes are often essed in a drive to work "to have something" or "to build a good life," while at the same time trying to "make do with what you have." This means working hard, saving money for material things, and raising children—any "child you touch"—to try to make something out of themselves. Decent families tend to accept mainstream values more fully than street families, and they attempt to instill them in their children. Probably the most meaningful description of the mission of the decent family, as seen by members and outsiders alike, is to instill "backbone" and a sense of responsibility in its younger members. In their efforts toward this goal, decent parents are much more able and willing than street-oriented ones to ally themselves with outside institutions such as schools and churches. They value hard work and self-reliance and are willing to sacrifice for their children: they harbor hopes for a better future for their children, if not for themselves. Rather than dwelling on the hardships and inequities facing them, many such decent people, particularly the increasing number of grandmothers raising grandchildren (see Chapter 6), often see their difficult situation as a test from God and derive great support from their faith and church community.

The role of the "man of the house" is significant. Working-class black families have traditionally placed a high value on male authority. Generally, the man is seen as the "head of household," with the woman as his partner and the children as their subjects. His role includes protecting the family from threats, at times literally putting his body in the line of fire on the street. In return he expects to rule his household and to get respect from the other members, and he encourages his sons to grow up with the same expectations. Being a breadwinner or good provider is often a moral issue, and a man unable to provide for a family invites disrespect from his partner. Many young men who lack the resources to do so often say, "I can't play house," and opt out of forming a family, perhaps leaving the woman and any children to fend for themselves.

Intact nuclear families, although in the minority in the impoverished inner city, provide powerful role models. Typically, husband and wife work at low-paying jobs, sometimes juggling more than one such job each. They may be aided financially by the contributions of a teenage child who works part-time. Such families, along with other such local families, are often vigilant in their desire to keep the children away from the streets.

In public such an intact family makes a striking picture as the man may take pains to show he is in complete control—with the woman and the children following his lead. On the inner-city streets this appearance helps him play his role as protector, and he may exhibit exaggerated concern for his family, particularly when other males are near. His actions and words, including loud and deep-voiced assertions to get his small children in line, let strangers know: "This is my family, and I am in charge." He signals that he is capable of protecting them and that his family is not to be messed with.

I witnessed such a display one Saturday afternoon at the Gallery, an indoor shopping mall with a primarily black, Hispanic, and working- to middle-class white clientele. Rasheed Taylor, his wife, Iisha, and their children, Rhonda, Jimmy, and Malika, wandered about the crowded food court looking for a place to sit down to eat. They finally found a table next to mine. Before sitting down, Mr. Taylor asked me if the seats were available, to which I replied they were. He then summoned his family, and they walked forward promptly and in an orderly way to take the seats. The three children sat on one side and the parents on the other. Mr. Taylor took food requests and with a stern look in his eye told the children to stay seated until he and his wife returned with the food. The children nodded attentively. After the adults left, the children seemed to relax, talking more freely and playing with one another. When the parents returned, the kids straightened up again, received their food, and began to eat, displaying quiet and gracious manners all the while. It was very clear to everybody looking on that Mr. Taylor was in charge of this family, with everyone showing him utter deference and respect.

Extremely aware of the problematic and often dangerous environment in which they reside, decent parents tend to be strict in their child-rearing practices, encouraging children to respect authority and walk a straight moral line. They sometimes display an almost obsessive concern about trouble of any kind and encourage their children to avoid people and situations that might lead to it. But this is very difficult, since the decent and the street families live in such close proximity. Marge, a slight, forty-three-year-old, married, decent parent of five who resides in such a neighborhood, relates her experience:

> But you know what happens now? I have five children. Or I had five children—my oldest son got killed in a car accident. My children have always been different [decent]. And sometimes we have to act that way [street] that other people act to show them that you're not gonna be intimidated, that my child is gonna go to the store, they're gonna come out here and play, they're gonna go to school. You don't wanta do that, but you can't go to them and talk. 'Cause I've tried that. I've tried to go to people and say, "Listen. These are children. Let's try to make them get along." I remember years ago my sons had some expensive baseball mitts and bats that was given to them. I didn't buy them. They got them from Mr. Lee because he had the baseball team. And so he gave my sons some baseball bats and gloves. At that time the park at Twenty-seventh and Girard was Fred Jackson Stadium; they call it Ruth Bloom now. My sons played baseball there. So one little boy wanted to borrow some of the gloves and the bat. I told my children, "Don't let him hold [use] the gloves and the bat." But they let him hold them anyway. So he told them that when he finished with them he would put them on the porch. I told them they were never going to see them again, and they were never put on the porch. So I went to his mother, that was my neighbor, and I approached her very nicely and I said, "Johnny didn't bring Terry and Curtis's gloves and bat back." You know, she cursed me out! I was shocked. [She said,] "He doesn't have to take a so-and-so bat and a ball." And that woman really shocked me and hurt my feelings. I said, "Forget it. Just forget it." She was really ignorant. But I had to—even though I didn't get ignorant [get on her level] 'cause my son was there—but I had to say *some* negative things to her to let her know that I was just shocked. But I've been here [residing in this neighborhood] twenty-two years, and in twenty-two years I've had at least ten different, separate incidents that I had to go out and talk to somebody, to the point that I told my children, "No more." Somebody's gonna get hurt 'cause they don't know when to stop.

OK, my daughter, Annette, she went to Germantown High. So she was in about the ninth grade, had never had a fight in her life. She came from the store one day, and she told me about this girl that kept pickin' on her. She came up on the porch, and she said, "Mommy, come to the door. I want to show you this girl that keeps picking on me." Of course. Anybody that bothered them, I always wanted to see who it was in case I had to go see their parents or whatever. So I came and looked over the railing on the porch, and me and my daughter were lookin' down the street in that direction, not really at her [which could have been taken as offensive]. The girl came up and said, "Who the fuck are you lookin' at?" I said to my daughter, "Don't say anything." So I said to the girl, "You better go home. You better take your little butt home." OK. So she did go home. That afternoon, my daughter was sitting on the steps of the porch and reading a book—now this is a child who never had a fight, gets good grades. I think I raised her extremely well. She's a biochemist now. She's sitting on the step, reading her little book, and the girl came up to her, said something to her. I wasn't even out there, and so by the time my sons came to get me, my daughter and her were fighting. That was the first fight that she ever had in her life, and she was in the ninth grade. So I went out there and separated them. The girl went around the corner. When she came back, she had twenty different people with her. But I knew what was gonna happen. So—those same baseball bats I told you about—I told my son to get the baseball bats from the hallway. I said, "We're not gonna get off the porch, but if we have to, if they come up here, we're gonna have to do something." So they came back, and I had to actually coax them off like I was a little tough, like I'm not gonna take it. And I said to my sons, "If they come up here, we're gonna pay they ass back," and all that kind of stuff. And that's how I got them off us. I mean, it was about twenty of them, friends, family, neighbors.

As I indicated above, people who define themselves as decent tend themselves to be polite and considerate of others and teach their children to be the same way. But this is sometimes difficult, mainly because of the social environment in which they reside, and they often perceive a need to "get ignorant"—to act aggressively, even to threaten violence.[2] For whether a certain child gets picked on may well depend not just on the reputation of the child but, equally important, on how "bad" the child's family is known to be. How many people the child can gather together for the purposes of defense or revenge often emerges as a critical issue. Thus social relations can become practical matters of personal defense. Violence can come at any time, and many persons feel a great need to be ready to defend themselves.

At home, at work, and in church, decent parents strive to maintain a positive mental attitude and a spirit of cooperation. When disciplining their children, they tend to use corporal punishment, but unlike street parents, who can often be observed lashing out at their children, they may explain the reason for the spanking. These parents express their care and love for teenage children by guarding against the appearance of any kind of "loose" behavior (violence, drug use, staying out very late) that might be associated with the streets. In this regard, they are vigilant, observing children's peers as well and sometimes embarrassing their own children by voicing value judgments in front of friends.

These same parents are aware, however, that the right material things as well as a certain amount of cash are essential to young people's survival on the street. So they may purchase expensive things for their children, even when money is tight, in order that the children will be less tempted to turn to the drug trade or other aspects of the underground economy for money.

## THE DECENT SINGLE MOTHER

A single mother with children—the majority of decent families in the impoverished sections of the inner city are of this type—must work even harder to neutralize the draw of the street, and she does so mainly by being strict and by instilling decent values in her children. She may live with her mother or other relatives and friends, or she may simply receive help with child care from her extended family. In raising her children, she often must press others to defer to her authority; but without a strong man of the house, a figure boys in particular are prepared to respect, she is at some disadvantage with regard not only to her own sons and daughters but also to the young men of the streets. These men may test her ability to control her household by attempting to date her daughters or to draw her sons into the streets. A mother on her own often feels she must be constantly on guard and exhibit a great deal of determination.

Diane, a single mother of four sons, three of whom are grown, offers a case in point. Diane is forty-six years old, of average height, heavyset, and light-complexioned. One of her sons is a night watchman at the utility company, and another is a security guard at a downtown store. Diane herself works as an aide in a day care center. In describing her situation, she has this to say:

It really is pretty bad around here. There's quite a few grandmothers taking care of kids. They mothers out here on crack. There's quite a few of 'em. The drugs are terrible. Now, I got a fifteen-year-old boy, and I do everything I can to keep him straight. 'Cause they [drug dealers and users] all on the corner. You can't say you not in it, 'cause we in a bad area. They be all on the corner. They be sittin' in front of apartments takin' the crack. And constantly, every day, I have to stay on 'em and make sure everything's OK. Which is real bad, I never seen it this bad. And I been around here since '81, and I never seen it this bad. At nights they be roamin' up and down the streets, and they be droppin' the caps [used crack vials] all in front of your door. And when the kids out there playin', you gotta like sweep 'em up. It's harder for me now to try to keep my fifteen-year-old under control. Right now, he likes to do auto mechanics, hook up radios in people's cars, and long as I keep 'im interested in that, I'm OK. But it's not a day that goes by that I'm not in fear. 'Cause right now he got friends that's sellin' it. They, you know, got a whole lot of money and stuff. And I get him to come and mop floors [she works part-time as a janitor], and I give him a few dollars. I say, "As long as you got a roof over yo' head, son, don't worry about nothin' else."

It's just a constant struggle tryin' to raise yo' kids in this time. It's very hard. They [boys on the street] say to him, "Man, why you got to go in the house?" And they keep sittin' right on my stoop. If he go somewhere, I got to know where he's at and who he's with. And they be tellin' him [come with us]. He say, "No, man, I got to stay on these steps. I don't want no problem with my mama!" Now, I been a single parent for fifteen years. So far, I don't have any problems. I have four sons. I got just the one that's not grown, the fifteen-year-old. Everyone else is grown. My oldest is thirty-five. I'm tryin'. Not that easy. I got just one more, now. Then I'll be all right. If I need help, the older ones'll help me. Most of the time, I keep track myself. I told him I'll kill him if I catch him out here sellin'. And I know most of the drug dealers. He better not. I'm gon' hurt him. They better not give him nothin'. He better not do nothin' for them. I tell him, "I know some of your friends are dealers. [You can] speak to 'em, but don't let me catch you hangin' on the corner. I done struggled too hard to try to take care of you. I'm not gon' let you throw your life away."

When me and my husband separated in '79, I figured I had to do it. He was out there drivin' trucks and never home. I had to teach my kids how to play ball and this and that. I said, "If I have to be a single parent, I'll do it." It used to be the gangs, and you fought 'em, and it was over. But now if you fight somebody, they may come back and kill you. It's a whole lot different now. You got to be street-smart to get along. My boy doesn't like to fight. I took him out of school, put him in a home course. The staff does what it wants to. [They] just work for a paycheck.

You tell the kid, now you can't pick their friends, so you do what you can. I try to tell mine, "You gon' be out there with the bad [street kids], you can't do what they do. You got to use your own mind." Every day, if I don't get up and say a prayer, I can't make it. I can't make it. I watch him closely. If he go somewhere, I have to know where he at. And when I leave him, or if he go to them girlfriends' houses, I tell the parents, "If you not responsible, he can't stay." I'm not gon' have no teenager making no baby.

These comments show how one decent inner-city parent makes sense of the breakdown in civility, order, and morality she sees occurring in her community and how she copes. When Diane was a child, and even when her older sons were growing up, gang fights were common, but they generally took the form of an air-clearing brawl. Today many community residents feel that if you run afoul of a gang or an individual, somebody may simply kill you. Note that the schools are included among the institutions seen to have abdicated their responsibilities, a widespread belief among many inner-city parents.

## THE STREET FAMILY

So-called street parents, unlike decent ones, often show a lack of consideration for other people and have a rather superficial sense of family and community. They may love their children but frequently find it difficult both to cope with the physical and emotional demands of parenthood and to reconcile their needs with those of their children. Members of these families, who are more fully invested in the code of the street than the decent people are, may aggressively socialize their children into it in a normative way. They more fully believe in the code and judge themselves and others according to its values.

In fact, the overwhelming majority of families in the inner-city community try to approximate the decent-family model, but many others clearly represent the decent families' worst fears. Not only are their financial resources extremely limited, but what little they have may easily be misused. The lives of the street-oriented are often marked by disorganization. In the most desperate circumstances, people frequently have a limited understanding of priorities and consequences, and so frustrations mount over bills, food, and, at times, liquor, cigarettes, and drugs. Some people tend toward self-destructive behavior; many street-oriented women are crack-addicted ("on the pipe"), alcoholic, or involved in complicated relationships with men who abuse them.

In addition, the seeming intractability of their situation, caused in large part by the lack of well-paying jobs and the persistence of racial discrimination, has engendered deep-seated bitterness and anger in many of the most desperate and poorest blacks, especially young people. The need both to exercise a measure of control and to lash out at somebody is often reflected in the adults' relations with their children. At the very least, the frustrations associated with persistent poverty shorten the fuse in such people, contributing to a lack of patience with anyone—child or adult—who irritates them.

People who fit the conception of street are often considered to be lowlife or "bad people," especially by the "decent people," and they are generally seen as incapable of being anything but a bad influence on the community and a bother to their neighbors. For example, on a relatively quiet block in West Oak Lane, on the edge of a racially integrated, predominantly middle-class neighborhood, there is a row of houses inhabited by impoverished people. One of them is Joe Dickens, a heavyset, thirty-two-year-old black man. Joe rents the house he lives in, and he shares it with his three children—two daughters (aged seven and five) and a three-year-old son. With patches on the brickwork, an irregular pillar holding up the porch roof, and an unpainted plywood front door, his house sticks out on the block. The front windows have bars; the small front yard is filled with trash and weeds; the garbage cans at the side of the house are continually overflowing.

Even more obtrusive is the lifestyle of the household. Dickens's wife has disappeared from the scene. It is rumored that her crack habit got completely out of control, and she gravitated to the streets and became a prostitute to support her habit. Dickens could not accept this behavior and let her go; he took over running the house and caring for the children as best he could. And to the extent that the children are fed, clothed, and housed under his roof, he might be considered a responsible parent.

But many of the neighbors do not view him as responsible. They see him yelling and cursing at the kids when he pays attention to them at all. Mostly, he allows them to "rip and run" unsupervised up and down the street at all hours, riding their Big Wheels and making a racket. They are joined by other neighborhood children playing on the streets and sidewalks without adult supervision. Dickens himself pays more attention to his buddies, who seem always to be hanging out at the house—on the porch in warm weather—playing loud rap music, drinking beer, and playing cards.

Dickens generally begins his day at about 11 A.M., when he may go out for cheesesteaks and videos for his visitors. In fact, one gets the impression that the house is the scene of an ongoing party. The noise constantly disturbs the neighbors, sometimes prompting them to call the police. But the police rarely respond to the complaints, leaving the neighbors frustrated and demoralized. Dickens seems almost completely indifferent to his neighbors and inconsiderate of their concerns, a defining trait of street-oriented people.

Dickens's decent neighbors are afraid to confront him because they fear getting into trouble with him and his buddies. They are sure that he believes in the principle that might makes right and that he is likely to try to harm anyone who annoys him. Furthermore, they suspect he is a crack dealer. The neighbors cannot confirm this, but some are convinced anyway, and activities around his house support this conclusion. People come and go at all hours of the day and night; they often leave their car engines running, dash into the house, and quickly emerge and drive off. Dickens's children, of course, see much of this activity. At times the children are made to stand outside on the porch while business is presumably being transacted inside. These children are learning by example the values of toughness and self-absorption: to be loud, boisterous, proudly crude, and uncouth—in short, street.

Maxine's family is another example. On a block that has managed to retain a preponderance of decent households, one house had stood vacant for some time. One day the absentee landlord showed up and started making minor repairs, painting the porch railings, and carrying out trash bags. Sometime later, Maxine, a large brown-skinned woman, was spotted sweeping up in the backyard, helped out by a heavyset middle-aged black man. The block's residents took note. Had the home been sold? Had the landlord found new tenants? Who were they? What were they like? Finally, move-in day arrived. Maxine and her friend, along with her six children, appeared on the block with an old blue pickup truck loaded down with old furniture, including beds, tables, lamps, and black plastic bags full of stuff. Anxious neighbors watched while they unloaded the truck and moved the belongings into the house.

After they moved in, Maxine's children were the first to make their presence felt on the block, spending a large part of the day playing noisily without supervision outside. Soon, however, a larger problem developed: a middle-aged male whose relationship to Maxine was unclear appeared to move in. After he did so, people began to notice a series of comings and goings at various times of the day and night. There were also exchanges on the front porch, on the sidewalk, and in the street. Though residents did not know the exact nature of these transactions, her neighbors assumed that they involved drugs, because everything else seemed to fit. In addition, at night those residing closest to Maxine could hear the sounds of a great commotion and the screams of her children. The block had become decidedly less peaceful—and dirtier. On trash-pickup day, Maxine's trash would often not be stored properly, and some of it would fall to the ground, where it would lie and fly around with the wind. She and her children would sometimes contribute to the litter by tossing empty bags and soda bottles from the porch as soon as they were done with them. This behavior further upset the neighbors.

But most upsetting of all was the blatant drug dealing now going on at Maxine's house. All of this came to a head one Saturday in May at about 1 P.M. On this nice spring afternoon, the peace of the block was disturbed by a young man who was wailing and banging on Maxine's front door. A few residents were out and about doing chores, and small children played and rode their tricycles and bikes up and down the block. "Gimme my drugs, bitch! Where my drugs at?" the young man cried as he banged on the door. The neighbors who were out began to look at Maxine's house. After hearing this noise and assessing the situation, one woman ran to collect her small daughter, who was in front of the house on her tricycle. Suddenly, a beat-up brown windowless van careened around the corner and came to a screeching halt in front of Maxine's house. Out jumped two young black men, who headed for Maxine's front door. Without knocking, they entered, as though they had been summoned to deal with the other young man. But no sooner had they entered than they emerged, running out, ducking and hiding behind nearby trees and cars. It was clear that they were afraid of being hit by some flying object—or possibly of being shot at. By now the commotion had brought together a small crowd. And after a little while the police were summoned, and they came. They parked their police van on the street near the brown van and proceeded to the front door. They entered and in a few minutes emerged with the first young man and placed him in the van. At this point the man began to scream and yell at Maxine. "I'll get you, bitch! You won't get away with this. I'll get you," he cried. "As soon as I get out, I'll get you!" The police van drove away, leaving the neighbors with their worst fears confirmed: Maxine had established the street lifestyle on their previously quiet block.

Street-oriented women tend to perform their motherly duties sporadically. The most irresponsible women can be found at local bars and crack houses, getting high and socializing with other adults. Reports of crack addicts abandoning their children have become common in drug-infested inner-city communities. Typically, neighbors or relatives discover the abandoned children, often hungry and distraught over the absence of their mother. After repeated absences a friend or relative, particularly a grandmother, will often step in to care for the children, sometimes petitioning the authorities to send her, as guardian of the children, the mother's welfare check, if she gets one. By this time, however, the children may well have learned the first lesson of the streets: you cannot take survival itself, let alone respect, for granted; you have to fight for your place in the world. Some of the children learn to fend for themselves, foraging for food and money any way they can. They are sometimes employed by drug dealers or become addicted themselves (see Chapter 3).

These children of the street, growing up with little supervision, are said to "come up hard." They often learn to fight at an early age, using short-tempered adults around them as role models. The street-oriented home may be fraught with anger, verbal disputes, physical aggression, even mayhem. The children are victimized by these goings-on and quickly learn to hit those who cross them.

The people who see themselves as decent refer to the general set of cultural deficits exhibited by people like Maxine and Joe Dickens—a fundamental lack of social polish and commitment to norms of civility—as "ignorance." In their view ignorance lies behind the propensity to violence that makes relatively minor social transgressions snowball into more serious disagreements, and they believe that the street-oriented are quick to resort to violence in almost any dispute.

The fact that the decent people, as a rule civilly disposed, socially conscious, and self-reliant men and women, share the neighborhood streets and other public places with those associated with the street, the inconsiderate, the ignorant, and the desperate, places the "good" people at special risk. In order to live and function in the community, they must adapt to a street reality that is often dominated by people who at best are suffering severely in some way and who are apt to resort quickly to violence to settle disputes. This process of adapting means learning and observing the code of the street. Decent people may readily defer to people, especially strangers, who seem to be at all street-oriented. When they encounter such people at theaters and other public places talking loudly or making excessive noise, they are reluctant to correct them for fear of verbal abuse that could lead to violence. Similarly, they will often avoid confrontations over a parking space or traffic error for fear of a verbal or physical altercation. But under their breaths they may mutter "street niggers" to a black companion, drawing a sharp cultural distinction between themselves and such individuals.

There are also times when decent people try to approach the level of the ignorant ones by "getting ignorant" themselves, as Diane's story illustrates, making clear by their behavior that they too are entitled to respect and are not to be messed with. In these circumstances, they may appear more than ready to face down the ignorant ones, indicating they have reached their limit or threshold for violent confrontation. From such seemingly innocent encounters, actual fights can and do erupt, but often there is an underlying issue—typically involving money. Don Moses is a sixty-year-old gypsy taxi driver who has lived in various local black communities his entire life. Don has the reputation of being a decent man, attending church when he can and trying to treat everyone with respect. He knows the city "like the back of my hand." He related to me the following story of the levels of violence in his neighborhood:

Somebody's mother, daughter, father, child got shot. I hear it all the time. Hardly a night goes by that I don't hear gunshots. Sometimes you hear live voices and gunshots. You get the paper the next day—I remember the other night I was in the bathroom, and somebody shot—boom!—between our yards. The next day, that shot I heard, it was somebody getting shot. He went to the door, this guy did this guy wrong, kicked the door open, bam!—shot the guy. I just had a feeling—sometimes you hear a shot and you say, "I wonder who went down behind that." Sure enough, somebody did go down. Could have been anything, the littlest thing. Could be somebody left the trash can with the lid off in front of his house. Anything.

A good example of that is a neighbor. I got along—and I've always prided myself on being able to get along with everybody, especially neighbors. I say you have to take care with your neighbors and look out for them because who else is going to look out for your property if you're not there or your children. My neighbor and I, we got along very well. Last winter, my neighbor, who was a woman, her mother started an argument. She used to have this little bickering with me for no reason at all. She'd say something to me—I left the flashers on on my car once: "Why don't you turn the flashers off? The first thing you wanta do if your battery runs down is ask Johnnie"—that's the girl's name—"to give you a jump: she can't be doing this." And I would politely say, "Thank you for telling me. I'll try my best to keep my thinking cap on."

It kept on until she finally found something to really jump on. Her son borrowed some money from me, and he didn't pay it back. Her daughter approached me and said, "Look, my brother hasn't paid you back the money. I feel responsible for him, I was there. I'm gonna give you the money." Now, if you tell me that, I'm gonna be looking for you. So when I would see her, and I'd see her a couple times, "I don't have it now." So one time I was walkin' in the house, she told me, "Look, you're gonna have to see my brother for that money." So, I said, "Sure, it's fine. I'll see. We'll cross each other's paths sometime." So as fate would have it, one day he shows up and he and I had a few words. And he didn't have it on him. Three or four times he said he was gonna have it, and he didn't have it. So then that led into the time I was home and her and her mother blowed up. Her mother lit into me: "I don't know why you keep harassin' "—I really hadn't said anything to her for about a month after she said her brother would take care of it, I'd have to see him—I'd say, "No problem. It wasn't your debt. It was your brother's debt. You just happened to be there. The transaction took place in your place." Jesus, her mother lit into me. Now, I know that she instigated that by tellin' her mother, "Every time I see Don, he's askin' me for the money." I knew that's what happened. I didn't wanta let her know that I knew. She knew it, and she was trying to hush her mother up and pull me aside and talk to me. I started to get real angry with her mother because her mother had already prodded and tried to get something started with me, so she finally succeeded. All I said to her was, "Look, it really wasn't any of your business. I don't have anything to say to you about this. I don't wanta hurt your feelings. I don't wanta be disrespectful to you 'cause you're older than I. I don't want anything negative to jump off, and I don't want any problems with your daughter or your son." He was on the porch, and he gets the attitude: "What are you doin' talkin to my mother?" I said, "I didn't say anything. I didn't use no profanity. I didn't raise my voice. I wasn't disrespectful to her. I think she was very disrespectful to me." So he jumps up off the porch and goes into the house. I walked back to say something to him. He jumps up and goes into the house. Now, he pulled a gun on several people and I was lookin' for him to come out with a gun, but he didn't. He didn't come out of the house. So after that—that's been a year ago—things kind of cooled off. We just started kind of talkin' to each other again. You don't wanta fight with your neighbor.

As Don's account indicates, respect or props are very much an issue in the community, and if a person determines that he or she is not getting the proper deference, there can be trouble. In this case the man Don had lent money to had not paid up, so his sister intervened, perhaps very much aware that her brother could be viewed as disrespecting Don by not paying off the debt. Then, on the porch, the man "copped" an attitude with Don about the supposed way he was treating his mother, but things cooled off and violence was averted. Meanwhile, Don is still waiting for his money, but he is prepared to wait for the man who owes him to pay up voluntarily, mainly because the person is potentially violent—and street—and Don does not want to give him an excuse to feel he has been wronged enough to resort to violence. For the time being, Don knows that the "price" of repaying the debt owed to him may well be too high.

The inner-city community is actually quite diverse economically; various people are doing fairly well, whereas others are very poor but decent and still others are utterly and profoundly suffering, alienated, and angry. Such is the social terrain the decent family must navigate and negotiate in order to remain whole as well as secure. This situation creates a major dilemma for decent families who are trying to raise their children to remain decent even though they must negotiate the streets. These parents want their children to value educations, jobs, and a future, but they also want them to get their fair share of respect and the props that go with it—and not to be dissed or attacked or shot.

## YVETTE'S STORY

Yvette is a young woman who grew up in a decent family in a drug-infested neighborhood. Her parents sheltered her from the public environment to such an extent that she was forbidden to go onto the street unless she had somewhere to go. Although they themselves were members of the working poor, the extended family was very poor and exhibited many of the characteristics decent people associate with the street. Yvette's parents thus sought to protect her from her own relatives. Their efforts, though extreme, seem to have paid off: today Yvette is a successful college student with plans to become a doctor. Her story brings into sharp focus many of the points discussed above.

I'm twenty now, and I've lived in North Philly all my life—Twenty-fifth and Girard; it's a pretty rough neighborhood. When I was growing up, the area wasn't as crime-ridden as it is now. When I was smaller, it was more like a decent neighborhood. I live on a block with a lot of older people, so I saw a lot of people who had [decent] values around me because they stayed in the house, they sat on the porch. But that's gone now. I didn't have too many people to play with on the block, because there weren't that many kids on the block. And my mother kind of kept me in the house most of the time, because she didn't want me getting mixed up with the wrong crowd or whatever.

I went to Valley Christian School, which is a private school. And she struggled to put me in that school, but she wanted to make it so that I wouldn't be in public schools, 'cause she thought that in public schools there is just a bad crowd there, and she didn't want me mixed up with that. So I went there, and at that point my whole family started thinking, "OK, there's a problem because Yvette is starting to think that she's better than everyone else because she's going to a private school." Whereas my cousins were going to public schools and getting in trouble, getting suspended, whatever. And I wasn't doing that, because I was in a private, Christian school. And I didn't even have to say anything. Just me being in that private school convinced my family, my aunts and uncles, that something was going on with me. I didn't have too many friends in the community, because, like I said, my mother kept me inside the house. I came home from school and I studied. When the studying was over, I had like ten minutes of phone time, watch a little TV, go to sleep. That was my daily regimen. I didn't really go outside.

Most of my family's on welfare—welfare recipients. And the people who do work—my uncle works for UPS, the delivery company. And my other uncle, he worked in some factory of some sort. And my family that are janitors, maintenance people—basically everyone works in low-skill jobs. Education is not stressed in my family at all. Most of the people haven't even completed high school; my mother is one of the few. She's the only one out of her people who graduated high school.

My mother's fifty-five, and now she owns her own home, but even that was a struggle. In doing that, my family criticized her as well. My family thinks my mother as well as me, we're both sellouts. Because my mother has a white-collar job. She's just an administrative assistant, it's not that prestigious, but compared to what they do, they think—they think that because they're blue-collar and she's white-collar, it's a different kind of work. A different kind of respect goes with that white collar. And they think that because she is white-collar, she kind of removes herself from them. I don't know how to say it right. And then when she went to buy a house—none of them own their own houses. So, "OK, she thinks she's better than us again." Just because she's making it, she's making something of her life, they think there's something wrong with that.

One thing that really stands out in my mind, one of my aunts, the least thing that I would do, she would try to blame me with stuff—that any normal kid would do, but she'd blow it up to make like it was bigger, and then her and my mom would get into fights over nothing. Today they look back on the things and think, "Why did we fight? What was the problem?" Smart remarks. In church they talk about us. Just animosity comes out in a lot of ways. This aunt was on welfare for about ten years. Now she's a maintenance worker downtown. She has three kids and she's married, but her husband died. She's kind of well-off now because she had a couple of insurance policies on him, so she has a lot of money. She still has the same values even though she has a lot of money. She still has that same animosity towards me and my mother. She has a sixth-grade education, and she sees me going to college as something, "Why are you doing this? You trying to be better than me?" And presently now she's trying to use the fact that she has a job, a maintenance job, that pays twelve dollars an hour—that's a very good job—and that she has this money from the insurance policy, she's trying to use that to say, "OK, you might think that you're better than me in regards that you're going to college, you're trying to get this degree and want to be a doctor. But you're really not. You're really not anything." This is the mentality that comes out on a daily basis. I mean, we hear rumors of it. It's a lot of gossip.

This summer there was an incident. I was tutoring her two children in math and science, just trying to help them out because they're kind of failing. One's at Simon Gratz High and one's at James Middle School. And I wanted to help them out. And she caught me one day when my mother wasn't there. She's like, "You know, Yvette, you make people hate you." And I'm like, "What are you talking about? What is the problem?" She was like, "You come around here. You think you're better than everybody else. Da-da-da." It's just a whole spiel that she goes on. But that just tells me—I didn't do anything, I tried to help her kids, and she saw me trying to help her kids as me thinking I'm better than her. Which is twisted. That's just wrong. So I don't really talk to this aunt anymore, because I've just had it, basically. I try to reach back and help, but it seems like it's just interpreted wrong.

My other aunts all feel the same way, but not as strongly as her. My cousins, too. My cousins threatened to beat me up once just because [they said] I thought I was better than them. They're older than me, too. Right now one's twenty-six and one's twenty-three, but when we were in school—they were in high school, I was in middle school—and they dropped out, as usual, since no one in my family stresses education, and I was still going, and it was like, "We just wanta beat you up because you are just a nerd." They would just tell me that. 'Cause I'm a nerd. 'Cause I'm going to school. I'm trying to get good grades. I had a baby-sitter till I was about fourteen. And my aunts were my baby-sitters. So they'd see me come over there and study, and that's when they'd say I was a nerd, they'd get mad at me for studying. 'Cause they dropped out, they're not doing anything with their lives, and I'm sitting in their house and studying. They see me as the enemy.

My mother kept me grounded, though. My religion keeps me grounded. I have a goal in life. I'm trying not to let anybody get in between that goal. So that's the only way I handle it. 'Cause I have a goal in mind, and I'm going to do this. People are going to try to get me down. I was told that—my mother told me, people will try to get in your way because they're going to think this and that about you. But you have to go on. So that's the only thing. That's all I have. My family is not a support for me at all.

Another thing that distinguishes me is that it's just me. I don't have any brothers and sisters. My cousins are one of whatever—five, six. And it's just me. So I get all the attention. My biological father was—I didn't know him. From what I hear, he wasn't all that stable. I have brothers and sisters that I don't know about by other women. But they got divorced when I was about two or three months. And my mother didn't want me growing up without a father figure, so—this is gonna sound kind of weird—one of my uncles who's really a nice person, she kind of recruited him in to be a father figure in my life. I never ever knew that he was not my father until I was about thirteen or fourteen years old. It was just kept a secret. They lived in the same house—they weren't in the same bedroom or anything like that, but I didn't make anything of that. As far as I knew, I just had a mom and I had a dad and I had this nice little family. And I went to private school. You know, a nice cute little family. I didn't know. Until one of my nice cute little cousins wanted to spoil that, so they were like, "Yvette, you know that's not your father. That's your uncle. You don't have a father." And they did it in such a nasty way that I was just really upset. My mom was upset. My dad who was my uncle was extremely upset, and that caused a lot of animosity in the family for about a year or so. Just fighting, bickering. But I think I needed that foundation with both of them there because by thirteen I had my goals in life. I wanted to be a doctor. I was getting straight A's in school. I was set at that point. I don't think I would have gotten to that point without both of them there.

My father's also one of the people who helped me just to realize, "Yvette, you've got to make something of yourself. You see your cousins. They're not doing anything." He used them as one of my motivating forces. I didn't stop thinking of him as my father after I found out. It was really too late. He had done so much and just been there. He was always Daddy. He did die about four years ago, and even in his obituary I'm listed as his daughter because that's just what I am. And all his friends recognize me as his daughter. It's just that my nice little family, with the animosity, faded. One of my aunts had three kids—the one who had the most animosity—her husband was an alcoholic, he wasn't really there. So these kids had a father, but he was there in name only. Every time my aunt had a baby, he wanted to say it wasn't his, even though it was his 'cause they all looked like him. He was always drunk all the time. So he was just a father in name only—unlike my father, he just did not put in the time, dedication, whatever. He was [just] a sperm donor to me. That's how I think of him. That's how I think of my biological father. That doesn't make a father to me. That seems to be—the father image in my family isn't strong as well. The responsibility just isn't there. They mostly put it on the women. So I guess my cousins got jealous that there was someone in my life who was actually paying my tuition to go to this school, who was actually picking me up from school every day, helping me do my homework. They didn't have it.

In my neighborhood a lot of the older people have the mother and the father and the kids, but of the younger generation, no, I see all of the weight shifted on the mother. And the mother really has to be strong if she wants her kids to be something in society. It really takes a lot to do it by yourself. All the people on my block are [in their] sixties and seventies now. We have a changing rotation, but generally there are no young people on my block. From forties to seventies, that's it. We have a Section 8 [government subsidized] home across the street from me where there are lower-class welfare-recipient families, and there're just mothers and children. The mothers have no control over their kids whatsoever. You see babies just walking back and forth on the street. They're little, they're little kids. They need attention. And their mothers are hanging in the house, on the phone, whatever. We see a constant flow of cars go by. Guys get out. They go in the house for a minute, throw some Pampers in there, and leave. That's not productive for me. That's the closest thing on my block or around Germantown Avenue that I see to decentness: "OK, we'll give you some Pampers. Here you go. Live on that." What about the kid? What about the kid needing to see their father? What about the kid needing to see their mother? Their mother isn't even paying any attention. It's not fair, and it makes me mad.

My mother is strong. She has a sense of humor, but she's serious about life. You have to have a goal in life, or else you're not going to go anywhere. She also had a horrible history. Her father was actually an alcoholic as well, and her mother had eight kids and wound up raising all of them basically by herself because my grandfather died and she was left with the kids. And when he was alive, he was always drunk. And then, when my mother was ten, her mother fell down the steps and died. So there was eight kids. They were left alone. They were spread out, raised by aunts, uncles, whatever. And she learned from her background; she said, "OK, it's not gonna be like this for my daughter." This is what she told me. So when she found that my biological father was no good, she was like, "OK, we've got to have some sort of stable environment for this girl because I don't want her to have to go through the things I did." So she's always instilled in me values first of all. And she's like, "You've got to have a goal." And I had a goal, I had values, I had the stable family, and that helped me to get where I'm at.

And now she's still working towards her goal. There's never a point that she gets to that she's satisfied. She's in an all-white department in her job now. And there's a lot of discrimination going on in that department. And she's very strong because she has to go to work and put up with this every single day. And it's just a struggle for her because she comes home and she talks about it constantly. What should she do? But she's persevering, and I just have to give her much respect for that because it's really hard to do that.

She's basically—it's a combination from both sides. They're basically cutting each other off. She's kind of isolated. She talks to one of her sisters. Out of seven other siblings, she only talks to one of her sisters because of the strong animosity in our family. Whatever she hears about her other brothers and sisters, it's through her aunt. We really don't get together that much because of the situation. And she's just accepted it. She's not gonna let them bring her down. So the best way to get away from it is just to cut them off. So that's exactly what she did. And I'm really kind of hurt because I want to have a family like everyone else, an extended family. But I can't, because there's just so much jealousy and animosity. We can't have a gathering without someone saying something. We [she and her mom] support each other. We have a strong relationship with God. God is our support. I don't know—it comes from within. We don't have too many supports. We just don't. They're not there.

My mother's on the younger side of the people on the block. It ranges from forty to seventy, so she's fifty-five. We're trying to fight against what's going on across the street, but that's really not working too well. As far as the welfare mothers—it's like eight of them in one house with all their kids—I don't know what kind of house it is. It's got about four bedrooms. It's a city house, I'm sure of that at least. Because we have a politician that lives on the street, and she knows exactly what type of house it is and what they're doing. It's maybe homeless women with children. They get their checks, and they can build up their money and then go out and live in a house or something like that. But they're all together, and there's a lot of them. And this certain type of behavior that comes with them, that is just ridiculous. As a block, we're concerned about the kids, basically. 'Cause the kids are just not being paid any attention at all.

My neighborhood is definitely drug-ridden. Violence too. I haven't exactly seen anyone get shot, but I always seem to get there just after something's happened. Last summer we just had three boys murdered on the corner of the block that I live on. They were all drug dealers. There was just some sort of fight over drug turf or whatever. Robbery—the pipers stole the flowerpot cemented onto our porch off the porch. I don't understand it, but they did it. Any car that doesn't move, in two or three days it's gone. We've had four cars stolen, and that's ridiculous. And if they can't steal the car, they'll lift the hood up and take the battery. Something. They steal everything. Mugging. Not too many fights break out. It's either you get shot or something gets stolen. That's basically it.

My mother has fortified herself into our house. She's got iron doors in the front and the back. Steel windows. Bars on the windows. Our house looks like a little prison. But she calls this her security. She doesn't want to get up and move. Even though she can, she doesn't want to do it. She wants to stay in her community. She wants to try to fight back, just like all the rest of the neighbors. They want to fight back. They want to protect what's theirs. I mean, it's going to be a tough fight. It doesn't look like they're winning at this point, but they don't want to get up and leave what's theirs.

It used to be more peaceful. The situation with the welfare house [Section 8] started about three years ago. And every year we have a different selection of women. They only stay there for a year, and then it's new people who come in. Somebody gives them a certain amount of time to build themselves up, and then they're out. The block isn't all that great, but that just adds to it. Other than that, we have the drugs—that's just all in our neighborhood.

My situation was kind of strict. My mom and my dad kept me in the house. I did not have any friends on my block. So my situation was very severe. In some aspects I might be seen as abnormal because I wasn't allowed to play outside. The only playtime I had was in school, in the playground or whatever. So they really did control who were my friends. My friends were the people who were in that private school. I had white friends, Asian friends, I had everybody. It just wasn't all black friends. People would come off of neighboring streets like Culver Street to ask me, "Can I play?" 'Cause my whole family lives in the same area. So my cousins or their friends would come over— "Can Yvette come outside?" "No." I'd stay in the house. So I was bred to be a nerd, I guess. Until the time when my aunt started taking care of me, being my baby-sitter. Then I had a little more freedom. But the rule was I couldn't go off the porch there. I could go outside, but I couldn't go off the porch. I could sit on the steps or something. At my own house I stayed in the house. This is the aunt where her children threatened to beat me up. So she watched me for a while, and they got jealous. So then I had to leave.

But I wasn't completely sheltered. I was thrown out of this sheltering environment when I went to high school. I went to Grant High School for Engineering and Science—a public magnet school. And that was different for me. The school had about six, seven hundred kids in it. Not really big compared to most public schools. It was about 60 percent black. I was used to maybe two hundred people in the whole school—that's what my other school was. And I was seen as a nerd there, too. When people would try to fight me, I did not know what to do, because I was so sheltered I just never had that situation, so I talked my way out of it most of the time. Just talking like, "This is not worth fighting over. This is something stupid." Just talk your way out of it. Kids would leave me alone because they would see I really had no interest in fighting over something that I thought was stupid. If they had hit me, I would've hit back of course 'cause you're taught to hit back, but I just never had that situation.

My mother told me, somebody tries to get in your way, fight back, get them out of your way. You have a goal, you've got to get there. She tells me that to this day, 'cause I'm like, "Oh my God, college is so hard. I can't deal with the stress." She's like, "You have a goal. Get to it." The good thing about it, with my parents I had an open line of communication. And I don't think a lot of people have that. And we talked about everything—my mom, my dad, and me. As a family, we talked about it. And that really helped me. It really did. Instead of just keeping it to myself or fighting just to get over, I talked it over with my parents and they helped me to have some direction as to what to do in that situation. Like, people don't like me, they think I'm a nerd, they think I'm trying to be snotty. I don't know, I just talked to them about it.

I had a small group of friends. Not everybody was a nerd. Not everybody was getting A's. But I did find a crowd. I think everyone finds the niche. Freshman year is always the worst because you don't know where you belong, if you belong. And my character is I'm never going to try to change myself to be what somebody else wants, so I didn't have a niche. I kind of made a niche for myself. And my small group of friends were just like me. That's it. I mean, everyone knew of me in the class, but I only had about seven or eight friends who I can really call friends. Most of them were from West Philly, and they had the same struggles as I did, so we had some common ground right there. And they were supportive to me as well because we talk about our situations and stuff. And if ever I got in a situation at school and they were there, they'd help me out.

I had problems, but I talked all of it out. I'm a real communication person. That's just something that was instilled in me. Your parents are there as support. The only way they can help you is if they know what's going on. If you keep it to yourself, then they can't help you. And that's another way I think that I'm blessed, because if I didn't have parents, that would be just one less support that I would have.

Yvette's account underscores the difficulties that the decent family encounters when trying to live among so many people who are committed to the street, not only neighbors but relatives as well. Increasingly, teenage girls, most often those associated with the street, become involved in group and individual fights. In many ways their fights are not unlike those of the boys. Their goal is often the same—to gain respect, to be recognized as capable of setting or maintaining a certain standard. They frequently try to achieve this end in ways that have been widely associated with young men, including posturing, abusive language, and the ready use of violence to settle disputes, but the issues for the girls are usually different. Although conflicts over turf and status exist among the girls, the majority of the disputes seem rooted in assessments of beauty (which girl in a group is "the cutest"), competition over boyfriends, and attempts to regulate other people's knowledge and opinions of a girl's behavior or that of someone close to her, including friends, siblings, and parents. Jealousy, as was shown in the case of Yvette, is often an issue, because it is extremely difficult for some young people existing in a sea of deprivation to "suffer" the advancement of someone assumed to be their social equal. Among many impoverished young people, any indication of an improvement in the person's status can be taken as a threat and cause for alarm, thus provoking a struggle at least to "stay even."

In this context a major cause of conflicts among girls is "he say, she say," particularly those involving issues of personal attribution, or name-calling. This practice begins in the early school years and continues through high school. It occurs when people, especially girls, talk publicly about others, thus putting their "business in the streets." Usually, one girl will say something derogatory about another in the group, most often in public, "behind her back." The remark will get back to the girl; she may retaliate, or her friends may feel required to "take up for" her. In essence, this is a form of group gossiping in which individuals are negatively assessed and evaluated. As with much gossip, the things said may or may not be true, but the point is that such imputations can cast aspersions on a person's good name. The accused is required to defend herself against the slander, a process that can result in arguments and fights, often over little of real substance. Here again one sees the issue of low self-esteem, which encourages youngsters to be highly sensitive to slights and to be vulnerable to feeling easily "dissed."

Because the street element so dominates the public spaces, even the decent people must show they are ready to meet the street ethic in order to survive unmolested. As a result, most decent parents encourage their children to hit back if challenged, particularly if the child is backed into a corner. It is difficult not to fight back, because status and esteem are often at issue. This makes the emphasis in Marge's family on talking one's way out of confrontations ("stuff") or walking away rather exceptional, but many young people try such a tack and engage in fighting only as a last resort. As one thirteen-year-old girl in a detention center for youths who have committed violent acts told me, "To get people to leave you alone, you gotta fight. Talking don't always get you out of stuff." In the case of Yvette, though her mother encouraged her to defend herself, sensibly, she was reluctant to fight.

Since their efforts to achieve upward mobility tend to be viewed as "disrespecting" their own community, decent people, particularly children, must often struggle to advance themselves. In fact, as Yvette's account shows, street-oriented people can be said at times to mount a policing effort to keep their decent counterparts from "selling out" or "acting white," that is, from leaving the community for one of higher socioeconomic status. This retaliation, which can sometimes be violent, against the upwardly mobile points to the deep alienation present in parts of the inner-city community. Many residents therefore work to maintain the status quo, and so the individual who tries to excel usually has a great deal to overcome.

The lengths to which Yvette's parents went to prevent her exposure to the street clearly show this dynamic at work. The account represents a general feeling among decent inner-city residents that the street is both dangerous and seductive—one misstep can cause a fatal fall—and so children, particularly those at an impressionable age, need to sheltered from it. However, as the story of Tyree in the next chapter will suggest, contact and involvement with the street is almost unavoidable, especially for young men.

# TWO

# Campaigning for Respect

I N the inner-city environment respect on the street may be viewed as a form of social capital that is very valuable, especially when various other forms of capital have been denied or are unavailable. Not only is it protective; it often forms the core of the person's self esteem, particularly when alternative avenues of self-expression are closed or sensed to be. As the problems of the inner city have become ever more acute, as the public authorities have seemingly abdicated their responsibilities, many of those residing in such communities feel that they are on their own, that especially in matters of personal defense, they must assume the primary responsibility. The criminal justice system is widely perceived as beset with a double standard: one for blacks and one for whites, resulting in a profound distrust in this institution. In the most socially isolated pockets of the inner city, this situation has given rise to a kind of people's law based on a peculiar form of social exchange that is perhaps best understood as a perversion of the Golden Rule, whose by-product in this case is respect and whose caveat is vengeance, or payback. Given its value and its practical implications, respect is fought for and held and challenged as much as honor was in the age of chivalry. Respect becomes critical for staying out of harm's way. In public the person whose very appearance—including his or her clothing, demeanor, and way of moving, as well as "the crowd" he or she runs with, or family reputation—deters transgressions feels that he or she possesses, and may be considered by others to possess, a measure of respect. Much of the code has to do with achieving and holding respect. And children learn its rules early.

## THE SOCIAL SHUFFLE

Children from even the most decent homes must come to terms with the various influences of the street. Indeed, as children grow and their parents' control wanes, they go through a social shuffling process that can affirm—or test or undermine—much of the socialization they have received at home. In other words, the street serves as a mediating influence under which children may come to reconsider and rearrange their personal orientations. This is a time of status passage,[1] a formative stage for social identity, as children sort out their ways of being. It is a critical period of flux, and a child can go either way—decent or street. For children from decent homes, the immediate and present reality of the street situation can overcome the compunctions against tough behavior that their parents taught them; as children learn to deal with their social environment, they may thus quickly put aside the lessons of the home. The child is confronted with the local hierarchy based on toughness and the premium placed on being a good fighter. As a means of survival, one often learns the value of having a "name," a reputation for being willing and able to fight. To build such a reputation is to gain respect among peers. And a physically talented child who starts down this track may find him- or herself increasingly committed to an orientation that can lead to trouble. Of course, a talented child from either a decent or a street-oriented family may discover ways of gaining respect without resorting unduly to aggressive and violent responses—becoming an athlete or, occasionally, a good student. Some parents encourage their children to become involved in dance, camp, Little League, and other activities to support a positive orientation. The important point here is that the kind of home a child comes from influences but does not always determine the way the child will ultimately turn out. The neighborhood and the surrounding environmental influences, including available social and economic opportunities and how the child adapts to this environment, are key.

Typically, in the inner-city poor neighborhood, by the age of ten, children from decent and street-oriented families alike are mingling on the neighborhood streets and figuring out their identities. Here they try out roles and scripts in a process that challenges their talents and prior socialization and may involve more than a little luck, good or bad. In this volatile environment, they learn to watch their backs and to anticipate and negotiate those situations that might lead to troubles with others. The outcomes of these cumulative interactions with the street ultimately determine every child's life chances.

Herein lies the real meaning of the many fights and altercations that "hide" behind the ostensible, as a rule seemingly petty, precipitating causes, such as the competitions over girlfriends and boyfriends and the "he say, she say" conflicts of personal attribution, including "signifying" and other name-calling games. Adolescents everywhere are insecure and trying to establish their identities. Young people from the middle and upper classes, however, usually have a wider variety of ways to express the fact that they consider themselves worthwhile. The negotiations they engage in may also include aggression, but they tend to be more verbal in a way unlike those of more limited resources. In poor inner-city neighborhoods, verbal prowess is important for establishing identity, but physicality is a fairly common way of asserting oneself.[2] Physical assertiveness is also unambiguous. If you punch someone out, if you succeed in keeping someone from walking down your block, "you did it." It is a fait accompli, and the evidence that you prevailed is there for all to see.

During this campaign for respect, through these various conflicts, the connections between actually being respected and the need for being in physical control of at least a portion of one's environment become internalized, and the germ of the code of the street emerges. As children mature and obtain an increasingly more sophisticated understanding of the code, it becomes part of their working conception of the world, so that by the time they reach adulthood, it has emerged as an important element of public social order. The rules of physical engagement and their personal implications become crystallized. Children learn the conditions under which violence is appropriate, and they also learn how the code defines their relationship to their peers. They thus grow to appreciate the give-and-take of life in public, the process of negotiation, as well as its implications for social identity. And to a degree they learn to resolve disputes mainly through physical contests that settle—at least for the time being—the question of who is the toughest and who will take, or tolerate, what from whom under what circumstances. In effect, they learn the social order of their local peer groups; this order, always open to change, is one of the primary reasons the youths take such a strong interest in the fight.

This reality of inner-city life is absorbed largely on the streets. There children gain, in the words of the street, valued "street knowledge." At an early age, often even before they start school and without much adult supervision, children from street-oriented families gravitate to the streets, where they must be ready to "hang," to socialize competitively with peers. These children have a great deal of latitude and are allowed to rip and run up and down the streets. They often come home from school, put their books down, and go right back out the door. On school nights many eight- and nine-year-olds remain out until nine or ten o'clock (teenagers may come home whenever they want to). On the streets they play in groups that often become the source of their primary social bonds.

In the street, through their play, children pour their individual life experiences into a common knowledge pool, mixing, negating, affirming, confirming, and elaborating on what they have observed in the home and matching their skills against those of others. They also learn to fight; in particular, they learn the social meaning of fighting. In these circumstances even small children test one another, pushing and shoving others, and they seem ready to hit other children over matters not to their liking. In turn, they are readily hit by other children, and the child who is toughest prevails. Furthermore, as the violent resolution of disputes—the hitting and cursing—gains social reinforcement, the child is more completely initiated into a world that provides a strong rationale for physically campaigning for self-respect.

In a critical sense, violent behavior is determined by specific situations, thus giving importance to the various ways individuals define and interpret such situations, which become so many public trials. The individual builds patterns as outcomes are repeated over time. Behaviors, violent or civil, that work for a young person and are reinforced by peers will likely be repeated, particularly as the child begins to build a "name," or a reputation for toughness.

Moreover, younger children refine their understanding of the code by observing the disputes of older children, which are often resolved through cursing and abusive talk, and sometimes through outright aggression or violence. They see that one child succumbs to the greater physical and mental abilities of the other. These younger children are also alert and attentive witnesses to the occasional verbal and physical fights of adults; later, they will compare notes among themselves and share their own interpretations of the event. Almost always the victor is the person who physically won the altercation, and this person often enjoys the esteem and respect of onlookers. These experiences reinforce the lessons many children have learned at home: might makes right; toughness is a virtue, humility is not. The social meaning of fighting becomes clarified as these children come to appreciate the real consequences of winning and losing. And the child's understanding of the code becomes more refined but also an increasingly important part of his or her working conception of the world.

The street-oriented adults with whom children come in contact at home and on the street—including mothers, fathers, brothers, sisters, boyfriends, cousins, neighbors, and friends—help shape and reinforce this understanding by verbalizing the messages these children are getting through public experience: "Watch your back." "Protect yourself." "Don't punk out." "Respect yourself." "If someone disses you, you got to straighten them out." Many parents actually impose sanctions if a child is not sufficiently aggressive. For example, if a child loses a fight and comes home upset, the parent might respond, "Don't you come in here crying that somebody beat you up; you better get back out there and whup his ass. I didn't raise no punks! If you don't whup his ass, I'll whup yo' ass when you come home." Thus the child gains reinforcement for being tough and showing nerve.

While fighting, some children cry, as though they are doing something they are at best ambivalent about. The fight may go against their wishes, yet they may feel constrained to fight or face the consequences—not just from peers but also from caretakers or parents, who may administer another beating if they back down. Some adults recall receiving such lessons from their own parents and justify repeating them to their children as a way to toughen them up. Appearing capable of taking care of oneself as a form of self-defense is a dominant theme among both street-oriented and decent adults who worry about the safety of their children. But taking care of oneself does not always involve physical fighting; at times it can involve getting "out of stuff" by outwitting adversaries, a tactic often encouraged by decent parents of the inner city. Marge, the hardworking decent woman and mother of five children whom we met in the preceding chapter, tells this story:

> My son that's bad now—his name is Curtis. And he was going to Linden Junior High School, and he was in the eighth grade. And my son Terry was in the same grade. Terry's a year younger, but Curtis had gotten put back in the second grade. They had never had a fight.
>
> So he [Curtis] called me at work one day and told me that somebody was bothering him, and he was afraid. He was thirteen or fourteen at the time. He said he was also afraid to tell the teacher because if he told the teacher, they were gonna pick on him more. And he didn't have any men in his life at the time— my husband was not his father, so that was another issue. So I said to him, "What are you gonna do? Are you gonna leave school?" He said he was afraid to leave school because if he left school, they would still pick on him. So I said to him, "Curtis, I'll tell you what you do. I'm gonna get off work early. What I want you to do, I want you to talk as bad as you can talk and don't act afraid. They don't know me. None of your friends in

your classroom know me." I said, "I want you to come out and talk as bad as you can talk, but don't hit anybody. And then walk away." I said, "If a fight breaks out, then I'll come and break it up." And that's what he did, and they left him alone. Isn't that something? See, he had to show nerve; it's very important for boys. It's easier for girls. The boys in the neighborhood—if you don't do some of the things they do, or even with the clothes, if you don't have nice things—at that time it was Jordache jeans and Sergio—if you don't have some of those things, people will pick on you and that type of thing.

Many decent parents encourage their children to stand up to those who might be aggressive toward them, but they also encourage their children to avoid trouble. Given their superior resources and their connections to the wider society, including schools, churches, and other institutions, the decent parents have the ability to see themselves beyond the immediate neighborhood; they tend to have more ways "to be somebody" than the typical street-oriented person. The difference in outlook has to do mainly with a difference in social class. Hence they tend to encourage their children to avoid conflict by talking or by turning and walking away. But, as was indicated above, this is not always possible, and as a last resort such children are usually taught to stand their ground.

## SELF-IMAGE BASED ON "JUICE"

By the time they are teenagers, most young people have internalized the code of the street, or at least learned to comport themselves in accordance with its rules. As we saw above, the code revolves around the presentation of self. Its basic requirement is the display of a certain predisposition to violence. A person's public bearing must send the unmistakable, if sometimes subtle, message that one is capable of violence, and possibly mayhem, when the situation requires it, that one can take care of oneself. The nature of this communication is determined largely by the demands of the circumstances but can involve facial expressions, gait, and direct talk—all geared mainly to deterring aggression. Physical appearance, including clothes, jewelry, and grooming, also plays an important part in how a person is viewed; to be respected, it is vital to have the right look.

Even so, there are no guarantees against challenges, because there are always people around looking for a fight in order to increase their share of respect—or "juice," as it is sometimes called on the street. Moreover, if a person is assaulted, it is essential in the eyes of his "running buddies" as well as his opponent for him to avenge himself. Otherwise he risks being "tried" (challenged) or "rolled on" (physically assaulted) by any number of others. Indeed, if he is not careful, he can lose the respect of his running buddies, thus perhaps encouraging one of them to try him. This is a critical consideration, for without running buddies or "homies" who can be depended on to watch his back in a "jam," the person is vulnerable to being rolled on by still others. Part of what protects a person is both how many people can be counted on to avenge his honor if he is rolled on in a fight and who these defenders are—that is, what their status on the street is. Some of the best-protected people in the environment are members not only of tough street-corner groups but also of families and extended families of cousins, uncles, fathers, and brothers who are known to be down with the street. Their family members, especially when the family's reputation is secure, "can go anywhere, and won't nobody bother them." Generally, to maintain his honor, the young man must show that he himself, as an individual, is not someone to be "messed with" or dissed. To show this, he may "act crazy"—that is, have the reputation for being quick-tempered. In general, though, a person must "keep himself straight" by managing his position of respect among others, including his homies; fundamentally, this task involves managing his self-image, which is shaped by what he thinks others are thinking of him in relation to his peers.[3]

Objects play an important and complicated role in establishing self-image. Jackets, sneakers, gold jewelry, even expensive firearms, reflect not just taste, which tends to be tightly regulated among adolescents of all social classes, but also a willingness to possess things that may require defending. A boy wearing a fashionable, expensive jacket, for example, is vulnerable to attack by another who covets the

jacket and either can't afford to buy one or wants the added satisfaction of depriving someone else of his. However, if a boy forgoes the
desirable jacket and wears one that isn't hip, he runs the risk of being
teased or even assaulted as an unworthy person. A youth with a
decency orientation describes the situation this way:

> Here go another thing. If you outside, right, and your mom's
> on welfare and she on crack, the persons you trying to be with
> dress [in] like purple sweatpants and white sneaks, but it's all
> decent, right, and you got on some bummy jeans and a pair of
> dull sneaks, they won't—some of the people out there selling
> drugs won't let you hang with them unless you dress like [in]
> purple sweatpants and decent sneaks every day . . .
>
> They tease 'em. First they'll tease 'em and then they'll try to
> say they stink, like they smell like pig or something like that,
> and then they'll be like, "Get out of here. Get out. We don't
> want you near us. You stink. You dirty." All that stuff. And I
> don't think that's right. If he's young, it ain't his fault or her
> fault that she dressin' like that. It's her mother and her dad's
> fault.

To be allowed to hang with certain prestigious crowds, a boy must
wear a different set of expensive clothes every day. Not to do so might
make him appear socially deficient. So he may come to covet such
items—especially when he spots easy prey wearing them. The youth
continues,

> You can even get hurt off your own clothes. Like, say I'm
> walkin' down the street and somebody try to take my hat from
> me and I won't let 'em take it and they got a gun. You can get
> killed over one little simple hat. Or if I got a gold ring and a
> gold necklace on and they see me one dark night on a dark street,
> and they stick me up and I won't let 'em, and they shoot me.
> I'm dead and they hid me. I'm dead and won't nobody ever know
> [who did it].

In acquiring valued things, therefore, an individual shores up his
or her identity—but since it is an identity based on having something,

it is highly precarious. This very precariousness gives a heightened sense of urgency to staying even with peers, with whom the person is actually competing. Young men and women who can command respect through their presentation of self—by allowing their possessions and body language to speak for them—may not have to campaign for regard but may, rather, gain it by the force of their manner. Those who are unable to command respect in this way must actively campaign for it.[4]

One way to campaign for status is to take the possessions of others. Seemingly ordinary objects can become trophies with symbolic value that far exceeds their monetary worth. Possessing the trophy can symbolize the ability to violate somebody—to "get in his face," to dis him—and thus to enhance one's own worth by stealing someone else's. The trophy does not have to be something material. It can be another person's sense of honor, snatched away with a derogatory remark. It can be the outcome of a fight. It can be the imposition of a certain standard, such as a girl getting herself recognized as the most beautiful. Material things, however, fit easily into the pattern: sneakers, a pistol, even somebody else's girlfriend can become a trophy. When a person can take something from another and then flaunt it, he gains a certain regard by being the owner, or the controller, of that thing. But this display of ownership can then provoke a challenge from other people. This game of who controls what is thus constantly being played out on inner-city streets, and the trophy—extrinsic or intrinsic, tangible or intangible—identifies the current winner.

In this often violent give-and-take, raising oneself up largely depends on putting someone else down. The level of jealousy and envy underscores the alienation that permeates the inner city. There is a general sense that very little respect is to be had, and therefore everyone competes to get what affirmation he can from what is available. The resulting craving for respect gives people thin skins and short fuses. Shows of deference by others can be highly soothing, contributing to a sense of security, comfort, self-confidence, and self-respect. Unanswered transgressions diminish these feelings and are believed to encourage further transgressions. Constant vigilance is therefore required against even giving the impression that transgressions will be tolerated. Among young people, whose sense of self-esteem is particularly vulnerable, there is an especially heightened concern about being disrespected. Many inner-city young men in particular crave respect to such a degree that they will risk their lives to attain and maintain it.

As was noted above, the issue of respect is thus closely tied to whether a person has an inclination to be violent, even as a victim. In the wider society, particularly among the middle class, people may not feel required to retaliate physically after an attack, although they are well aware that they have been degraded or taken advantage of. They may feel a great need to defend themselves *during* an attack, or to behave in a way that deters aggression, but they are much more likely than street-oriented people to feel that they can walk away from a possible altercation with their self-esteem intact. Some people may even have the strength of character to flee without thinking that their self-respect will be diminished.

In impoverished inner-city black communities, however, particularly among young males and perhaps increasingly among females, such flight would be extremely difficult. To run away would likely leave one's self-esteem in tatters, while inviting further disrespect. Therefore, people often feel constrained not only to stand up and at least attempt to resist during an assault but also to "pay back"—to seek revenge—after a successful assault on their person. Revenge may include going to get a weapon or even getting relatives and friends involved. Their very identity, their self-respect, and their honor are often intricately tied up with the way they perform on the streets during and after such encounters. And it is this identity, including a credible reputation for payback, or vengeance, that is strongly believed to deter future assaults.

## THE STAGING AREA

In Philadelphia as in other urban areas, young people especially become associated with the parts of the city, including streets and blocks, from which they come, gaining reputations based on the "character" of such areas. People are likely to assume that a person who comes from a "bad" area is bad.[5] The reputation of the neighborhood affects the reputation of the school, particularly the high school, that the youth attends. The school's reputation is shaped by its history, including the records of its sports teams, the achievements of its students, the levels of violence and of entrenched and persistent poverty associated with the area, and the number of staging areas in and around it.

Staging areas are hangouts where a wide mix of people gather for various reasons. It is here that campaigns for respect are most often waged. Three types of staging areas can be distinguished. One is quite local, revolving around neighborhood establishments such as carry-outs, liquor stores, and bars. The staging area might be inside, on a street corner outside, or at a house party with little or no adult supervision, where alcohol and drugs are available. The second type is a business strip whose stores cater to street-oriented working-class and poor people. Buzzing with activity, it draws people from a larger area. The third type—multiplex theaters, sporting events, and concerts—brings together large crowds from throughout the city. Such areas are the most volatile, especially at places such as roller-skating rinks or dances where there is music, alcohol, drugs, and rough crowds of young people inclined to "act out" what they have seen or heard others do.

People from other neighborhoods who come to a staging area and present themselves are said to be "representing" both who they are and the "world" or " 'hood" from which they hail. To represent is to place one's area of the city on the line, to say to outsiders, "Hey, this is what's to me [what I am made of] and my neighborhood," compared with other neighborhoods of the city. For the boldest young people, it is to put oneself on the line, in effect, to put a chip on one's shoulder and dare others to knock it off. It is to wage a campaign for respect, but with the added elements of dare and challenge. There are often enough young people in the staging area to provide the critical mass of negative energy necessary to spark violence, not just against people like themselves but also against others present in the staging area, creating a flashpoint for violence. At sporting events (where a school's prestige can be on the line) and at other public events like movies at the multiplex, some people are looking for a fight, making the place something of a tinderbox.

In representing, material goods play an important and complicated role in establishing self-image. Youths typically place a high premium on eyewear, leather jackets, expensive sneakers, and other items that take on significance as status symbols. An impoverished inner-city youth who can acquire these material things is able to feel big and impress others, but these others may then attempt to relieve him of his property in order to feel big themselves and impress still others. The wise youths of the neighborhood understand that it is better not to opt for the more expensive items, because they realize that by doing so they make themselves into targets for theft and robbery. But for those who go for bad the staging area is a place to show off, to represent, even to dare someone to mess with you. Just visiting the staging area can be quite satisfying, and risky. The person goes to the "block" or the staging area to see what is the latest trend, what is happening, who is doing what with whom, or who did what to whom, and when.

But the staging area is also a densely populated place where young people hang out and look to meet members of the opposite sex. Here young men and women out to be "with it" or "hip" smoke cigarettes or drink "forties" or other alcoholic beverages, or perhaps they are there to get high on "blunts" (drug-laced cigars). As people represent, their demeanor may serve as a kind of dare. Young men may taunt others by joking with them, saying directly, "Now, start something!" as though they are ready for anything. At an event with large crowds from all around the city, heterogeneous groups vie for social position. People can become touchy, and a fight can start over seemingly minor incidents, but what happens is anything but minor, because an injury or death may result, rearranging the social order of the group and setting the stage for payback-inspired feuds. With so much at stake a man, or a woman, can easily feel disrespected by another who looks at him for "too long" or simply by being cut off in the concession line. Such a "cut," which might also be viewed as an advance at someone's girl- or boyfriend, may be taken as a "statement." Challenging the statement creates a "beef," and a confrontation can erupt. As the situation deteriorates, it may be very difficult for either party to back down, particularly if members of an audience are present who have, or are understood to have, a significant social investment in who and what each participant pretends to be.

The fight over the beef can begin within the confines of the multiplex or athletic event, first with words that can quickly escalate into shouting, name-calling, or fisticuffs. A peace officer or security guard is usually there, or is sent for, to break up the altercation. Bystanders may also try to break it up, but this is becoming increasingly rare, as people assume that a fight in a public place is likely to erupt into warfare with guns or knives; a stranger trying to intervene may be risking his or her life, and most people will not do so unless they are very sure of themselves or have a stake in the outcome.

If violence occurs, matters are not always settled on the spot. If one person gets the better of the other, there often must be a payback. Everybody knows this, and certain people may wait. Mainly for protection, young people who attend such events may carry "equalizers" or "shit"—firearms or other weapons—but because of security, only the boldest will try to enter the event armed. Most people will leave their shit in the trunk of the car, or hidden in accessible bushes or a trash can, to be retrieved if the need arises. A young man with a publicly known beef will feel there is a chance that he will have to go get his shit. For this to happen, the young man's life does not always have to be in danger; pride, how he feels about his homies, low feelings, or having gotten the bad end of an altercation may be enough for him to prepare to settle things or to try to avenge the offense. So after the security guard or others have stopped the fight, the participants may want to take it outside, where their shit is, and where there is a lot less security. While the staging areas of the city are often the places where beefs spontaneously develop and fights to settle them occur, the code itself germinates, emerges, and grows on the streets, in the alleys, and on the playgrounds of the inner-city neighborhood, where in the interests of social survival small children begin early in life their campaign for respect.[6]

## TYREE'S STORY*

Tyree is a young black man of fifteen, a high school student, and his story illustrates the intricacy of the rules of the code. Until recently, he lived in a poor section of South Philadelphia with his mother, Rose, a nurse's aide at a local hospital. Then their house burned down, and they lost much of what they owned. Tyree never knew his father, but his mother has had a number of boyfriends who have served as a male presence in his life. These men have come and gone, leaving a bit of themselves here and there. He has known Richard, a man who worked as a security guard; Reece, a parking lot attendant who sold drugs on the side; and Mike, who worked as a janitor at the hospital. Mike continues to come around, and at this point he is Tyree's mom's "main squeeze," the man with whom she keeps company the most. Tyree likes Mike the best. Mike has taken Tyree to Eagles games in the fall and Seventy-sixers games in the winter. Steady and decent, Mike has been most like a real father to Tyree.

After the fire Tyree and Rose moved in with his grandmother, who lives in Southwest Philadelphia, one of the most distressed neighborhoods in the city. Along Fifty-eighth in Southwest, a local staging area, small groups of teenage boys hang out, talking, milling, and passing the time. On the side of a dilapidated building is a graffiti memorial reading, "Barry, we love you, RIP." Particularly at night, prostitutes hustle their wares on the corners. A drug dealer hangs near the pay telephone, standing there as though this is his corner, which for all intents and purposes it is. Public, open-air drug marketing goes on here—in broad daylight or at night. Buyers, some with out-of-town license plates, stop their cars, seeming not to care who might be looking on. Some are white, others are black, but they have one thing in mind—to "cop" their drugs and go on about their business.

Drug dealing is big business here. The trade is carried out in public, but also in the homes of certain proprietors, who charge dealers

---

*This account of "Tyree's Story" is based on an extended ethnographic interview. It is dramatized in places to represent vividly the intricacies of the code of the street.

to sell in the house and rent rooms to whores or johns who want to get "tightened up." There are also crack houses, where people simply go to buy or smoke their drugs. The neighbors are aware of this situation, but they are often demoralized, feeling there is little they can do about it. They sometimes call the police, but the police require proof that the place is what the neighbors know it to be. But such proof is not easy for the police to gather. It is sometimes easier, though frustrating, for the residents simply to "see but don't see," trying their best to ignore what is much more than a nuisance.

This is the neighborhood Tyree has moved into, and he has been here only a few days. His major concern at this point in his young life is "to get cool" with the boys who run the neighborhood. He refers to these boys as "bols." He refuses to call them boys. Part of this may have to do with the fact that for so long the term "boy" was so demeaning that young black men replaced the term with one considered to be "cool" from the standpoint of the code. At any rate, Tyree says "bols," spelling it "b-o-l-s" and pronouncing it "bulls." A particular meaning of the term is "friend." On the streets of his new neighborhood, Tyree's biggest problem now is to get cool with these bols.

What does that entail? Here, as in almost any working-class to impoverished inner-city neighborhood, the bols are known to run the neighborhood. Tyree understands what the deal is. He used to run with the bols from his old neighborhood, where he himself was in charge, where he had established himself as a main bol of the neighborhood. The task before him now is to get to know the new bols—but also to allow them to get to know him. They must be able to take his "measure" up close, to see what he will or will not stand in his dealings with others, how much nerve and heart he possesses, whether he will defend what he claims is his. Tyree has a general idea of what he has to do here to survive or to have any semblance of a decent existence.

On Saturday, while his mom is at work, Tyree's grandmom quite innocently asks him to run to the store for her.

"Yeah, Grandmom. What you want?"

"I need a loaf of bread and a quart of milk."

Tyree dutifully takes the money and heads out the door. It is two o'clock on a nice, sunny afternoon. He leaves the house and begins to walk up the street toward the store. He can't help being somewhat tense, given his familiarity with the code of the street. He knows that eventually he will encounter the bols. And sure enough, after about five minutes, he spies about twenty bols walking up the street toward him. He sees them, and they see him. Their eyes meet. It is too late to turn back, for that would mean he would lose face, that he had acted scared, and his sense of manhood will not allow him to do that. He must face this situation.

As he approaches the bols, he feels himself tensing up even more, but he continues. As they come face-to-face, they stop and begin to talk. He knows they want to know what his business is. What is he doing here? Where does he come from? What gang is he from? Even before the questions are fully asked, Tyree tries to respond, "Well, uh, my grandmom, uh . . ." But the bols do not really want an answer. They want to roll on him (beat him up). Before he realizes it, the bols begin to punch him out, allowing most of the group to "get a piece." One boy punches—then another and another.

It is important to understand that these are almost ritual punches, with "good licks" and some kicking, pushing, and slapping "upside the head." Soon Tyree loses his balance and falls to the ground. "[This] really scared me," he said. Falling in such a fight is very risky, for then the worst can happen: someone "could really get messed up." There is an important distinction between rolling on someone and messing someone up. To roll is simply to take advantage of someone, to act as the aggressor in the fight. To mess someone up is actually to hurt him physically to the point where blood is spilled and he might have to go to the hospital. In this instance, the bols are not out to mess Tyree up.

The bols leave Tyree lying on the ground in a fetal position. As they move away, they smirk and say things like, "Who do he think he is?" and "We showed the motherfucker, think he gon' come up in here bigger than shit!" Tyree is bruised and hurt, but his pride is hurt much more than his body. For Tyree is a man, and it is extremely important not to let people do this to you. But there was really little that he could do to prevent this. He has been rolled on and utterly dissed. He is very angry, but also sad and dejected. He knows that they could have seriously hurt him. They wanted to put something on his mind, to show him whose turf this is. And Tyree understands the profound meaning of this incident, for he understands the code and has himself lived by it.

Tyree picks himself up and, without completing his errand, walks back to his grandmom's house with his head down. He is angry, for he has been violated. When he arrives at his grandmom's house, she says, "Where you been? Where are the groceries?" He mumbles a reply and goes to sit on the living room stairs and peer out the window. "What's wrong, boy?" she asks.

"Aw, nothin'," he says.

"Wha—you been fightin'?" she presses.

With this, he mumbles, "I met some bols."

"You hurt!? I'll call the police!" she exclaims.

"Naw, don't call the police."

"But you hurt."

"Don't call no police, I'll take care of it myself," he pleads.

This is something of a revelation to his grandmom. She hadn't known that the young men on the streets were this way, because she has never had Tyree with her for so long. She's an elderly woman, and old people are sometimes deferred to and protected by the same bols who violated Tyree. This is part of the code. She had never been aware that Tyree was so vulnerable, so she now worries about what to do.

Tyree goes to the bathroom to clean himself up. He showers and then sits and mopes around the house. He knows his grandmom still needs her groceries, and pretty soon, without saying a word, he leaves for the store. As he travels the distance to the store, he is somewhat edgy, circumspect, trying to watch his back, peeping around the corners and hoping to see any of the bols *before* they see him. He makes it up the two blocks to the store, walks in, and looks around. And over by the ice cream freezer he spies one of the bols who rolled on him earlier. The bol sees him. What does Tyree do now? Full of nerve, he rushes over to the bol and punches him in the face. Tyree gets in a couple of licks before the boy's nose begins to bleed, which was really all Tyree wanted to do; he wanted to pay him back, to let him know he has been punched and violated back. At that point the bol looks at Tyree and acknowledges aloud, "You got me that time, but I'll be back!"

Tyree looks in the bol's eyes and says, "Yeah, you and yo' mama." And with that he exits the store, without getting what he came for. He walks away. Tyree now feels good, as though he is getting his respect back.

With all the punches and hits, and particularly the public dissing he underwent at the hands of the bols, Tyree suffered a serious loss of respect. To settle scores as he did with the bol at the store is to begin to get his respect back. He retrieves self-esteem at the expense of another, in this case, the bol he publicly punched out. Tyree feels so good, in fact, that he walks (with some care) on to another store—through the turf of the bols—to get his grandmom's groceries. He buys what he wants and heads home carefully, watching out for the bols. Tyree feels under some obligation to punch out every bol he sees until he can avenge himself and regain his respect.

This is the code of the street. The code is not new. It is as old as the world, going back to Roman times or the world of the shogun warriors or the early American Old South.[7] And it can be observed in working-class Scotch-Irish or Italian or Hispanic communities. But profound economic dislocation and the simultaneous emergence of an underground economy that thrives on the "law of the jungle" implicit in the code have exacerbated conditions in many communities. Equally important, the proliferation and availability of guns have further exacerbated such conditions. Tyree could easily acquire a gun. Most of the young boys he knows from his old neighborhood know where they can get a gun without too much trouble.

Tyree arrives home with the groceries, and his grandmom is pleased. Although relieved that Tyree hasn't gotten into more trouble, she now has a new worry—how Tyree will get along with the young men of her neighborhood. She asks him more about his altercation, and he tries to assure her that he can take care of himself. But when he leaves the house, his grandmother worries, and this worry is shared by his mother. Increasingly, given the local news reports of street crime, shootings, and drugs, Tyree's mother questions her decision to move in with her own mother, although she really had little choice; the alternative would have been homelessness. Now

Tyree spends much of his energy trying to persuade his mother and grandmother not to worry him as he ventures outside in the streets. And while he tries to reassure them, he is really not very sure himself. For he knows that when he leaves the house he must watch his back.

The young men are very aware of Tyree's presence in the neighborhood; they are much more sensitive to the presence of interlopers than are the adults. (This fact is relevant to an understanding of Tyree's mother's and grandmother's ignorance of or indifference to the implications of their move into the new neighborhood.) When leaving home, Tyree steps from his house into the street and then looks up and down, trying to spot a bol before the bol spots him. His orientation is one of studied defensiveness. He wants to avoid contact with those who might be inclined to roll on him. He peeks around corners, travels through alleys, and basically does what he feels he must do—lie low.

There is pressure on Tyree to get cool with these bols, if only in the interest of safety. A few weeks later, on a Saturday afternoon, he is again walking down a street in his new neighborhood, heading to Center City to meet some friends from his old neighborhood. As he approaches the bus stop, he sees a group of bols coming up the street. They are about a block and a half away, and Tyree thus has a choice of running or staying. But something inside him—his concern about being manly, his quest to be defined as a person with nerve, heart, or simply street knowledge—makes him hesitate. They see him, and now it is too late. They know that he sees them. Now he can't run or dodge them; he must meet this situation head-on. Tyree must do what a man has to do. He knows he must deal with them, because the situation has been building for a while. He tenses up, for he feels caught in the wrong place, but he is unable to flee. He knows that if he runs today, he'll always be running. His manhood is on the line. Therefore he goes and meets the bols. But it is almost as though both parties have been expecting this day. He knew it was coming eventually. They knew it was coming, and all the while they have been keeping tabs on him, maybe even keeping score on him, particularly noting the way he rolled on the bol in the convenience store (whose name he later found out was Tiny). This is a showdown.

As they come face-to-face, Tyree says, "What's up!"

They return his greeting, "Hey!" The situation is tense. Tyree says, "Look, y'all. I can't fight no twenty bols." There is a short silence. Then he says, "Can we be bols? Can I be bols with y'all?"

Summoned by Calvin, who seems to be the leader, the group huddles. A few talk to one another, while the others remain quiet. Calvin soon emerges and says, "You gotta fight J C." J C steps forward. He is about six one, eighteen years old, and weighs about 180 pounds. Though Tyree is daunted by the prospect of fighting J C, he tries not to display any signs of fear. He has been expecting to have to fight someone, and he has been dreading this for four weeks; he just didn't know how this would work out—when it would be, whom he would fight, or whether he could trust that others would not jump in. The showdown, therefore, is something of a relief. So he doesn't hesitate. He simply and quickly agrees, saying, "All right," trying to disabuse others of the notion that he is scared.

Calvin says, "Let's go behind this building." So the group of young men go behind a building on Walton Street for what promises to be a fair fight. Tyree is only five seven and weighs about 140 pounds, but he is muscular and quick, and he knows how to hold his hands in a pose to block any shots. J C does the same, and they begin to spar, dancing around, swinging now and then. Their eyes are riveted, following each other's every move. They watch each other's hands, looking for weaknesses and trying not to show any of their own. Much is at stake here. They spar and keep their eyes on each other but also on the audience that eggs them on. J C, of course, is the favorite, but Tyree seems not to care.

They begin to fight. Tyree lands the first punch to J C's midsection, breaking the tension. J C feints and swings at Tyree with a right cross. Finally J C grabs Tyree and begins to pummel him. But Tyree hangs in there, swinging, punching, scratching, even biting. This is supposed to be a "fair fight," but the distinction soon gets blurred. J C is clearly getting the best of Tyree, and Tyree becomes increasingly angry, while feelings of humiliation loom. Yet, in addition to the nerve he showed in taking J C on, he shows just as much heart by hanging in there with the larger boy, for J C is not only larger but also quick with his hands and quite agile. What Tyree lacks in strength and ability, he makes up for in guts. And this is on display for everyone to observe.

After about twenty minutes, the fight ends, and apparently J C has won. "The bol was just too big and too fast, but I showed them that I had heart," says Tyree. He might have added that J C also had much at stake in this fight; he had a lot to lose if he had gotten whipped, particularly in front of his bols. It is also clear that J C knows he has been in a fight. He has lost a shoe, and his eye is badly bruised. Tyree's shirt collar is almost completely torn off, his arms and neck now bear deep scratches and scrapes, and his nose is bleeding. He put up a very good fight, which was impressive to all. He lost, but he lost to a worthy opponent.

Tyree has now won the respect of the bols, and he is thus allowed to be—in a limited way—a member of the group. The fight with J C has been a step in a long process that will allow him to get cool with the bols and to establish himself in the neighborhood. In the next few days and weeks, people will talk about the fight and how Tyree, though he did not win, gave a good account of himself. And since J C had such a strong reputation or "name" in the neighborhood, Tyree benefits from the encounter. So Tyree gets known around the 'hood. The bols will now greet him on the streets and not bother him, at least on certain conditions. Tyree may be carrying a box of chicken, and if a bol says, "Hey, Tyree, what's up. Gimme some of that," Tyree is obligated to share it. This is true not just for food but for virtually anything Tyree displays as his own. If he is wearing a nice jacket or a nice pair of sneaks, he must be ready to "loan" them. If he has money, he is expected to be generous with the others. And as he does so, he negotiates his place in the group. This is the code.

As he meets the demands of his new role, he gets cool with the others, establishing, maintaining, and controlling his share of respect. As the young men learn to relate to others, they learn, in effect, their place. But in an environment of such deprivation, respect is in short supply and cannot be taken for granted; trials and contests continue, day in, day out. Status in the group is continually being adjusted, and this dynamic allows bols who are cool with one another to live in relative peace.

## I GOT YO' BACK

In the process of working his way up in the group, Tyree makes friends with Malik. Malik is Tyree's age, fifteen, and is physically about the same size; they are pretty evenly matched. Both young men are marginal to the group, not yet completely established as members. Both have fought other boys but have never fought each other. This observation is significant because fighting is such an important part of residing in the neighborhood, of being a part of the neighborhood groups that dominate the public spaces. Physical prowess and ultimately respect itself are in large part the coin of the social order. Certain boys appoint themselves as defenders and protectors of their turf—of their neighborhood—against bols from other neighborhoods; in so doing, they claim the area as their domain, making it known that anyone and anything going down in the neighborhood is their business, particularly in matters involving young women.

Malik and Tyree hang together. They traverse the city together, occasionally going downtown to the Gallery, to Thirtieth Street Station, or to one of the staging areas dominated by other bols; in these other areas of the city, people might jump them without a moment's hesitation, mainly because if someone is not in his own neighborhood, there may be a virtual price on his head. This means that anyone out to make a name for himself might jump outsiders for the honor of it, or simply on "GP"—general principle. So in order to travel in peace, or to believe they are traveling in peace, Malik and Tyree often dress to look mean or cool, as though they are "not for foolishness"—not to be messed with. They try to be ready, working to impress others with the notion that they are deadly serious, "that we don't play." When they travel out of the 'hood, they charge each other with watching their backs, and by taking on these critical responsibilities, they bond and become "tight," at times "going for brothers," or "cousins."[8]

These fictive kinship relationships involve a close connection between the two boys, so close that they are ready and willing not only to watch each other's back but to take up for the other in time of need. But this is not always an easy relationship.

For instance, one day Malik and Tyree are walking down a street in the neighborhood and encounter a group of young women. In his characteristic way, Tyree begins to "rap" or "hit on" one of the young women, trying out his conversational game. As so often happens when young women are present, the boys can become downright silly, acting out in ways that at times surprise both themselves and their companions. The girls giggle and laugh at Tyree, and Malik, too, laughs at his "silly" conversation in front of the young women. Tyree's "jaws get tight"—that is, he becomes perturbed by Malik's show of disrespect.

As they leave the girls and walk about a block down the street, Tyree stops and confronts Malik. "Say, man. Why you always squarin' me off. You always dissin' me. I'm tired of yo' shit, man."

"Aw, man. I didn't do nothin'," responds Malik.

"Yes you did. You always gettin' on my case, and I'm tired of yo' shit. Put up yo' hands, man. Put up yo' hands," challenges Tyree.

"Aw, man. I don't wanta fight you, man," responds Malik.

"Naw, man. I ain't bullshittin'. Put up yo' hands," presses Tyree.

"Well, I ain't gon' fight you here, let's go behind this building," offers Malik, finally accepting Tyree's challenge.

The two young men walk behind the building they are standing next to and begin to square off. Almost on cue, the two friends put up their hands in the fighting position in an attempt to settle their differences in the man-to-man manner they know. With no audience present, they commence battle, sparring and dancing about.

Tyree and Malik have agreed to a contest that is somewhere between a fair fight and a real fight. Such fights are part of a long and honorable tradition of settling disputes between men, and this tradition has a justice that is its own result, effectively settling things for the time being. The fights are characterized by elaborate rules, including "no hitting in the face," "you got to use just your hands," and "no double-teaming." No one can tell beforehand, however, whether a fight will remain "fair" or change in the course of battle. A change can result simply from audience reaction, which serves to interpret each blow and indicate who is winning or who is beating whom. Audience reaction can sometimes tilt the scale from fair to unfair, and it can determine who wins and loses and thus who must then get even. For instance, a loud slap to the face, even if accidental and quickly followed by apologies, can alter the character of the contest. Young boys can start off joking and wind up fighting to the death, all because of a reaction to a miscalculation that pushed the contest hopelessly off-balance.

Malik and Tyree dance and spar, huffing and puffing, dodging and feinting. To the onlooker, it appears to be a game, for real blows seem hardly to be exchanged. But suddenly Malik lands a blow to Tyree's shoulder and another to his stomach, and he follows this up with this taunt: "I gotcha." Dropping his guard, Tyree acknowledges this, but then he quickly resumes his fighting stance, again putting up his hands. They go at it again, punching, dancing, dodging. Tyree lands a good punch to Malik's stomach and then, with a right cross, catches him on the chest, but Malik counters with a kidney punch and a knee to the crotch. Tyree checks his opponent with, "Watch that shit, man." They continue trading punches, hits, and feints. They are getting tired. Tyree, hands up, accidentally lets an open hand to to Malik's face with the sound of a slap. Tyree knows instinctively what he has done, that he has seriously violated the rules of the fair fight, and just as quickly he says, "Aw, 'cuse me, man." The apology must come quickly and must be sincere, otherwise such a blow can escalate the fight to the point of a serious exchange. Malik responds, "Watch yourself, man. Watch yourself."

They continue their dancing and sparring for about twenty minutes and then stop. They have fought and, for the moment, settled their differences. But, actually, something much more profound has occurred as well. To be sure, the two boys can now smile at each other again, knowing that if they have a disagreement, they can settle it man to man. Through this little fight, they have bonded socially. They have tested each other's mettle, discerned important limits, and gained an abiding sense of what each one will "take" from the other. With this in mind they adjust their behavior in each other's presence, giving the other his "props," or respect. In this context they learn to accept each other, or pay the consequences; in effect, they learn the rules of their relationship. After consummating their bond through a fight, they can now walk together again, while expecting that if someone was to try to jump Malik, Tyree would likely be there to defend his friend, or vice versa. They informally agree to watch each other's back. When this very strong—and necessary in the inner city—expectation is met, powerful bonds of trust are formed and, with repeated supportive exchanges, ever more firmly established. Essentially, this is what it means to "get cool" with someone, and when the story gets out, each is now more cool with the wider group of bols as well.

## MANHOOD AND NERVE

On the neighborhood streets, many of the concerns of Tyree, Malik, and other young males relating to respect and identity have come to be expressed in the concept of "manhood." Manhood on the streets means assuming the prerogatives of men with respect to strangers, other men, and women—being distinguished as a man. It implies physicality and a certain ruthlessness. Inner-city men associate manhood with this concept in large part because of its practical application: if others have little regard for a person's manhood, his very life and the lives of his loved ones could be in jeopardy. But there is a chicken-and-egg aspect to this situation: one's physical safety is more likely to be jeopardized in public *because* manhood is associated with respect. In other words, an existential link has been created between the idea of manhood and one's self-esteem, so that it has become hard to say which is primary. For many inner-city youths, manhood and respect are two sides of the same coin; physical and psychological well-being are inseparable, and both require a sense of control, of being in charge.

For many young men, the operating assumption is that a man, especially a "real" man, knows what other men know—the code of the street. And if one is not a real man, one is diminished as a person. Moreover, the code is seen as possessing a certain justice, since everyone supposedly has the opportunity to learn it, and thus can be held responsible for being familiar with it. If the victim of a mugging, for example, does not know the code and thus responds "wrong," the perpetrator may feel justified in killing him and may not experience or show remorse. He may think, "Too bad, but it's his fault. He should have known better."

A person venturing outside must adopt the code—a kind of shield—to prevent others from messing with him. In crime-ridden parts of the inner city, it is easy for people to think they are being tried or tested by others even when this is not the case. For something extremely valuable on the street—respect—is at stake in every inter-action, and people are thus encouraged to rise to the occasion, par-ticularly with strangers. For people unfamiliar with the code—generally people who live outside the inner city—this concern with respect in the most ordinary interactions can be frightening and incomprehensible. But for those who are invested in the code, the clear object of their demeanor is to discourage strangers from even thinking about testing their manhood, and the sense of power that comes with the ability to deter others can be alluring even to those who know the code without being heavily invested in it—the decent inner-city youths. Thus a boy who has been leading a basically decent life can, under trying circumstances, suddenly resort to deadly force.

Central to the issue of manhood is the widespread belief that one of the most effective ways of gaining respect is to manifest nerve. A man shows nerve by taking another person's possessions, messing with someone's woman, throwing the first punch, "getting in some-one's face," or pulling a trigger. Its proper display helps check others who would violate one's person, and it also helps build a reputation that works to prevent future challenges. But since such a show of nerve is a forceful expression of disrespect toward the person on the receiving end, the victim may be greatly offended and seek to retaliate with equal or greater force. The background knowledge that a display of nerve can easily provoke a life-threatening response is part of the concept.

True nerve expresses a lack of fear of death. Many feel that it is acceptable to risk dying over issues of respect. In fact, among the hard-core street-oriented, the clear risk of violent death may be pref-erable to being dissed. Conveying the attitude of being able to take somebody else's life if the situation demands it gives one a real sense of power on the streets. Many youths, both decent and street-oriented, try to create this impression, both for its practical defense value and for the positive way it makes them feel about themselves. The difference between them is that the decent youth often can code-switch: in other settings—with teachers, say, or at his part-time job—he may be polite and deferential. The seriously street-oriented youth has made the concept of manhood part of his very identity and has difficulty manipulating it.

## THE SCHOOL AS A STAGING AREA

The inner-city school is an outpost of the traditions of the wider society. Racially segregated and situated in an impoverished inner-city community in which violence, drugs, and crime are rampant, it is characterized by the street/decent dynamic.[9] During their early years, most of the children accept the legitimacy of the school, and then eagerly approach the task of learning. As time passes, however, in their relentless campaign for the respect that will be meaningful in their public environment, youth increasingly embrace the street code. By the fourth grade, enough children have opted for the code of the street that it begins to compete effectively with the culture of the school, and the code begins to dominate their public culture—in school as well as out—becoming a way of life for many and eventually conflating with the culture of the school itself. Such a school becomes a primary staging area for the campaign for respect.

In this social setting, decent kids learn to code switch, while street kids become more singularly committed to the street. Such a division, as previously stated, is largely a function of persistent poverty and local neighborhood effects, which include social isolation and alienation, but it is also strongly related to family background, available peers, and role models. For many alienated young black people, attending school and doing well becomes negatively associated with acting white. In what is essentially a racially black street-world, as shown in Tyree's case, one develops a strong need to show others he can handle himself socially and physically on the ghetto streets, a powerful community value in and of itself. This "street knowledge" is esteemed, and the quest for it and the consideration for those who have it begin to predominate, ultimately competing with, if not undermining, the mission of the school.

With each passing year the school loses ground as more and more students adopt a street orientation, if only for self-defense in the neighborhood. But often what is out on the streets is brought into the classrooms. The most troublesome students are then encouraged by peers to act out, to get over on the teacher, to test authority by probing for weaknesses. Particularly during mild weather, many students in the upper grades attend school sporadically or stop coming altogether, because street activities effectively complete for their time. Even while in school, they walk the halls instead of attending class, and their encounters there often mirror those on the street, marked by tension and fights.

Some of the seriously street-oriented kids may have mental health issues; some have been abused by their parents; others are depressed. The most troubled may fight with teachers, bring guns and knives to school, and threaten people. The idea of deprivation and anger is important here. In this highly competitive setting, the most deprived youths, who can easily be made to feel bad, sometimes become jealous of peers. To avoid feeling bad, these kids may lift themselves up by putting others down. A common tactic is to "bust on" or "signify" at someone, verbally teasing the person, at times to the point of tears. Sometimes the prettiest girls can get beaten up out of jealousy. From so much envy and jealousy, beefs easily erupt, beginning with ritual "bumping" and ending in serious physical confrontations to settle things. Bumping rights are then negotiated, determining who is allowed to bump whom, to pick on whom, and in what circumstances. In essence, these young people are campaigning for place, esteem, and ultimately respect.

In this situation, the school becomes transformed in the most profound sense into a staging area for the streets, a place where people come to present themselves, to represent where they come from, and to stay even with or to dominate their peers. Violence is always a possibility, for the typically troubled school is surrounded by persistent poverty, where scarcity of valued things is the rule, thus lending a competitive edge to the social environment. However, the trophies to be won are not of an academic kind, rather they are those of the street, particularly respect. In this campaign, young people must be prepared not only to fight, but also to take great care with their appearance. The right look means *not* wearing old or "bummy" clothes, or sneakers that are worn or dirty or out of style. Esteem is so precarious that it can be taken away with just a word, and kids are constantly challenged to defend what they have. Social life becomes a zero-sum scenario: "If you have something and exhibit it, it means I'm less. Who do you think you are by doing that?" The decent kids mimic the street ones, behaving in street ways that often confuse teachers (and also prospective employers and police who might be incapable of distinguishing the decent from the street). Some teachers are unable to differentiate between the two groups. Overwhelmed by clothes, the look, or the swagger, they cannot discern the shy kid underneath, which may be why teachers classify the majority of young people as "street."

To be sure, much of the students' behavior may be purely defensive, which requires significant expenditures of social energy. This situation tends to victimize the weakest players and certainly disrupts the business of the school. In time, when unattended, the street element (and those who would be "street") dominates the school and its local terrain. In the most troubled schools, the street element becomes so powerful that beefs and scores can only be settled by death. Again, most of the young people in these settings are inclined toward decency, but when the street elements rule, they are encouraged to campaign for respect by adopting a street attitude, look, and presentation of self. In this context, the decent kids often must struggle to maintain their credibility, like the fifteen-year-old boy I observed who typically changed his "square" clothes for a black leather jacket (thereby adopting a street look) after he got around the corner from his home and out of his mother's view. In order to preserve his own self-respect and the respect of his peers, he would also hide his books under his jacket while walking to school, bidding to appear street.

In school as in the neighborhood, adolescents are concerned with developing a sense of who they are, what they are, and what they will be. They try on many different personas and roles, and they experiment with many scripts. Some work, others don't. How do the roles of decent and street play in their search for an identity, and what parts do others play? What stages do the young people go through? What is the "career" of identity as this career takes shape?

Observing the interactions of adolescents in school and talking with them reveal how important school authority is to young people, but too often the authority figures are viewed as alien and unreceptive. The teachers and administrators are concerned that their own authority be taken seriously, and claims to authority are always up for grabs—if not subject to out-and-out challenge.

Young people, of course, do not go about developing their identities based solely on privileges and rewards granted by teachers, but this dynamic does exist to some degree. Often students perceive (more or less accurately) that the institution and its staff are utterly unreceptive to their street presentations. Mixed with their inability to distinguish the decent child from the street child, the teachers' efforts to combat the street may caused them to lump the good students with the bad, generally viewing all who display street emblems as adversaries. Here, their concerns might be as much with teaching as with controlling their charges.

In response, the decent children place ever greater stock in their ability to code-switch, adopting one set of behaviors for inside the building and one for outside. But, as indicated above—particularly in the heat of the campaign for respect—the two roles often merge, and what is considered proper in either setting can become one and the same. When this confusion goes unchecked, discipline in the school situation becomes elusive, particularly for those children who seem "to get away with it."

When students become convinced that they cannot receive their props from teachers and staff, they turn elsewhere, typically to the street, encouraging others to follow their lead, particularly when the unobtainable appears to be granted only on the basis of acting white. The sour grapes attitude notwithstanding, a powerful incentive for young people then emerges, especially for those sitting on the cultural fence, to invest themselves in the so-called oppositional culture, which may be confused with their "black identity." Such a resolution allows these alienated students to campaign for respect on their own terms, in a world they control.

Impacted by profound social isolation, the children face the basic problem of alienation. Many students become smug in their lack of appreciation of what the business of the school is and how it is connected with the world outside. In addition, they seldom encounter successful black people who have gone through school and gone on to do well.

Education is thus undermined because the mission of the school cannot equal the mission of the kids. To accept the school would be to give in and act white, to give up the value of the street for some other thing. And the value of that other thing has not been sufficiently explained to the children to make them want to give up the ways of the street and take on the ideology of the school. So the outpost of mainstream society tries to deliver its message to kids in an environment that has little regard for that society. In fact, the code of the street, and by extension the oppositional culture, competes very effectively with traditional values. As the young people come to see the school and its agents as unreceptive to them, embracing the oppositional culture becomes more important as a way to salvage self-esteem. The mission of the school is called into question, if not undermined.

Alienated black students take on the oppositional role so effectively that they often become models for other disaffected students. They do it because they are profoundly at odds with the white culture and can see themselves as visibly different. But other alienated students may mimic them because they are such strong models.

The culture of the street doesn't allow backing down. When the boys at the Youth Study Center (Philadelphia's juvenile detention facility) saw a video on conflict resolution as an alternative to fighting, they just shook their heads. They knew that you never back down. That is to set yourself up as a doormat. You have to be tough. If you show fear, others will exploit it. So you always have to give the impression that you are strong, that you are a "thorough dude." Even a teacher who shows fear becomes vulnerable and can be emotionally undone by the kids. When that happens, the kids know they've won.

So there is an adversarial relationship between the teachers and the students. The teachers' role is to keep the kids in line. The students' role is either to behave or to try to get over on the teacher.

The school is a microcosm of the community in a sense. Although police and disciplinarians are on patrol, kids are parading up and down the halls, socializing, even buying and selling drugs. The same things are going on inside the school as outside it. Yet it remains a haven, a place where one can go and expect relative order.

## THE DILEMMA OF THE DECENT KID

At a certain critical point in development, sometime around ages five through eight, the child of a decent inner-city family ventures into the street, away from home, out of the view and immediate control of his family. Here children begin to develop an identity beyond the family, one that is helped along by the way they go about meeting the exigencies of the streets. They find their level, get cool with others, and adjust to the situation as they swim about the environment "looking for themselves" and trying to "be real." Essentially, such youth face the dilemma of how to obtain their props—and keep them—on the streets while building a reputation for decency as well.

They often experience a certain tension between what they learn at home and what they find in the streets. The family often becomes mildly concerned about the kinds of children their child is playing with. At this stage the child's peer group becomes extremely important. Often the child must go with what groups are available, and a child from a decent home can easily be sucked up by the streets. The child may learn to code-switch, presenting himself one way at home and another with peers.

Many children are left on their own for long periods of time. Others in the neighborhood, including "big brothers," "cousins," and neighborhood friends of the family, may be encouraged to look out for them. But at the same time the children want to try new things, to find themselves, and to grow into independence. The child encounters the street in the form of peers, cousins, and older children—and begins to absorb the experience.

To many residents the negative aspects of the street are exemplified by groups of young men like those who harassed Tyree. These young men often come from homes ravaged by unemployment and family disorganization. On the streets they develop contacts and "family" ties with other youths like themselves, as did Tyree and Malik. The groups they form are extremely attractive to other youths, and not simply to those whose lives have been seriously compromised by poverty. These groups dominate the public spaces, and every young person must deal with them. Even the decent young people must make their peace with them.

The connection these decent young people have with the street is not simply a matter of coercion. Often they strongly aspire to feelings of self-worth. And to achieve their goal, they must do more than make peace with the street group; they must actually come to terms with the street. Like Tyree, they must get cool with the people who dominate the public spaces. They must let others know how tough they are, how hard they are to roll on, how much mess they will take. The others want to know what will make such a person's jaws tight, what will get him mad. To find out, they may challenge the person to a fight or test his limits with insults to his family. Some of the most decent youths reach their limits rather quickly, thus allowing others to see what's to him, or what he's made of. Often a fight ensues: as the young men say, "It's showtime."

So the streets, or at least the public spaces, are extremely important to young people, because these are places where they are involved in the process of forging their own local identities—identities that carry over into other critical areas of their lives, including school, church, employment, and future family life. This is an issue for all the children in the environment, decent and street. Even the most decent child in the neighborhood must at some point display a degree of commitment to the street.

Life under the code might be considered a kind of game played by rules that are partly specified but partly emergent. The young person is encouraged to be familiar with the rules of the game and even to use them as a metaphor for life—or else feel left out, become marginalized, and, ultimately, risk being rolled on. So the young person is inclined to enact his own particular role, to show his familiarity with the game, and more specifically his street knowledge, so as to gain points with others.

It is essential that the child learn to play well. This ability is strongly related to who his mentors and homies are and how much interest and support they show for the child. How "good" he is corresponds to a large degree to how "bad" his neighborhood is viewed to be. The tougher the neighborhood, the more prestige he has in the minds of outsiders he encounters. This prestige also presents a challenge to newcomers, as was the case with Tyree.

Young people who project decency are generally not given much respect on the streets. Decency or a "nice" attitude is often taken as a sign of weakness, at times inviting others to "roll on" or "try" the person. To be nice is to risk being taken for a sissy, someone who can't fight, a weakling, someone to be rolled on. And to roll on someone once is not always enough for those in search of respect. It is often done repeatedly to establish a pattern of dominance in a group. Young people who are out to make a name for themselves actively look for others to roll on. Once achieved, a name must be sustained and sometimes defended; its owner must then live up to his reputation, or be challenged. A strong reputation wards off danger from others. In this context the decent kids with low self-esteem, little social support, and a perceived unwillingness to be violent become especially vulnerable to being rolled on, their occasional defeats and resultant deference feeding the reputations of others.

With some number of campaigns to his credit, the winner may feel self-confident enough to challenge someone who has already established himself. Defeating such a person may be the ultimate trophy for a boy seriously campaigning for respect. But he is likely to roll on decent youths first. In self-defense, otherwise decent youths will sometimes mimic those who are more committed to the street. On the streets and in the halls at school, they sometimes adopt the "street look," wearing the street uniform, but also swaggering, using foul language, and generally trying to "go for bad," all in the interest of acquiring respect. Presenting this street side of themselves may blur the line distinguishing decency from the street in the eyes not only of their peers but also of outsiders like prospective employers and teachers, and perhaps in the eyes of the young people themselves—though it is a public confusion they often desire.

For in this environment respect is sometimes especially necessary for getting along, and many of the decent kids will play along, code-switching when the situation demands it. Occasionally, though, a decent kid will sit on the fence, impassively, not knowing which way to turn. As luck may have it, attracted by the right peer, he may become overly impressed by the "cool" behavior of his more street-oriented peers. As was indicated above, such a youth is apt to be respect-needy, since decent values and behavior are generally not held in high esteem. An especially solicitous member of the street group might bring such a person around to his group. But for the decent acquaintance there may be the attraction of elusive social acceptance, of being able to get cool with people on this side of the playground or classroom. The youth may approach this opportunity with some ambivalence, however; such children have heard the many warnings from parents, teachers, and school authorities about "not getting with the wrong crowd."

In this environment, depending on the circumstances, the decent kid gets a taste of the street culture, the ways of the street group, and these ways—always at odds with the conventional world—can "get good" to him. Particularly satisfying may be the new shows of deference he experiences, as well as the expectations of respect and friendship. Acceptance by the "in crowd" may be too attractive to let pass. In time the decent group may gradually lose its hold on or attraction for the kid. With the taste of the street and social acceptance may come higher self-esteem.

At the same time a fifteen-year-old boy also faces the issues of coming of age and manhood. Here he is encouraged to try out his newfound size and strength to see what they will win him in the game of social esteem. If he has been beaten up and pushed around once too often by a vulnerable target, he may now stand up, particularly if his adolescent growth spurts have left him bigger than others who have been tormenting him. He now begins to relate to them differently. A youngster who can gain some support for his new way of relating to the group of tough guys may be inclined to test his new strength on others. With the help of his acquaintances, he is able to see himself in a different light, and people are now seeing *him* differently. Respect-needy, and on a campaign, he is inclined to practice his new ways not just on other street kids but also on decent kids he knows well, closely noting the social reaction to his new, if provisional, identity. If he is encouraged, he gains points for going for bad as he tries out and forges this new identity by gaining social support. As he grows confident, he settles old scores and may well challenge others. And, as a person, he changes.

If he once sought to be loved, he now seeks to have others fear him. The street code says it is better to be feared than loved. Here he models himself on the street kids, notes how he can put fear in the hearts of others, and is encouraged by his successes to continue. On the street he goes for bad, challenging others, picking fights, and, in the words of the old heads, "selling wolf tickets."[10] At about this time an old head, a neighborhood mentor, who has been following this youngster's career, may "pull his coat," intervening and warning him about what will happen to him if he does not change his ways. But such intervention is less likely to happen today than in years past, mainly because of the general disengagement of such mentors, largely as a result of the spreading economic dislocation and social distress of many ghetto communities. Allowed to continue, he refines his skills, gaining a taste of respect, and comes to crave more: it gets good to him, and slowly he develops a different attitude about himself. He changes from a person who code-switched to go for bad to one who increasingly doesn't seem to have to put up a front in order to assume a street posture in defense of himself and of what belongs to him.

This "coming of age" process has implications for relations with parents, teachers, coaches, and other meaningful adults in the child's life. If he used to do his homework, he may now be less attentive to it. He may have a problem obeying teachers. His grades perhaps begin to suffer. When his mom asks him to go to the store or to run some other errand, he resists. He develops difficulty in doing as he's told. He increasingly gives authority figures back talk. Slowly, his stance changes from that of a cooperative child to that of an adversary. Arguments erupt more easily.

The changes are clear to those looking on, those people who once depended on the image they had of him as a nice and decent youngster. But those closest to him, particularly mothers, aunts, uncles, and adult neighbors, who remember his formative years, may resist any other definition of the person they know and love—that is, a young man who to them is the same person. They are often incredulous when they hear of something terrible the boy is accused of doing.

Once such a street-oriented person has established himself or made a name for himself, he has some disincentive for code-switching, for now he has much to lose by letting the wrong people see him do so. He is not inclined to sell out to appease "white people or striving blacks." On the streets he has respect precisely because he has opposed that wider society, and to switch back is to undermine his name or reputation as bad. Here the alienation so many young people feel has taken on a life of its own and become established. Those deeply involved in the code of the street sometimes find themselves proselytizing, urging others to join them. (We seldom hear of decent kids saying to street kids, "Hey, why don't you come join us?") A common entreaty is, "Hey! When you gon' get legal?" (meaning, "When are you gon' come and sell drugs with us?").

In contrast, youngsters with a strong decency orientation attempt to avoid falling victim to alienation while still living in an environment rife with its consequences. Lee Hamilton, an eighteen year old, exemplifies this problem of how to obtain props in a street-oriented environment while maintaining decency.

Raised in an impoverished inner-city community, Lee grew up with two older brothers and a younger sister. His father lived with them for a while, but he drank and was physically abusive to the children. Eventually he moved out of the house, though not out of the neighborhood. As a young teenager, Lee found he could go to his father for money, but they would always get into arguments. For a time he took friends with him to avoid the fights until his father got angry about that too.

Lee's older brother, meanwhile, gravitated toward the street and ended up in prison for robbery. This hurt their mother, a nurse's aide and a churchgoer, very much, and Lee resolved to go a different way from his brother in order to spare her any more grief. Growing up in the community, he had learned the code but was determined not to get sucked into it, and so he searched out friends who were similarly inclined. He found them on the basketball court. Although only five nine and 150 pounds himself, Lee learned to play well enough to hang out with this group.

In addition to playing basketball, the members of the group are distinguished by the larger plans they have. Some are looking to get a job after graduating from high school. Shawn is very good on the court and hopes to make basketball a serious pursuit. Pete and Lee himself get good grades and are planning to attend community college. Even now, when their game is over, these boys go home rather than hanging around on a street corner. In fact, the whole group stands in contradistinction to the street group.

Nonetheless, Lee wears the same clothes as his street-oriented neighbors. When the police cruise his drug-infested neighborhood and see him in his Timberland boots, his striped shirt, and his hooded sweatshirt, they stop him and ask him where his drugs are, and this makes him bitter. The knowledge that the wider system in the person of cops, teachers, and store managers downtown is instantly ready to lump them with the street element takes a psychological toll on boys like Lee. At the same time, there is so little support for decency on the streets that they have to mimic the street kids in order to get by. Some kids handle this by hiding their books when walking home from school or even by changing their jacket, say, once out of view of their mother. It is vital that the wider system identify these youths and pluck them out of the street environment, for they can easily be lost. Lee is already angry at the police.

One way Lee and his friends pass muster on the street is by wearing clothes approved by the street. Another is to act out in judicious ways, cussing or acting tough in situations in which it is not likely to lead to real trouble. But the pressure to be street is always there. One area in which it is keenly felt is in dealing with girls. Many of the girls in poor communities are looking for a boy with money who will buy them gold jewelry and clothes and have their hair tracked. A nice car alone can snare many a girl. Lee's good looks compensate somewhat for his lack of money, but some other decent boys find it hard to get a girl interested in them. That in itself can lure a boy into becoming a drug dealer. Lee prefers to seek out more serious girls whose interests are not purely material, but it does help his self-image that he can attract the attention of some of the more street girls without flashing gold.

Crucial to resolving the dilemma of being decent in a street-oriented environment is the ability to code-switch. I might add that the serious street element has no need for a put-on; rather, the street is in the person, consuming his being, so much so that he has a limited behavioral repertoire. A decent youth like Lee tends to have a wide array of styles from which to choose how to act, and certainly with which to gauge and understand the conduct of others. With such street knowledge the young person may avoid being taken advantage of on the streets (not a small accomplishment). To be more appealing to those of the street, however, he must present himself in opposition to adult authority and, to some degree, make his peace with the oppositional culture. And this behavior is reinforced by the street group.

It is important to appreciate here that the code of the street and the street knowledge it implies are essential for survival on the inner-city streets. The code works to organize publicly the community, limiting violence and street crime. It thus serves as a kind of policing mechanism, encouraging people to trust others with a certain respect or to face the consequences.

By a certain age a young person may become proficient on the streets and accumulate a certain amount of capital. This kind and form of capital is not always useful or valued in the wider society, but it is capital nonetheless. It is recognized and valued on the streets, and to lack it is to be vulnerable there.

The issues here—those of credibility and social belonging—raise other issues and questions. Would the decent kid resolve his dilemma differently if more decent kids were present? If there were a critical mass of decent kids, could he get by with his decency—in deed as well as behavior—intact? But in the impoverished pockets of the inner city, the decent-acting kids do not form a critical mass. There may be overwhelming numbers of youths who in some settings—at home, at work, in church, or in the presence of significant adults about whose opinions they care—display a commitment to decency, but they cannot always do so here. They are encouraged by the dominant youths here to switch codes and play by the rules of the street, or face sanctions at the hands of peers about whose opinions they also care.

And, as has been indicated, there is a practical reason for such a tack. To avoid being bothered, decent and street youths alike must say through behavior, words, and gestures, "If you mess with me, there will be a severe physical penalty—coming from me. And I'm man enough to make you pay." This message must be delivered loudly and clearly if a youth is to be left alone, and simply exhibiting a decent orientation does not do so forcefully enough. During the altercations between Tyree and his newfound friends, much of this was being worked out, and as a result Tyree got cool with the others, and they got cool with him. This outcome is essential for Tyree's well-being—and perhaps even for his physical survival.

# THREE

# Drugs, Violence, and Street Crime

N 1899 W. E. B. Du Bois published *The Philadelphia Negro*, which made a major contribution to our understanding of the social situation of African Americans in cities, although this was not appreciated at the time. Like so much significant ethnography, this description has become part of the wider historical record, describing social life in the period under study.

In today's ghetto there appears to be much more crime and higher levels of violence and homicide than in the earlier period. In addition, an ideology of alienation supporting an oppositional culture has developed; this can be seen with particular clarity in the rap music that encourages its young listeners to kill cops, to rape, and the like. Nowhere is this situation better highlighted than in the connection between drugs and violence, as young men involved in the drug trade often apply the ideology glorified in rap music to the problem of making a living and survival in what has become an oppositional if not an outlaw culture.

Du Bois was concerned with the reasons why black Americans were poorly integrated into the mainstream system in the wake of their great migration from the rural South to the urban North after the abolition of slavery. The situation he discovered was one of race prejudice, ethnic competition, and a consequent black exclusion and inability to participate in mainstream society, all in the social context of white supremacy. This pattern of exclusion resulted in deep and debilitating social pathologies in the black community, the legacy of which persists to this day.

In making sense of the social organization of the black community, Du Bois developed a typology made up of four classes. The first were the well-to-do; the second, the hardworking, decent laborers who were getting by fairly well; the third, the "worthy poor," those who were working or trying to work but barely making ends meet; and the fourth, the "submerged tenth," those who were in effect beneath the surface of economic viability. Du Bois portrayed the submerged tenth as largely characterized by irresponsibility, drinking, violence, robbery, thievery, and alienation. But the situation of the submerged tenth was not a prominent theme in his study as a whole. Today the counterpart of this class, the so-called ghetto underclass, appears much more entrenched and its pathologies more prevalent, but the outlines Du Bois provided in *The Philadelphia Negro* can be clearly traced in the contemporary picture.

The growth and transformation of this underclass is in large part a result of the profound economic changes the country—especially urban areas like Philadelphia—has undergone in the past twenty to thirty years. Deindustrialization and the growth of the global economy have led to a steady loss of the unskilled and semiskilled manufacturing jobs that, with mixed results, had sustained the urban working class since the start of the industrial revolution.[1] At the same time "welfare reform" has led to a much weakened social safety net.[2] For the most desperate people, many of whom are not effectively adjusting to these changes—elements of today's submerged tenth—the underground economy of drugs and crime often emerges to pick up the slack.[3] To be sure, the active participants in this economy are at serious risk of violence, death, and incarceration. Equally important, those living near drug dealers and other hustlers are often victimized. Decent and law-abiding people at times become victims of random violence or are otherwise ensnared in the schemes of the underground economy's participants. Sometimes even those from decent families, particularly the young, become seduced by the ways of the street.

In *The Philadelphia Negro*, Du Bois pointed to the problem that kept young African American men from finding jobs: the lack of education, connections, social skills, and white skin color, as well as the adoption of a certain outlook, an unwillingness to work, and a lack of hope for the future. Today it is clear what that persistent state of affairs has led to.

The severe problem of racial discrimination Du Bois uncovered certainly persists in Philadelphia and other cities, but, as will be discussed below, it has been transformed and at times taken on a more practical form. More conventional people often seek to place much social distance between themselves and anonymous black people they encounter in public. And many young blacks sometimes in direct response find it difficult to take white people or even conventional black people seriously, and they actively live their lives in opposition to them and everything they are taken to represent. Lacking trust in mainstream institutions, many turn to "hustling" in the underground economy. This has implications for middle-class blacks, many of whom have remained in Philadelphia and often work hard to defend themselves and their loved ones not only from those espousing oppositional values but also from the criminal element.

In many working-class and impoverished black communities today, particularly as faith in the criminal justice system erodes, social behavior in public is organized around the code of the streets. Feeling they cannot depend on the police and other civil authorities to protect them from danger, residents often take personal responsibility for their security. They may yield, but often they are prepared to let others know in no uncertain terms that there will be dire consequences if they are violated. And they tend to teach their children to stand up for themselves physically or to meet violence with violence. Growing up in such environments, young people are sometimes lured into the way of the street or become its prey. For too many of these youths, the drug trade seems to offer a ready niche, a viable way to "get by" or to enhance their wealth even if they are not full-time participants.

Because the drug trade is organized around a code of conduct approximating the code of the streets and employing violence as the basis for social control, the drug culture contributes significantly to the violence of inner-city neighborhoods. Furthermore, many inner-city boys admire drug dealers and emulate their style, making it difficult for outsiders to distinguish a dealer from a law-abiding teenager. Part of this style is to project a violent image, and boys who are only "playing tough" may find themselves challenged and honor bound to fight. In addition, the trappings of drug dealers (the Timberland boots, the gold chains) are expensive, encouraging those without drug profits or other financial resources simply to steal.

## THE CULTURAL ECONOMIC CONNECTION

As I indicated above, anyone who wants to understand the widespread social dislocation in the inner-city poor community must approach these problems—along with other urban ills—from a structural as well as a cultural standpoint.[4] Liberals and conservatives alike today tend to stress values like individual responsibility when considering such issues as drugs, violence, teen pregnancy, family formation, and the work ethic. Some commentators readily blame "welfare" for poverty and find it hard to see how anyone, even the poor, would deliberately deviate from the norms of the mainstream culture. But the profound changes our society is currently undergoing in the way it organizes work have enormous cultural implications for the ability of the populations most severely affected by these developments to function in accordance with mainstream norms.

The United States has for some time been moving from manufacturing to a service and high-tech economy in which the well-being of workers, particularly those with low skills and little education, is subordinated to the bottom line. In cities like Philadelphia certain neighborhoods have been devastated by the effects of deindustrialization. Many jobs have become automated, been transferred to developing countries, or moved to nearby cities like King of Prussia. For those who cannot afford a car, travel requires two hours on public transportation from the old city neighborhoods where concentrations of black people, Hispanics, and working-class whites live.[5]

With widespread joblessness, many inner-city people become

stressed and their communities become distressed. Poor people adapt to these circumstances in the ways they know, meeting the exigencies of their situation as best they can. The kinds of problems that trigger moral outrage begin to emerge: teen pregnancy, welfare dependency, and the underground economy. Its cottage industries of drugs, prostitution, welfare scams, and other rackets are there to pick up the economic slack. Quasi-legal hustling is part of it; people do odd jobs under the table and teach young people to follow their lead. Some people have a regular second or third job entirely off the books.

The drug trade is certainly illegal, but it is the most lucrative and most accessible element of the underground economy and has become a way of life in numerous inner-city communities. Many youngsters dream of leading the drug dealer's life, or at least their highly glamorized conceptions of this life. Of course, drugs have been around for a long time, but they have become deeply rooted in the inner-city black community, a situation largely tolerated by civic authorities and the police. As law-abiding residents witness this situation, they become ever more cynical and alienated.

Here it is important to underscore the connections between jobs, drugs, and alienation. Many of the young blacks who have difficulty obtaining a job feel victimized by prejudice and discrimination. Such feelings of victimization may lead to a greater understanding, if not tolerance, of those who resort to dealing drugs to "survive." In these circumstances the drug trade, so dangerous and problematic for local communities and for society, becomes normal happenstance. In destitute inner-city communities, it is in fact becoming increasingly difficult to distinguish poverty from drug involvement. For example, many welfare mothers have become intimately connected with the drug trade, either as users or as what might be called support personnel, by allowing drug-dealing boyfriends or male relatives to use their homes as crack houses or drug depots in exchange for money or favors.

In addition, the young man who sells drugs is often encouraged and motivated to create new markets, sometimes recruiting his own family members into the drug culture, thus at times leading to their drug dependency. Why? Because he has come to covet the material things he sees dangled before him, things that become important not simply as practical items but as status symbols among his peers. A particular brand of eyeglasses or shoes or pants can indicate a person's social standing, bestowing on him a certain amount of self-esteem. Timberland boots, for example, which support a roughneck or macho image, are now being worn by many drug dealers and have come to be considered hip. The owner of such items, through his exhibitions and displays, is thus able to gain deference from and status among his peers. Media images—television, movies, the consumer mentality—fuel these desires as well. And when the regular economy cannot provide the means for satisfying them, some of the most desperate people turn to the underground economy.

But the despair, the alienation, and the distress are still there, and this condition encourages the development and spread of the oppositional culture. For those living according to the rules of that culture, it becomes important to be tough, to act as though one is beyond the reach of lawful authority—to go for bad. In this scenario, anything associated with conventional white society is seen as square; the hip things are at odds with it. The untied sneakers, the pants worn well below the waist, the hat turned backward—all have become a style. These unconventional symbols have been taken over by people who have made them into status symbols, but they are status symbols *to the extent that* they go against what is conventional.

Exacerbating the antagonism toward the conventional is the way residents of the ghetto become personally victimized by all this. Not only does their community get a bad reputation, but the people themselves, particularly black males, become demonized. They are stereotyped; everyone from that community who dresses and who looks that way is a priori seen as being at odds with conventional society. The anonymous law-abiding black male is often taken as a threat to it. Yet many ghetto males are caught in a bind because they are espousing their particular ways of dressing and acting simply to be self-respecting among their neighborhood peers. A boy may be completely decent, but to the extent that he takes on the *presentation* of "badness" to enhance his local public image, even as a form of self-defense, he further alienates himself in the eyes of the wider society, which has denounced people like him as inclined to violate its norms, values, rules, and conventions—to threaten it.

Such cultural displays in turn make young people even less employable. Beset with negative stereotypes, employers sometimes discriminate against whole census tracts or zip codes where impoverished people live. The decent people are strongly associated with the indecent people, and the employers often do not worry about making distinctions. They just want to avoid the whole troublesome situation, selecting whites over blacks. Joleen Kirschenman and Kathryn Neckerman conducted a study in Chicago to discover the extent to which employers discriminated against young black people.[6] They found that discrimination was rife: many of the employers much preferred white women and immigrants to young black people.

Similarly, in Philadelphia, a great many black boys and girls, especially the boys, are feared by employers. Even when they do get work, there is often a racial division of labor in the workplace. Inner-city black boys and girls tend to get stuck in entry-level jobs and are rarely promoted. One very clear example of this in present-day Philadelphia is the restaurant business, in which an obvious division of labor exists. In upscale and moderately priced restaurants, blacks are conspicuously absent from the wait staff but overrepresented among the kitchen help. In addition, if a problem with stealing or some other trouble on the job arises, they are prime suspects and are sometimes summarily dismissed.[7] Such experiences, and the reports of them, contribute to their working conception of the world. Their resulting bitterness and alienation then nurture the oppositional culture. To be self-respecting, many young men and women must exhibit a certain contempt for a system they are sure has contempt for them. When such factors are added to the consequences of deindustrialization, the result is an incendiary situation, as Du Bois appreciated.[8]

The attraction of the violence-prone drug trade thus results from a combination of inadequate opportunity in the regular economy, on the one hand, and the imperatives of street life, on the other. The interplay between these two factors is powerfully at work in the social organization of the underground economy in inner-city neighborhoods.

•   •   •

## CLOCKING: THE DRUG TRADE AS A LIVING

The transition from the regular economy to the underground economy, particularly to the drug trade, is not simple. Some young people are able to dabble in it for a while and then return to the regular economy, or they operate simultaneously in both. But the drug trade and the wages it pays sometimes become overwhelming and downright addictive. People may manage to quit when a better opportunity appears or when they confront death or jail (for themselves or for loved ones or friends) and begin to have second thoughts. More likely, however, working in the drug trade becomes a regular occupation for the most desperate, who are then said to be "clocking."

The introduction of crack has exacerbated the problem. Because it is cheap and readily available, it can support many dealers. Boys can acquire the needed skills—"street knowledge" and the ability to act on it—just by growing up in the impoverished inner-city neighborhood. Whatever a boy's home life is like, growing up in the 'hood means learning to some degree the code of the streets, the prescriptions and proscriptions of public behavior. He must be able to handle himself in public, and his parents, no matter how decent they are, may strongly encourage him to learn the rules. And because of various barriers he can often parlay that experience into a place in the drug trade much more easily than into a reasonable job. The relative ease of that transition speaks volumes about the life circumstances of inner-city adolescents.

For many impoverished young black men of the inner city, the opportunity for dealing drugs is literally just outside the door. By selling drugs, they have a chance to put more money into their pockets than they could get by legal means, and they can present themselves to peers as hip, in sharp contrast to the square image of those who work in places like McDonald's and wear silly uniforms. In fact, the oppositional culture has dubbed opting to sell drugs "getting legal." Martin, the decent, law-abiding young man referred to earlier, was often accosted by his drug-dealing peers as he stepped outside his door and headed for his regular job with the remark "Hey, Martin. When you gon' get legal?" He would simply reply, "Later for that. Later for that."[9] When one needs money, which is always, this way of making it can seem like a godsend, and other boys encourage him to sell.

A common way of getting into the drug trade is to be part of a neighborhood peer group that begins to sell. A boy's social group can be easily transformed from a play group or a group that hangs around the corner listening to rap music or playing basketball—relatively innocuous activities—to a drug gang. The change requires a drug organizer to approach the group and consult the leader or "main man." The leader then begins to distribute opportunities to deal drugs—which is a kind of power—to various of his friends, his "boys." In time the small neighborhood group becomes a force to be reckoned with in the community, while taking an ever sharper interest in issues of turf and territory. The group then works to confuse concerns having to do with money and with protecting turf. The leader can paint an enticing picture for these boys, and he has an incentive to do so because the deed enhances his power. With "top dogs," "middle dogs," and "low dogs," the system resembles a pyramid scheme.[10]

Youths who have strong family grounding—very decent folks, churchgoing families with a nuclear or quasi-nuclear structure and with love and concern for the younger people—are often the most resistant. But those who are drawn by the group, who get caught up with the responsibilities of breadwinning, with little opportunity to do so in the regular economy, sometimes resolve the tension by joining the drug trade. In turn, as they become serious dealers, these boys will often sell drugs to anybody who will buy them, including their own relatives; money and group loyalty become paramount issues. In this connection they may develop not only an excuse but a whole rap, a way of cajoling people to try crack just to get them hooked, because they know how quickly one can become addicted. For instance, they may approach someone as a friend and invite him or her to share some of their own supply, saying things like "It's not going to hurt you, it's not bad, you can handle it."

Strikingly, they may even become customers themselves—it is easy enough to become hooked by trying it once. Through the posturing required to prevail in the street life, many young people come to feel invincible, or they develop a profound need to show others they feel this way. And the power that accrues to dealers compounds the sense that they can control anything, even a crack cocaine high. In these circumstances they become "the man." Sometimes such a dealer does manage on crack off and on for a couple of years. Getting high now and then, he feels he is handling it, but, as the wiser dealers say, there is a fine line between handling it and having it handle you. At some inopportune moment he may be suddenly overcome with an insatiable need for the drug. Such a person is said to be "jonesing" for it; he is filled with such an intense desire for a high that he loses control of his actions. The predator becomes the prey—a common occurrence.

Like any marketing enterprise, the drug trade requires production and distribution networks.[11] Another requirement is social control. Among drug dealers that requirement is satisfied by the use and threat of violence. Violence is not always intended, but it occurs easily as a result of both the intense competition for customers and the general disorganization that marks the lives of so many young dealers. Misunderstandings easily arise, such as "messing up" somebody's money—not paying for drugs that one has been advanced, thus squandering the dealer's investment. The older and established dealers are obligated to "do in" the people who have messed up their money, because otherwise they would lose credibility and status on the streets. Attemped takeovers of the business of rival dealers are also common. Though there is room in the system for more people now than there was before crack, competition remains fierce, especially as the belief that anyone can get rich dealing drugs becomes increasingly prevalent. The push to get in on the drug trade can in this sense be likened to the gold rush.

It is understood on the streets that the drug trade itself is unforgiving. To make a misstep is to risk getting roughed up, shot, or killed. When a seemingly senseless killing occurs, people in the community immediately assume it is drug-related. Those who get into the trade realize they are playing with fire but, given the presumed financial stakes, may feel they have no choice or are up to the challenge. Often the people who get hurt "deserved it," in terms of the code of the drug trade: they "crossed somebody big," or they "thought they were slick." People in the community understand this rationale, and it seems that the police acknowledge it too. Once a crime is drug-related, there often seems to be little interest and accountability in bringing the people who perpetrated it to justice.

Arguments over "business" are frequently settled on the spot, typically on the basis of arbitrary considerations, unfounded assumptions, or outright lies. There is also an ongoing fight for turf because of the large number of dealers, some connected with an organization, others freelancing. When a gang is set up in a particular area, its members know the streets and control the turf. As the trade becomes profitable, however, would-be dealers from outside the gang may want to do business in the same area or even take it over. A person who tries to muscle in, however, is threatening not just the current dealer's economic well-being but that part of the community as well. The connections of many of these boys go deep in the community through extended families, who may rely on the money. If a dealer is pushed out, he and a portion of the community can face financial disaster. As a result, some dealers are ready to fight to keep their turf, and people often get wounded or killed in the process.

There are major and minor turf wars. A major turf war often spawns smaller ones. In a major fight—whether the weapons are words, fists, or guns, but especially if they are guns—the dispute gets settled, at least for the time being. But everyone has an interpretation of what happened. The interpretations are exchanged in the various neighborhood institutions, including barbershops, taverns, and street corners, where people gather and talk, and an understanding of the original fight is negotiated. Since at least some of the people involved know the principal participants personally, they may take sides, becoming emotionally invested in having their version of the event prevail, and the discussions themselves can become heated and lead to violence.

Some boys simply crave the status associated with being a dealer. They want to wear a beeper, to be seen to be "clocking," to be associated with something hip and lucrative, even though it is an underground enterprise. Drug dealers are living the fast life; they are living on the edge. Older people will give young dealers advice, telling them that they are "living too fast." But everyone knows that once a person gets into that world, it is very hard to get out. The dealer can get hooked on the money and the material things it can buy, just as someone can get hooked on the drug; the adventure, the thrill of danger, and the respect people give him are also addictive. Furthermore, his associates in the trade may not let him out, because he knows too much and might pass information on to the wrong people, or they may want to make him an example. Much of his ability to maneuver depends on his identity and connections (his cousins, brothers, uncles, his other associates in the trade, his gang members, his boys) and on his status. Often the higher his status, the more leeway and independence he has—the more "juice" he has. The truly independent people, those who have achieved a high level of respect, may be able to get out in ways other people cannot, because they have established that they can be trusted. But often the only sure way of getting out is to get out of town.

## VIOLENT FALLOUT

Drug users also engage in violence. Many users start out as victims— when family members or boyfriends who deal drugs actively get them hooked in order to expand their markets—but they then become victimizers, robbing others to support their habits. Although some of the violence is focused and some is not, the result is a constant sense of uncertainty, a belief that anything can happen at any time. The successful dealer must be ever vigilant, but of course this makes him jittery and prone to react violently at the slightest perceived provocation. Furthermore, under the influence of drugs people's behavior may become unpredictable or truly dangerous. In these situations innocent bystanders, sometimes small children, can be shot or killed. Since drug trafficking permeates so much of the inner-city community, all its residents, whether involved with drugs or not, are at risk of finding themselves the unintended target of a stray bullet. The awareness of this constant danger fosters anxiety and skittishness even among the decent people, who therefore become more likely themselves to overreact in an uncertain encounter; these people may move, if they can.

Also fueling the violence that attends the drug trade is the proliferation of guns, which have become for many people easily accessible.
Guns were in the community in the past, but mostly in the hands of
adults. Today kids fourteen and younger have guns, or they know
how and where to get them. In the inner-city community, one can
often hear gunshots in the distance but no sirens afterward. The
likelihood is that the shots are being fired by young boys playing with
guns, at times just shooting them off for the fun of it, usually in the
middle of the night. Guns can have personality and status attached
to them; they even have records. The price of a used gun indicates
its history. A gun that "has a body on it" (was used to kill someone)
is cheap because the person who is ultimately caught with it might
be held responsible for murder. Moreover, in a society where so
much economic inequality exists, for the severely alienated and desperate a gun can become like a bank card—an equalizer. Such a boy—
or, increasingly, girl—who desperately needs money may use a gun
to stick somebody up without a second thought. In a peculiar way,
however, the prevalence of and ready access to guns may keep certain
strangers honest and more careful in how they approach others. In
these circumstances a kind of Wild West mentality obtains in some
of the more dangerous neighborhoods, in which the fear of getting
shot can constrain people from violating others.

As a result of the general atmosphere of danger, even people with
a nonviolent orientation buy guns for protection. In Philadelphia not
long ago, a black minister and resident of an inner-city community
shot and killed an intruder. The incident sparked a good deal of
discussion, but the general reaction of his blacks neighbors was,
"Well, he did what he had to do." In fact, such incidents do not occur
just in the inner city. In the gentrified neighborhood adjacent to the
minister's, a white doctor going to bed one night heard a rumbling
downstairs. He came down with his gun and in the darkness
announced, "I have a gun." The rumbling continued, so he fired,
killing an intruder in his kitchen with a bullet to the back of the head.
He and his wife went to the police station, returned home at two in
the morning, and cleaned up the blood. It turned out that the intruder
was apparently trying to steal the small kitchen television set to sell
on the street, which could have brought a few dollars for crack. But

this white doctor was so disturbed at having killed a young black man in those circumstances that he immediately moved out of his house and left the community. Thus the casualties of violence include people who simply get caught up in it—not just those who get shot but sometimes those who perpetrate the violence as well.


## THE CRACK CULTURE: RATIONALE AND CONSEQUENCES

It must be continually underscored that much of this violence and drug activity is a reflection of the dislocations brought about by economic transformations, shifts that are occurring in the context of the new global economy. As was indicated above, where the wider economy is not receptive to these dislocated people, the underground economy is. That does not mean that anyone without a job is suddenly going to become a drug dealer; the process is not that simple. But the facts of race relations, unemployment, dislocation, and destitution create alienation, and alienation allows for a certain receptivity to overtures made by people seeking youthful new recruits for the drug trade.

Numerous inner-city black people continue to be locked out of many working-class occupations. Lack of education and training are often at issue, but, as Du Bois noted long ago, so is the problem of employers' racial preferences and social connections with prospective co-workers. For example, the building trades—plumbing, carpentry, roofing, and so forth—are often organized around family connections: fathers and uncles bring in their sons and nephews. To get a certificate to work in these trades, a young man requires a mentor, who not only teaches him skills but legitimizes him as a member of the trade. So the system perpetuates the dominance of ethnic groups that have been organized a long time. Now, the inner-city drug trade is composed of uncles and nephews too. From this perspective working-class Italians and Irish and others have their niche, and many severely alienated and desperate young blacks, at least those who are enterprising, can be said to have their niche too—in the drug trade.

As Du Bois would have appreciated, such behavior, while not to be condoned, is understandable as a manifestation of racism and persistent poverty.

In the inner-city community, drug dealing thus becomes recognized as work, though it is an occupation that overwhelming numbers of residents surely despise. Yet there are Robin Hood types among the drug dealers, who distribute some of their profits in the community, buying things for people, financially helping out their friends and relatives, as well as complete strangers. One drug dealer told me how bad he felt when he found out that a woman who had bought crack from one of his underlings had kids and had used all her welfare money for the drugs. He sought the woman out and gave her half her money back. His rationale was that business is business but that the kids shouldn't go hungry.

Crack's addictive quality has led to the rapid establishment of a crack culture and makes it easy to maintain a clientele.[12] The belief in the community is that crack addiction is immediate and permanent. Once you try crack, it is said, you're always "chasing the ghost"—the high that you get the first time is so intense that you can never achieve it again, but the desire to do so is strong enough that you keep pursuing it. One drug dealer told me that he has never seen anybody walk away from crack permanently; even if a user gets off it for two years, he said, the right drug dealer can easily hook him again by talking to him in the right way. I said to this dealer, "Knowing this, why do you sell crack? Isn't this like killing people, annihilating your own people?" He replied nonchalantly, "Well, if I wasn't doing it, somebody else would." To many inner-city residents, crack has become a seemingly permanent fixture of life, and dealing is a way to earn a living—even, for a few, to become rich.

## ALVIN AND JOYCE

When the young man obtains money, life can be very sweet. First, when it gets to be known in the neighborhood that he is clocking or "rolling," it is said that everyone wants to be his friend. Why?

Because he has money, but also because he is a "pusher-man," a man with the drugs. In the impoverished and distressed community, these two items are very powerful. They often signify the fast life, "what's happenin' "—the latest and hippest thing. And if he has charisma, the style, and the material things to go with this new status, such as a new Jeep Cherokee or Bronco, or the right clothes, then many people want to be associated with him. As Don Moses said, "The kids are making the money off of the drugs—they're the only ones who have money. Everybody wants to be associated with somebody who has money, and they're the only ones who have the money to really show the girls a good time. A lot of the nice girls that are looking for something, you'll find a lot of times that they end up with the drug addicts, and the drug addicts are about turning them on to that stuff. Then they move on to the next one. And it's sad, really sad. All part of the streets. The street is like a vacuum."

The drug dealer style impresses many young women. It signifies the fast life, but also the café life. These women may expect to be wined and dined, clothed, and showered with various material things. For many young women to have such a boyfriend is the next best thing to hitting the lottery; he competes very effectively with other young men who may possess much more decency but little cash.

Joyce was seventeen when she and Alvin began going together. Alvin, twenty-six and handsome, was a "big-time drug dealer." Joyce lived with her mother and two sisters in one of the poorest communities in the city. Joyce's mother, a hardworking woman whose husband had been killed in an automobile accident a few years earlier, was not on welfare. She worked as a cleaning woman in a downtown office building.

When Joyce began seeing Alvin, her mother worried, for she knew Alvin lived the fast life. He worked at a downtown hotel but seemed always to be around the neighborhood. There were rumors that he was "in the life," and he had the props and money to prove it. He never denied it; he would just smile and walk away.

After they had been going out for about six weeks, Alvin announced to Joyce's mother, Johnnie, "You ain't got to worry about her. I'll take care of her. You ain't got to worry about her, hear." It was almost as though Alvin had bought himself a wife, although they had not married—but were "going to." Johnnie felt she could do nothing. Alvin was good to her daughter, and she did not want to jeopardize the relationship. He continued to shower Joyce with love and affection and gave her almost anything she wanted. He moved her from her mother's house into their own apartment, although he was there only sporadically, because he divided his time between this place and a place he needed for "space."

Alvin bought Joyce a brand-new white Nissan automobile for her birthday, and this made her very happy. It indicated his commitment to her, and she liked that. She needed to be reassured, for it was known that Alvin had "other ladies" he liked to see. But even though there were rumors, it was clear to many that Joyce was Alvin's heart— the love of his life. She was a very attractive woman who knew how to dress and had style and a certain class that Alvin appreciated. He continued to dress her in expensive clothes and take her out to fancy downtown restaurants. The relationship was about two years old, the couple was much admired and the talk of the community, and everyone knew about Alvin's involvement in drugs.

One day Alvin brought home a large diamond engagement ring that blew Joyce's mind. She was beside herself with joy, she said. And they set an actual date to be married. But about a month afterward, Alvin was gunned down in a dispute over drugs. His death left Joyce embittered and sad, but with a car, some furs, and a diamond ring. To support herself, she sold or pawned everything and made out as best she could. Now she is reluctant to revisit their old haunts and places, not because she fears for herself but because the people there remind her of things she would rather put behind her.

In the impoverished neighborhood, many of the young women aspire to have such a man, at times thinking and hoping things will work out: it is to approach easy street, particularly if the woman can feel she has the love and the respect of the man. A streetwise young woman is likely to require that the man in her life "have something" before he "spends her time." He must be prepared to show his love by buying her material things, by paying for her to have her hair tracked (corn rows) or her nails done, and generally by being ready to give something up for her. Hence many young men become strongly motivated to obtain "crazy" money, and legal means of doing so may be too slow or nonexistent.

Under these conditions law-abiding and decent youths will imitate aspects of the fast life. In waging their campaigns for status and identity, they pretend to have money, pretend to have freedom and independence, and pretend to be violent: they go for bad. Unfortunately, as has been noted often, prospective employers and decent law-abiding people, including white people and black middle-class people who live in adjacent communities, are easily confused about who is a drug dealer and who is not. Out of a perceived need for protection, they are reluctant to employ these youths, and they may try to avoid anyone who resembles them. Such responses in turn further alienate inner-city young people.

It is worth noting that imitating the fast life is not peculiar to black inner-city teenagers. White middle-class teenagers also emulate this style. Images of hipness grounded in the inner-city subculture, which is so driven by the drug trade, move by cultural diffusion through the system into the middle class, white and black. But the middle-class versions are usually not so deadly. Middle-class youths have other forms of capital—more money and many more ways of effectively expressing themselves. When it comes to violence, such youth generally are much more willing to back down than to engage in a fight to the death. In situations involving the wrong mix of people and a large amount of posturing, there exists a slippery slope that can quickly turn make-believe into the real thing.

## THE STICKUP

The stickup is a variation on the code of the street, and often at issue are two elements that give the code its meaning and resonance: respect and alienation. The common street mugging involves a profound degree of alienation, but also requires a certain commitment to criminality, nerve, cunning, and even what young men of the street call heart. As a victim, a person with "street knowledge" may have a certain edge on one who lacks it. The edge here is simply the potential ability to behave or act ad lib in accordance with the demands and emergent expectations of the stickup man. In effect, such knowledge may provide the victim with the background knowledge of "how to get robbed"; it may even allow him or her the presence of mind to assist the assailant in his task, thus defusing a dangerous situation.

Stickups are particularly feared by law-abiding people in the ghetto, decent or street. They may occur in one manner in areas of concentrated poverty but in another in middle-class or "changing" neighborhoods. Perhaps the crucial difference is whether the victim is willing and able to defer or is bound by his or her own socialization to respond in kind. It may be that a stickup between peers requires a model different from the one for a stickup between culturally different parties. But wherever they occur, stickups have two major elements in common. The first is a radical redefinition of the situation—of who has the power—for everyone concerned, especially if a gun is involved. A drawn gun is a blunt display of power. The victim immediately realizes that he must give something up or, as the corner boys say, "pay some dues," because otherwise the perpetrator will hurt him. The second is social exchange—"your money or your life."

The code holds that might makes right and that if qualified, a person who needs anything may be moved simply to take it by force or stealth. Only the strongest, the wiliest, the most streetwise will survive, and so when people see an opportunity, they go for it. A generalized belief in the inner-city ghetto is that perpetrators choose their victims according to certain known factors and that it is therefore up to the individual to avoid placing him or herself in a vulnerable position. There is some truth to this notion, although in reality many people often find themselves at the wrong end of a stickup no matter what precautions they take. But if inner-city residents accepted the notion that assaults are utterly random, they would feel they had little control and would likely become too overwhelmed by fear to go out at all. So the belief that they can avoid stickups is an important defensive mechanism for people who are besieged by violence on a daily basis; this belief allows them to salvage a sense of freedom in a seemingly inexorable environment.

This section attempts to delineate the social processes involved in the stickup—how the deed is done.[13] These processes encompass both choice of victim and the etiquette of the event itself. One view is that if a streetwise person is foolish enough to allow himself to be robbed, he will understand that the assailant has power over him and so will defer to that power. When both parties thoroughly understand the situation, the stickup can resemble a ballet, in which each side smoothly performs a choreographed part. In such cases the victim's life is usually safe. If one person is street-dumb, however, or loses his head, things can easily go amiss and the victim may pay with his life or suffer a serious injury.

Most often in the inner-city community, the perpetrator of the crime and the victim are both black, so they have limited confidence in the agencies and agents of social control. The criminal transaction is often a matter for them to deal with on their own and on the spot. They must negotiate with each other, settling the score in the best way they know.

The potential perpetrator's first consideration is the selection of the right social setting and victim. He must assess the general surroundings, such as how secluded and dark the spot is and whether the potential victim appears able to handle himself. He may size up his prey. In the right circumstances a seemingly ordinary individual can become a predator.

In the holdup a profound power transaction occurs. The holdup man wants first to relieve the victim of his property. The victim often does not want to give it up, despite the holdup man's demands. Some stickup men use language calculated to override resistance. "Give it up," they say, "I got to have it." The streetwise victim fully cooperates with this command and may even help the perpetrator rob him. He knows the chances are good that the perpetrator is quite nervous about this whole transaction. In fact, the adrenaline is flowing strongly for both individuals, and so things can very easily go amiss. The wise victim knows this and so may seek to help the person attain his objective.

So the victim says, "All right. There it is. Please don't hurt me." In saying this, he is effectively submitting to the power of the holdup man and giving him his props. Such deferential behavior is itself often a large part of what the stickup man wants. He wants the person "with something" to recognize him, to acknowledge his power resources and what he can do to the victim. The wise victim, recognizing this, submits.

This submission is what the perpetrator wants, but it is also what he understands. After all, he has the power in these circumstances, a power that anyone should perceive. He has a gun and is pointing it at the victim, threatening to shoot. Or he may have a knife, threatening serious bodily harm. He further knows—as does the victim—that he is an anonymous stranger and more than likely will get away. Here the perpetrator often makes assumptions based on race and the concentrated poverty all around him. Also built into his act is the assumption that the police will not expend very much energy trying to bring him to justice, and he may assume that any thinking black person would assume the same thing. Therefore, he reasons, it is certainly easier for the person to give it up. The perpetrator's need to remain anonymous is acknowledged by the street-smart victim when the victim goes out of his way not to look at the perpetrator. Such a victim will absolutely not look the assailant in the eye, for though it is unlikely that the victim could actually recognize the perpetrator again, the look in the eye both introduces a certain level of ambiguity into the situation and could be taken as a direct challenge to the perpetrator's newly won authority. Once the victim and the perpetrator lock eyes, a bond that could be deadly has been established, and the event takes on the quality of being memorable. In that event, what started as a simple effort to relieve the victim of his money turns into an ambiguous transaction that may now require the victim's life.

At issue here are the participants' claims on human dignity, claims that have been thrown into furious competition. In order to get out of the situation unscathed, the victim must find a way to allow his assailant to exit with his (the assailant's) dignity intact—which in these circumstances is a goal quite difficult to accomplish. Not only are there competing notions of what constitutes enough dignity, but there is also the problem of just how to grant it—insofar as the vehicle for granting it can become part of its definition, shaping how little or how much is being granted. The wisest victim in such circumstances simply defers, agreeing with and "yessing" the assailant beyond reason. Yet even then it is not clear that the victim can avoid harm. The victim is clearly at the mercy of the assailant, who holds the power in this situation.

After the stickup the perpetrator may even attempt to "cool out" the victim of the crime. A stickup man with style and wiliness might go so far as to give the victim a big hug, mainly for the benefit of potential onlookers, in an attempt to give the impression that a stickup has *not* just occurred, that "we're all right." Some will make excuses or even offer apologies for their behavior, explaining that they or a relative was just robbed.

Thus there is an etiquette of the stickup. Assailant and victim must both know and play their roles. At issue is a core tenet of the code of the street: respect. Primarily, the assailant wants his victim's money, but he also wants things to go smoothly. He wants to wield his power undisputed; he wants his possession of that power to be recognized. Nothing conveys this recognition better than the clear act of total deference. Not to defer is to question the authority, the worth, the status, even the respectability of the assailant in a way that easily suggests contempt or even arrogance. Such a resistant victim is "acting uppity" (for the moment), and such behavior can utterly confuse the assailant. In these circumstances the assailant usually wants a simple way out of the situation: he may use his gun or knife, or he may simply flee. The victim's resistance—or inability to play along—thus may "flood out" the situation with too much information, rendering it unpredictable. If the assailant is not ready to "raise the ante," he may turn tail and run—or he may shoot. Few victims, streetwise or not, take this risk by flooding out the situation intentionally. If they do so inadvertently and survive, they have good fortune or luck to thank for it. It may be much safer to acquire the street knowledge of the etiquette and then help the assailant carry out his job of robbery.

Of course, the victim is most often surprised by the robbery and has no time to act deliberately. In fact, most stickup men greatly appreciate the element of surprise in pulling off their jobs. They may approach from the dark shadows of the street or from another car in a parking lot, or they may stalk their victim, choosing an opportune moment to announce, "Give it up."

The phenomenology of the stickup allows us to see that the assailant is not always identifiable as such; at most times and in most circumstances, he is part of the cultural "woodwork," revealing himself only at the opportune moment. Up to the point at which the stickup begins, the assailant has managed to be taken as a "law-abiding" citizen, someone who might even offer a helping hand to a person in distress. However, not everyone can pull off such deception. Young black, Hispanic, or even white men are often second-guessed in public, making it difficult for them to "get the drop" on a victim. To get the drop requires a certain cunning and stealth. The argument can be made that given the greater defensiveness of the potential victims, the assailants, in order to survive as a species, have had to adapt, becoming ever more creative in the manner in which they pull off their jobs.

Robert Hayes, a thirty-year-old black security guard who works at a Center City CVS, lives in the West Oak Lane section of Philadelphia. On a warm June day, on a busy section of Girard Avenue, he had just left a "cash exchange" after cashing a check. It was the middle of the afternoon, and people were all about. As he began walking away from the cash exchange, he heard a voice say, "Hey, excuse me, wait up." As Robert looked up, he saw a young black man trotting toward him holding up a brown paper sack, as if he had something to show him. Robert, suspecting nothing amiss and curious about what might be in the bag, waited for the man. As the man approached Robert, he directed him to look into the bag. Robert complied with the man's request and saw a black 9-millimeter pistol with the man's finger on the trigger. The man then said, "Give it up. Don't be no fool." Robert replied, "Well, I don't have any money." The man then said, "I just saw you leave the cash exchange. Le' me hold that fat wallet in your back pocket." Robert complied. And the man smiled at him and said, "Have a nice day," and went on about his business, clearing out of the area very quickly. In these circumstances Robert knew better than to resist, though a part of him wanted to. He says that he thought of his two young children and his wife and that he could always get more money and a wallet. What most upset him was the fact that this "young boy" had chumped him, had gotten the drop on him, and made a fool of him. "That hurt more than anything else," he says. But he adds, "I know in my heart that I did the right thing."

One of the greatest fears of people in the inner-city community is to be on the wrong end of a stickup, and they fear the stickup man, or, as he is known in the community, the stickup boy. (The term "stickup boy" initially referred to those who held up drug dealers, but it has come to refer to young holdup men in general.) In dealing with this fear, residents have developed a working conception of the proclivities of the stickup boy. As was indicated above, their belief that he "picks his people," allows residents to move at least some of the responsibility for a successful robbery from the stickup man to the victim by averring that it is up to those who use the streets—particularly themselves—not to be "picked" for a stickup. So residents, especially those who present themselves as streetwise, try to behave in ways that let potential stickup boys, as well as anyone else, know that they are not "the one" to be targeted for a stickup. They become preoccupied with giving the right signal to people with whom they share the neighborhood streets and other public spaces.

For young people this means being prepared to meet challenges with counteractions. When they are hit or otherwise violated, they may hit back. Or they may even "pay back" later on by avenging transgressions. An important part of the code is not to allow others to chump you, to let them know that you are "about serious business" and not to be trifled with. The message that you are not a pushover must be sent loudly and clearly.

Of course, this does not always work. There are circumstances in which the stickup boy will try anyone, including those who have proved they do not deserve to be tested. For instance, the victim could be absentmindedly walking down a street at the wrong time or simply be unlucky. But the belief on the street is that the stickup boy generally knows who is vulnerable and who is not.

Around the streetcorners and carryouts—the staging areas—where so many drug dealers and corner boys hang out, the would-be stickup boys generally know who is who, who "can fight" and who cannot, who has nerve and heart and who is a chump. Around such places, in various social arenas, and on the streets more generally, the chump gets little or no respect, and those who resemble him are the ones who most often get picked on, tried or tested, and become victims of robbery and gratuitous violence. Some people so labeled readily report such offenses to the police, a cardinal sin among those strongly invested in the street code.

Stereotypically, the chump is the "quiet" person who, as they say on the corner, "minds his business and don't bother no one. Dresses nice." He is also often "decent" and kind. But in this area of so much deprivation, onlookers are very inclined to take his displays of kindness for weakness, thus degrading a positive force in the public community. However, for personal security and standing around the carryout, it is important to demonstrate to all others that one is not a chump; but in order to do so a man must often present a street front, moving and acting in certain ways that more clearly identify him with the street. One common way is to swagger, display a quick temper, and a foul mouth, but also to let others know in no uncertain terms that he is prepared and able to defend himself or, as the young men say, to show them he "can hold his hands." The person must be ready and willing to fight, to "get physical," if the situation demands it, or to display the nerve and heart to engage in a standoff when necessary. In a word, he must be able through his demeanor to send the message that he will stand up to others and not let others roll on him. Such an image may require wearing the latest styles, including the "drug dealer look," and having a hip and ready "conversation"— knowing just what to say to keep others from moving on him verbally (the proper reply to someone who tests you)—although actions almost always speak louder than words. The posture at the opposite extreme of that associated with the chump has come to be described as "thorough" or being "a thorough dude"—knowing "what time it is," or being exceptionally streetwise. But for many, such an image is often just that—a front, a posture, a representation—and it is very difficult to enact so as to convince or fool those who are streetwise.

The smarter stickup boys, however, are increasingly coming to fear the chump because of the likelihood that he is precisely not down or knowledgeable about the code of the street. Such a person out of fear, so the reasoning goes, could cause a stickup to go wrong by carrying a gun or knife or by losing his composure and physically contesting the dominance of the stickup boy during a robbery. When a stickup has progressed to a certain point, the chump, through his inexperience with the streets, may misread the situation and believe he is in more danger than he actually is. He may then panic, flooding the situation out and effectively bringing what began nonviolently to a violent end. If the chump becomes nervous and tries aggressively to protect himself and/or his loved one, he may in reality be raising the stakes to a dangerous level.

The thorough dude, in contrast, may understand intuitively when the assailant is in control, but until the moment when there is a shift in who controls the situation, he may be able to alter the outcome. Such a person is seldom a passive player, rather, he knows what time it is; and at the right time, he defers to the power of the assailant. He understands that when a gun is put in your face, you do what you can to defer to or appease the person with the gun. You then "give it up," saying something like, "Here it is. It's all yours. Please don't hurt me." Effectively, he cuts his losses, saying, "You got me that time," and he tries to learn from his mistake and to make sure that this never happens to him again.

## SEE BUT DON'T SEE

People residing in the drug-infested, depressed inner-city community may understand the economic need for the drug trade. Many residents become demoralized yet often try to coexist with it, rationalizing that the boys who deal drugs are not necessarily bad boys but are simply doing what they think they need to do to make money. They themselves, however, don't want to be victimized by the trade, nor do they want their friends and loved ones to be harmed. Many have come to believe that the police and the public officials don't care about their communities, and this belief encourages them to give up any hope of doing something about the drug trade. As a result, they may condemn the dealing but also tolerate it. They become inured to it. They also understand that some local people rely on it for financial support. The Robin Hood phenomenon helps the justification process. As was mentioned above, some dealers try to assist their community by surreptitiously donating money to various organizations and helping to support their families and friends with drug profits. One drug dealer told me he paid for his aunt's surgery as well as for all his mother's bills, and he was very proud of having done that. He was proud of having taken his girlfriend out to fancy restaurants, proud of everything he had become. He knew drug dealing was wrong, but he accepted his role in it. Of course, not everybody in the community is so accepting of the drug trade. Most people have very, very negative feelings about dealing, feelings that are most obviously on display when violence occurs. That is an important point— some people object only when violence erupts.

Another reason for seeing and yet not seeing drug transactions is that as people walk the streets of the community, they cannot help seeing what's going on, but are afraid to get involved. Concerned for their own safety, they don't even want people to notice them witnessing what is going on. After an incident like a shooting or a gang war, people tend to clam up for fear of retribution, especially where the authorities are concerned. If a bust occurs, anyone who is considered to have been paying too much attention to the drug activity might be suspected of having told the police about it. The way people deal with this fear and the need to protect themselves is by seeing but not seeing.

Many parents see but don't see for another reason: they realize that their own son is probably involved in the trade. They disapprove of it, but they also benefit from it. A mother who receives money, sometimes even large sums of money, from her son may not ask too many questions about its source. She just accepts the fact that the money is there somehow. Since it is sorely needed, there is a strong incentive not to interrupt the flow. Some people are so torn over what they are tolerating that they pray and ask forgiveness from the Lord for their de facto approval. Yet they cannot bring themselves to intervene.

The economic unraveling in so many of these communities puts people up against the wall and encourages them to do things that they would otherwise be morally reluctant to do. A boy who can't get a job in the regular economy becomes a drug dealer not all at once but by increments. These boys make a whole set of choices and decisions based in part on what they are able to do successfully. A boy who grows up on the streets thoroughly invested in the code of the street is also closer to the underground economy. Once mastered, the savoir faire of the street world—knowing how to deal coolly with people, how to move, look, act, dress—is a form of capital, not a form middle-class people would respect, but capital that can nonetheless be cashed in.

Since the code of the street is sanctioned primarily by violence and the threat of violent retribution (an eye for an eye and a tooth for a tooth), the more inner-city youths choose this route in life, the more normative the code of the street becomes in the neighborhood. Neighbors are encouraged to choose between an abstract code of justice that is disparaged by the most dangerous people on the streets and a practical code that is geared toward survival in the public spaces of their community.

Children growing up in these circumstances learn early in life that this is the way things are and that the lessons of those who might teach them otherwise become less and less relevant. Surrounded by violence and by indifference to the innocent victims of drug dealers and users alike, the decent people are finding it harder and harder to maintain a sense of community. Thus violence comes to regulate life in the drug-infested neighborhoods and the putative neighborhood leaders are increasingly the people who control the violence.

The ramifications of this state of affairs reach far beyond inner-city communities. A startling study by the Sentencing Project revealed that 33 percent of young black men in their twenties are under the supervision of the criminal justice system—in jail, in prison, on probation, or on parole. This astounding figure must be considered partly responsible for the widespread perception of young black men as dangerous and not to be trusted. This kind of demonization affects all young blacks—those of the middle class, those of the dwindling working class, as well as the street element.

One might ask, "What can account for the disproportionate percentage of blacks among the adjudicated?" African Americans have been overrepresented in the prison population since the first studies were done, but the jump in their numbers over the past generation has been exponential. Part of the answer would have to be crack cocaine. The prison terms for the possession and sale of crack cocaine are stiffer than those for powder cocaine, a drug that is more expensive and more prevalent in the middle class. Another factor is that proportionately more blacks are dealers, and this speaks to the overall inability of young black men to get into the workforce. The glamorous hipness of dealing that certifies one as firmly in the oppositional culture is also a factor. When jobs disappear, leaving people poor and concentrated, the drug economy becomes an unforgiving way of life, organized around violence and predatory activity.

## THE VIOLENT DEATH

Television images portray and even glamorize the fast life, and movies such as *The Godfather*, *Set It Off*, *Boyz 'n the Hood*, and *Menace II Society* that feature gratuitous violence help legitimize violence for many young men.[14] The films have a certain realism and deal with the complex problems that emerge every day on the ghetto streets. When young men see a leading man resort to violence to settle a dispute, they can ask, "What does it do for him? Was he right? Did the victim deserve what he got?" The answers help them deal with their own problems: "How bad should I be? Should I take that jacket off that guy?"

But probably most important, the films, along with rap music as well as their everyday experiences, help youths become inured to violence and, perhaps, death itself. Those residing in some of the most troubled areas typically have witnessed much street violence that has at times resulted in maiming or death. All of this contributes to the posture that dying "ain't no big deal." One must understand that some young people bereft of hope for the future have made their peace with death and talk about planning their own funerals. They sometimes speak in euphemistic phrases like "going out" or "checking out." After experiencing the deaths of so many young friends, the hopeless conclude that life is bound to be short "for the way I'm living," or "if the deal go down, dying ain't no big thing." The high death rate among their peers keeps many from expecting to live beyond age twenty-five.

With such an outlook, "living fast and large" in the present makes sense, for "tomorrow ain't promised to you." Young men like this tend to lead an existential life that may acquire meaning only when faced with the possibility of imminent death. Not to be afraid to die is by implication to have few compunctions about taking another's life, for the right reasons, if the situation demands it. The youths who have internalized such attitudes and convincingly display them in their bearing are among the most threatening people of all. The most aggressive develop "beefs," and harbor grudges, at times with complete strangers, and gain a reputation for being "touchy" or "crazy." And they convey the message that they fear no one. With credibility for this position, supported by words and deeds, a young man can gain a sense of respect and power on the streets. This is what many youths strive to achieve, whether they emerge from a decent or a street-oriented background, for its practical defensive value, but also for the positive way it makes them feel about themselves as men.

At times a parent, particularly one steeped in the teachings of the church, will say to the young person directly, "Son, you living too fast. You living too fast. Better slow down. You gon' die." Some young people take it as a kind of warning, even as a sign from above, that "Mother would speak to me that way. Maybe I better heed what she is saying." But for this kind of message to be taken seriously, other events generally have to come together so that it seems prudent and wise for the young man to try to make a change. Of particular importance is the support or example of friends. If they have suffered severe setbacks like arrests, assaults, or serious drug-related health problems, their example may serve as a sign—and it can be a powerful influence in encouraging the person to try to change. What he needs then is a serious helping hand: a caring old head can make a real difference. Without such support the young person may simply muddle along, perhaps hitting on or missing an opportunity to be saved from the streets.

Sometimes young people are looking for an excuse to change, and a sign can be enough. They are often strongly if passively religious, at times invoking "God" or "the Lord" in conversations with peers. They may reflect on the notion that there is a higher power to be reckoned with, and that can be a support in the effort to change. Such people may also invoke the notion of fate, particularly when confronting things they cannot fathom or fully understand. Fate can be used to explain failure in a way that cushions disappointment. A young man can respond to a love affair that does not work out, a loss in the lottery, a fight that does not go his way, or material things that are totally out of reach by simply saying, "That wasn't meant for me," or "That wasn't for me." With feelings of deep resignation, he may let go of the desire to acquire or to achieve the particular objective, at least for the present.

On the other hand, the notion of fate can also encourage a person to be reckless in meting out violence. The belief that whatever one does or says was meant to be allows one to take chances that are not perceived as chances, risks that are not seen as risks, because what will be will be. Hence the person is able to walk the streets almost fearlessly, knowing that "when my time is here, it is here, and there's nothing I can do about it." Thus one can live life to the fullest, believing that it is just not "my time"—for now. In the heat of the moment, during an altercation, this belief can determine the outcome of a fight to the death, giving an individual the advantage that only profound faith in his or her ability to prevail can provide.

When a violent death does occur, it affects not just the victim and his or her family but the entire community. Something terrible has happened, and the community grieves and mourns. Many ask, "Why?" Johnny, Robert, Marcel, Kevin, or Rashawn was such a wonderful person, with so much promise, so much to give. Why was he "taken out like this"? The family often tries to accept the explanation that it is "the Creator's will." Its members may question "the Supreme Being," but always with the understanding that His authority is legitimate. For them, the fact that the young boy died must say something about the living, but also about the way the young boy lived his life. There is a strong belief in fate and the notion that a person has a time to be on the planet, but that people can "rush" their time by "living fast" or "running in the fast lane."


## THE AFTERMATH OF DEATH

When a young life is cut down, almost everyone goes into mourning. The first thing that happens is that a crowd gathers about the site of the shooting or the incident. The police then arrive, drawing more of a crowd. Since such a death often occurs close to the victim's home, his mother or his close relatives and friends may be on the scene of the killing. When they arrive, the women and girls often wail and moan, crying out their grief for all to hear, while the young men simply look on, in studied silence; they are there to help the young women if they require assistance. Soon the ambulance arrives and takes the person to the nearest hospital. If he is still alive, the mother or a relative or a neighbor will ride along inside the ambulance. At times, though, it is too late, and the ambulance will go to the morgue.

The next day, the relatives and neighbors and friends look for a report of the crime in the local newspaper. Friends and relatives may already be angry, and they sometimes vent this anger at the newspaper for not running a long enough story of the shooting or the death of their loved one. They sometimes vent at the police, calling them incompetent, racist, or worse. They may wonder why the person responsible for this deed has not been brought to justice. In the community there is profound sadness. People talk about the victim. "It is such a shame." "Why did he have to go this way?" "All he wanted was a decent life in this world." And there are many questions. Some people begin to question their faith. "Is there a God?" People who haven't spoken to one another in many months now find something to talk about. They speak of the deceased. Community residents develop a bond based on their links to this person.

The younger people take it especially hard. They wonder aloud why this happened, but in fact they know why. They know the boy was a drug dealer. They know that he violated in some way the code of the street and possibly messed up someone's money. "He did somebody wrong," or he "thought he was slick." It was something. Otherwise, the youth's death simply makes no sense. "Why do people have to be like that?" they ask. The girls sit on their stoops and cry. Some people pass by and say not a word. Everyone knows that the community is in mourning. Nothing has to be said. All is communicated by the sad looks on people's faces. Girls and boys, friends of the deceased, hug one another spontaneously. Again they bond. This is a terrible thing, a tragedy.

These feelings persist all week. Then there is the wake, as friends and relatives gather at the boy's home. They sit with the family members and try to comfort them. They recall the boy's positive points. Even though they all know the negative things about him, they almost never mention them. It is widely known that the boy was a drug dealer, but nobody will speak about his drug dealing or how it might have led to his death. They all know the boy was involved in "the life," yet at this moment they deny it. It is not good to speak of the boy's negative attributes, even though, deep down inside, everyone is aware of them. They may even know who killed him. But no one comes forward to tell the authorities, because the police are not to be trusted; they are alien forces in the community. The people in the community discuss this among themselves. The boys, his homies, make oblique threats to the people who did this. It is their obligation to get even, to deal with the assassin, and they say as much by their looks. But in reality, over the next days and weeks, nothing is done. Most people leave it to the police, the authorities, although it is important to act as though they will get the person who did this. Around the stoops, they talk big. At the spot where this "went down," they talk big. Over time, though, nothing happens, and they really want to leave it alone.

Of course, whether they do in fact leave it alone depends on what kind of homie the boy was. If he was very popular, then a group might try to do something to pay back, and a deadly feud can start. More often, there is just talk about getting even. They say, "This wasn't the first shooting, and this won't be the last on these streets." As they are saying these things, gathering together and bonding, various graffiti artists of the neighborhood erect memorials for the young man. Some will paint their car windows with messages of hope like "Rock, RIP." Some make T-shirts with the boy's picture emblazoned across the front as a memorial to him.

The day of the funeral arrives. At 11 A.M. on a Monday, the community of friends and relatives gathers at the local funeral parlor. Many are dressed in black; the young people are mainly in black leather. Most people are young, from fifteen to twenty-eight or so, but there are also older women and men, some very well dressed, others not. Some of the people appear to be quite poor. There are ladies with big gold earrings and girls whose hair needs fixing. There are girls with babies in tow. A two-year-old walks about the lobby of the funeral home, and the mother has to run after him as others look on. A number of homeboys in Timberland boots and black leather jackets stand outside in the light rain, suspiciously eyeing everyone who arrives. They talk to one another and mill about. Two or three police cars are also there, just in case of trouble. It is the police's job to protect the peace, to maintain order, and the cops sit and watch the crowd come and go. They ask no questions, but people think they are there to investigate, too. Both the cops and the residents have seen this all before, and everyone knows what to expect.

An old head in the community says,

> I knew the boy well. I always warned him about these drugs, but he couldn't resist. He knew. I told him I'd come to his funeral. And this is what I'm doing. It is a shame. But you know, it is the system. It is the system. No jobs. No education. And the drugs are all about. You realize what amount of drugs come in here [the neighborhood]. That's not us. It is them. The white people. They bring the drugs in here. They don't want us to have nothing. But this is what they give us. All this death and destruction. I know a boy did shoot him, but it was really the system. The system.

Inside, it is standing room only. This must give the young man's mother and other family members some support. His father is nowhere to be seen, however, and the old head says, "He's in jail." The old head adds that most of the men are in jail. That's where they are. That's what happens to the men. The victim was just nineteen years old. His friends are here, his homeboys and-girls. The girls wail and cry. The boy's mother cries and wails; this is a "drama for his mama," as community residents say. People whisper. A number of girls become so distraught that they get up and walk out of the service, tears streaming down their faces. The minister preaches about the young man. People sing sweet songs. There are testimonials about the boy's life, but here, too, nothing is said about the drugs or any of the other negative things he was involved with. Only the positive is accentuated.

# FOUR

# The Mating Game

T HE problem of teenage pregnancy in the inner city draws as much attention and expressions of puzzlement from the wider community as do the problems of drugs and violence. These kinds of behavior appear to work against everything for which decent young Americans strive: education, good jobs, a stable household, and middle-class values. Yet they make sense of a sort in the world of the street and in relation to the code that dominates it. Chapter 3 explored the relationship between the code and the underground economy of drugs and violence; this chapter looks at what young people, both decent and street, face as they grow up and find one another in this same world. It needs to be made clear that for these teenagers the benefits they perceive as deriving from their sexual behavior outweigh the risks. Their outlook on sex and pregnancy, like their outlook on violence, is strongly affected by their perceived options in life, and their sexual behavior follows rules very much shaped by the code of the street. Such perceptions are formed by the fortunes of immediate peers, family, and others with whom the youths identify. Among teenagers one of the most important factors working against pregnancy is their belief that they have something to lose by becoming parents at an early age; many believe they have something to gain.

## THE SOCIAL CONTEXT

In many of these neighborhoods it is the strong, financially stable, tightly knit, "decent" family, often but not always nuclear, that works to instill high aspirations in children and expectations of a good future that would be undermined by youthful parenthood. With the connections and examples of such families and their representatives in a neighborhood, a youth may hope to prevail in life despite presumed obstacles—financial, cultural, or other. The presence of these models can serve as a powerful inspiration to those who may be otherwise disadvantaged, and it can work socially as a bastion against the street culture. This street culture is characterized by support for and encouragement of an alternative lifestyle that appears highly attractive to many adolescents, despite their family background. Its activities are centered on the "fast life" and may include early sexual activity, drug experimentation, and other forms of delinquency. But while relatively advantaged youths with clear options may dabble in this culture, becoming hip enough for social approval and then moving on, those with fewer apparent options and a limited sense of the future may more fully invest themselves in the culture, attempting to gain status according to its principles and norms. The relative prominence of this culture in the poorest inner-city neighborhoods brings about not only a prevalence of much antisocial behavior but the high incidence of teenage parenthood as well.

As has been an important theme throughout this volume, working poor residents, for social purposes, distinguish values they see as decent from those they associate with the street. Generally, decency is a highly regarded personal quality, and the assigning of a street orientation to a person is usually deeply discrediting. In the impoverished neighborhood the meanings of the terms sometimes overlap, compete, and even support one another; their interaction is highly complex. In fact, though, these distinctions operate more or less to identify social polarities; and particularly among the young their social referents may be used to distinguish the socially "lame" from the "hip."

Among residents of the impoverished inner-city neighborhood, the culture of decency is usually represented by close and extended families, often characterized by low-income financial stability. It emphasizes the work ethic, getting ahead, or "having something" as important goals. Decency becomes an organizing principle against which others are then judged. The family unit, often with the aid of a strong religious component, instills in its members a certain degree of self-respect, civility, and propriety and even, despite prevailing impoverished living conditions, a positive view of the future. Many such decent families become highly protective of their children and motivated to leave the neighborhood. Those who cannot afford to leave try to accomplish socially what they cannot accomplish otherwise: they attempt to isolate their children from the children whom they associate with the street, for they believe that teenage pregnancy, early involvement with drugs, crime, and violence, and other difficulties begin in early childhood, in deep involvement with the play groups on the streets. Decent local role models, male or female "old heads," sometimes through direct mentoring, encourage young people to see possibilities and take advantage of opportunities available to people like themselves.

To negotiate this setting effectively, particularly its public places, one must to some degree be hip or down or streetwise, showing the ability to see through troublesome street situations and to prevail. To survive in the setting is thus to be somewhat adept at handling the streets, but to be streetwise is to risk one's claim to decency; for many youths decency is often associated with being lame or square. In growing up, young people of the neighborhood must therefore walk something of a social tightrope, coming to terms with the street. For instance, youths who go away to college and return are sometimes taunted and challenged by their more street-oriented peers with the mocking question "Can you still hang?" (Can you still handle the streets?) Those who would be socially mobile often feel they must be hip enough to get along with their more street-oriented peers, but square enough to keep out of trouble or avoid those habits and situations that would hurt their chances for social mobility or even simple survival. It is in this sense that many adolescents, simply by growing up in an underclass neighborhood, are at special risk.

Youths are at risk in other ways as well. Many observe the would-be legitimate role models around them and tend to find them unworthy of emulation. Conventional hard work seems not to have paid off for the old, and the relatively few hardworking people of the neighborhood appear to be struggling to survive. At the same time unconventional role models beckon the youths to a thriving underground economy, which promises "crazy" money, along with a certain thrill, power, and prestige. Streetwise and severely alienated young men can easily deal in the drug trade, part-time or full-time, as was shown in the preceding chapter. They may even draw their intimate female counterparts along with them, "hooking them up," and smoothly initiating them into prostitution.

Given that persistent poverty is so widespread in the neighborhood, for many residents, particularly the young, values of decency and law abidingness are more easily compromised. Needing money badly, these people feel social pressure and see the chance for making sometimes huge sums outside their front door. Because of all the vice and crime in the neighborhood, those who can leave tend to do so, isolating the very poor and the working poor even more. This exodus further demoralizes neighborhood residents and makes them more vulnerable to a number of ills, including rising drug use and teenage pregnancy.

The manufacturing jobs that used to provide opportunities for young people in inner-city neighborhoods and strongly, although indirectly, supported values of decency and conventionality have largely vanished from the economy, replaced by thousands of low-paying service jobs often located in the suburbs, beyond the reach of poor neighborhoods. These changes have damaged the financial health of the inner city and undermined the quality of available role models. The trust and perceptions of decency that once prevailed in the community are increasingly absent. In their place, street values, represented by the fast life, violence, and crime, become more prominent.

The consequences of these changes can be illustrated by their effect on one of the community's most important institutions, the relationship between old heads and young boys. The old head was once the epitome of decency in inner-city neighborhoods. Thanks to a vibrant manufacturing economy, he had relatively stable means. His acknowledged role in the community was to teach, support, encourage, and, in effect, socialize young men to meet their responsibilities regarding work, family life, the law, and common decency. Young boys and single men in their late teens or twenties had confidence in the old head's ability to impart practical advice. Very often he played surrogate father to those who needed his attention and moral support.

But as meaningful employment becomes increasingly scarce for young men of the neighborhood and the expansion of the drug culture offers opportunities for quick money, the old head is losing prestige and authority. Streetwise boys are concluding that his lessons about life and work ethic are no longer relevant, and a new role model is emerging. The embodiment of the street, this man is young, often a product of the street gang, and indifferent, at best, to the law and traditional values.

Traditional female role models, often paragons of decency, have also suffered decreased authority. Mature women, often grandmothers themselves, once effectively served the community as auxiliary parents who publicly augmented and supported the relationship between parent and child. These women would discipline children and act as role models for young women, exerting a certain degree of social control. As the neighborhoods grow ever more drug infested, ordinary young mothers and their children are among the most obvious casualties. The traditional female old head becomes stretched and overburdened; her role has become more complicated as she often steps in as a surrogate mother for her grandchildren or a stray neighborhood child.

These women universally lament the proliferation of drugs in the community, the "crack whores" who walk the neighborhood, the sporadic violence that now and then claims innocent bystanders. The open-air drug sales, the many pregnant girls, the incivility, the crime, the many street kids, and the diminished number of upstanding (as the residents say) role models make it difficult for old and young alike to maintain a positive outlook, to envision themselves beyond the immediate situation. As neighborhood deterioration feeds on itself, decent law-aiding people become increasingly demoralized; many of those who are capable leave, while some succumb to the street.

This is the social context in which the incidence of teenage pregnancy must be seen, complicated by peer pressure, ignorance, passion, luck, intent, desire for conquest, religion, love, and even deep hostility between young men and women. It is nothing less than the cultural manifestation of persistent urban poverty. It is a mean adaptation to blocked opportunities and profound lack, a grotesque form of coping by young people constantly undermined by a social system that historically has limited their social options and, until recently, rejected their claims to full citizenship.

The lack of family-sustaining jobs denies many young men the possibility of forming an economically self-reliant family, the traditional American mark of manhood. Partly in response, many young black men form strong attachments to peer groups that emphasize sexual prowess as proof of manhood, with babies as evidence. These groups congregate on street corners, boasting about their sexual exploits and deriding conventional family life. They encourage this orientation by rewarding members who are able to get over the sexual defenses of women. For many the object is to hit and run while maintaining personal freedom and independence from conjugal ties; when they exist, the ties should be on the young man's terms. Concerned with immediate gratification, some boys want babies to demonstrate their ability to control a girl's mind and body.

A sexual game emerges as girls are lured by the (usually older) boys' vague but convincing promises of love and sometimes marriage. At the same time the "fast" adolescent street orientation presents early sexual experience and promiscuity as a virtue. But when the girls submit, they often end up pregnant and abandoned. However, for many such girls who have few other perceivable options, motherhood, accidental or otherwise, becomes a rite of passage to adulthood. Although an overwhelming number may not be actively trying to have babies, many are not actively trying to prevent having them. One of the reasons for this may be the strong fundamentalist religious orientation of many poor blacks, which emphasizes the role of fate in life. If something happens, it happens; if something was meant to be, then let it be, and "God will find a way." With the dream of a mate, a girl may be indifferent to the possibility of pregnancy, even if it is not likely that pregnancy will lead to marriage. So the pregnant girl can look forward to a certain affirmation, particularly after the baby arrives—if not from the father, then from her peer group, from her family, from the Lord.

Thus, if it becomes obvious that the young father's promises are empty, the young woman has a certain amount of help in settling for the role of single parent. A large part of her identity is provided by the baby under her care and guidance, and for many street-oriented girls there is no quicker way to grow up. Becoming a mother can be a strong play for authority, maturity, and respect, but it is also a shortsighted and naïve gamble because the girl often fails to realize that her life will be suddenly burdened and her choices significantly limited.

In these circumstances outlook, including a certain amount of education, wisdom, and mentoring from decent role models, becomes extremely important. The strong, so-called decent family, often with a husband and wife, sometimes with a strong-willed single mother helped by close relatives and neighbors, may instill in girls a sense of hope. These families can hope to reproduce the relatively strong family form, which is generally regarded in the neighborhood as advantaged. The two parents or close kin are known as hard workers, striving to have something and strongly emphasizing the work ethic, common decency, and social and moral responsibility. Though the pay may be low, the family often can count on a regular income, giving its members the sense that decent values have paid off for them.

A girl growing up in such a family, or even living in close social and physical proximity to some, may have strong support from a mother, a father, friends, and neighbors who not only care very much whether she becomes pregnant but are also able to share knowledge about negotiating life beyond the confines of the neighborhood. The girl may then approach social mobility or at least delay pregnancy. In these circumstances she has a better chance to cultivate a positive sense of the future and a healthy self-respect; she may come to feel she has a great deal to lose by becoming an unwed parent.

Contributing strongly to this outlook are ministers, teachers, parents, and upwardly mobile peers. At times a successful older sister sets a standard and expectations for younger siblings, who may attempt to follow her example. The community and the decent family help place the successful one high in the sibling hierarchy by praising her achievements. At the very least, such support groups can strongly communicate their expectations that the girl will do something with her life other than have a baby out of wedlock—that is, they subscribe to and seek to pass on middle-class values.

Although the basic sexual codes of inner-city youths may not differ fundamentally from those of other young people, the social, economic, and personal consequences of adolescent sexual conduct vary profoundly for different social classes. Like all adolescents, inner-city youths are subject to intense, hard-to-control urges. Sexual relations, exploitive and otherwise, are common among middle-class teenagers as well, but most middle-class youths take a stronger interest in their future and know what a pregnancy can do to derail it. In contrast, many inner-city adolescents see no future that can be derailed—no hope for a tomorrow much different from today—hence they see little to lose by having a child out of wedlock.

Sexual conduct among these young people is to a large extent the product of the meshing of two opposing drives, that of the boys and that of the girls. For a variety of reasons tied to the socioeconomic situation, their goals are often diametrically opposed, and sex becomes a contest between them. As was noted above, to many boys sex is an important symbol of local social status; sexual conquests become so many notches on one's belt. Many of the girls offer sex as a gift in bargaining for the attentions of a young man. As boys and girls try to use each other to achieve their own ends, the reality that emerges sometimes approximates their goals, but it often brings frustration and disillusionment and perpetuates or even worsens their original situation.

Each sexual encounter generally has a winner and a loser. The girls have a dream, the boys a desire. The girls dream of being carried off by a Prince Charming who will love them, provide for them, and give them a family. The boys often desire either sex without commitment or babies without responsibility for them. It becomes extremely difficult for the boys, in view of their employment prospects, to see themselves taking on the responsibilities of conventional fathers and husbands. Yet they know what the girls want and play that role to get sex. In accepting a boy's advances, a girl may think she is maneuvering him toward a commitment or that her getting pregnant is the nudge he needs to marry her and give her the life she wants. What she does not see is that the boy, despite his claims, is often incapable of giving her that life, for in reality he has little money, few prospects for earning much, and no wish to be tied to a woman who will have a say in what he does. His loyalty is to his peer group and its norms. When the girl becomes pregnant, the boy tends to retreat from her, although, with the help of pressure from her family and peers, she may ultimately succeed in getting him to take some responsibility for the child.

## SEX: THE GAME AND THE DREAM

To many inner-city male youths, the most important people in their lives are members of their peer groups. They set the standards for conduct, and it is important to live up to those standards, to look good in their eyes. The peer group places a high value on sex, especially what middle-class people call casual sex. But though sex may be casual in terms of commitment to the partner, it is usually taken quite seriously as a measure of the boy's worth. A young man's primary goal is thus to find as many willing females as possible. The more "pussy" he gets, the more esteem accrues to him. But the young man not only must "get some"; he also must prove he is getting it. This leads him to talk about girls and sex with any other young man who will listen. Because of the implications sex has for their local social status and esteem, the young men are ready to be regaled with graphic tales of one another's sexual exploits.

The lore of the street says there is a contest going on between the boy and the girl even before they meet. To the young man the woman becomes, in the most profound sense, a sexual object. Her body and mind are the object of a sexual game, to be won for his personal aggrandizement. Status goes to the winner, and sex is prized as a testament not of love but of control over another human being. The goal of the sexual conquests is to make a fool of the young woman.

The young men describe their successful campaigns as "getting over" young women's sexual defenses. To get over, the young man must devise a "game," whose success is gauged by its acceptance by his peers and especially by women. Relying heavily on gaining the girl's confidence, the game consists of the boy's full presentation of self, including his dress, grooming, looks, dancing ability, and conversation, or "rap."

The rap is the verbal element of the game, whose object is to inspire sexual interest. It embodies the whole person and is thus crucial to success. Among peer-group members, raps are assessed, evaluated, and divided into weak and strong. The assessment of the young man's rap is, in effect, the evaluation of his whole game. Convincing proof of effectiveness is the "booty": the amount of sex the young man appears to be getting. Young men who are known to fail with women often face ridicule from the group, having their raps labeled "tissue paper," their games seen as inferior, and their identities devalued.

After developing a game over time, through trial and error, a young man is ever on the lookout for players, young women on whom to perfect it. To find willing players is to gain affirmation of self, and the boy's status in the peer group may go up if he can seduce a girl considered to be "choice," "down," or streetwise. On encountering an attractive girl, the boy typically sees a challenge: he attempts to "run his game." The girl usually is fully aware that a game is being attempted; but if the young man is sophisticated or "smooth," or if the girl is inexperienced, she may be duped.

In many instances the game plays on the dream that many inner-city girls harbor from their early teenage years. The popular love songs they listen to, usually from the age of seven or eight, are imbued with a wistful air, promising love and ecstasy to someone "just like you." This dream involved having a boyfriend, a fiancé, or a husband and the fairy-tale prospect of living happily ever after with one's children in a nice house in a good neighborhood—essentially the dream of the middle-class American lifestyle, complete with nuclear family. It is nurtured by daily watching of television soap operas, or "stories," as the women call them. The heroes and heroines may be white and upper middle class, but such characteristics only make them more attractive. Many girls dream of becoming the comfortable middle-class housewife portrayed on television, even though they see that their peers can only approximate that role.

When a girl is approached by a boy, her faith in the dream clouds her view of the situation. A romantically successful boy has a knack for knowing just what is on a girl's mind, what she wants from life, and how she hopes to obtain it. The young man's age—he may be four or five years older than the girl—gives him an authoritative edge and makes his readiness to "settle down" more credible. By enacting this role, he can shape the interaction, calling up the resources he needs to play the game successfully. He fits himself to be the *man* she wants him to be, but this identity may be exaggerated and temporary, maintained only until he gets what he wants. Essentially, he shows her the side of himself that he knows she wants to see, that represents what she wants in a man. For instance, he will sometimes "walk through the woods" with the girl: he might visit at her home and go to church with her family or even do "manly" chores around her house, showing that he is an "upstanding young man." But all of this may only be part of his game, and after he gets what he wants, he may cast off this aspect of his presentation and reveal something of his true self, as he flits to other women and reverts to behavior more characteristic of his everyday life—that which is centered on his peer group.

The girl may refuse to accept reports of the boy's duplicity; she must see for herself. Until she completely loses confidence in the young man, she may find herself strongly defending him to friends and family who question her choice. She may know she is being played, but given the effectiveness of the boy's game—his rap, his presentation of self, his looks, his age, his wit, his dancing ability, and his general popularity—infatuation often rules.

Aware of many abandoned young mothers, many a girl fervently hopes that her man is the one who will be different. In addition, her peer group supports her pursuit of the dream, implicitly upholding her belief in the young man's good faith. When a girl does become engaged to be married, there is much excitement, with relatives and friends oohing and aahing over their prospective life. But seldom does this happen, because for the immediate future, the boy is generally not interested in "playing house," as his peers derisively refer to domestic life.

While pursuing his game, the boy often feigns love and caring, pretending to be a dream man and acting as though he has the best intentions toward the girl. Ironically, in many cases the young many does indeed have good intentions. He may feel profound ambivalence, mainly because such intentions conflict with the values of his peer group and his lack of confidence in his ability to support a family. At times this reality and the male peer group's values are placed in sharp focus by his own deviance from them, as he incurs sanctions for allowing a girl to "rule" him or gains positive reinforcement for keeping her in line. The group sanctions its members by pinning on them demeaning labels such as "pussy," "pussy whipped," or "househusband," causing them to posture in a way that clearly distances them from such characterizations.

At times, however, a boy earnestly attempts to *be* a dream man, with honorable intentions of "doing right" by the young woman, of marrying her and living happily ever after according to their version of middle-class propriety. But the reality of his poor employment prospects makes it hard for him to follow through.

Unable to realize his vision of himself as the young woman's provider in the American middle-class tradition, which the peer group often labels "square," the young man may become even more committed to his game. In his ambivalence he may go so far as to make plans with the girls, including going house-hunting and shopping for furniture. A twenty-three-year-old woman who at seventeen became a single parent of a baby girl said this:

> Yeah, they'll [boys will] take you out. Walk you down to Center City, movies, window shops. [laughs] They point in the window, "Yeah, I'm gonna get you this. Wouldn't you like this? Look at that nice livin' room set." Then they want to take you to his house, go to his room: "Let's go over to my house, watch some TV." Next thing you know, your clothes is off and you in bed havin' sex, you know.

Such shopping trips carry important psychological implications for the relationship, serving as a salve that heals wounds and erases doubt about the young man's intentions. The young woman may report to her parents or friends about her last date or shopping trip, describe the furniture they priced and the supposed payment terms. She continues to have hope, which he fuels by "going with" her, letting her and others know that she is his "steady"—though for him to maintain status within his peer group, she should not be his only known girl. For the young man, however, making plans and successive shopping trips may be elements of the game—often nothing more than a stalling device to keep the girl hanging on so that he can continue to receive her social sexual favors.

In many cases the more the young man seems to exploit the young woman, the higher is his regard within the peer group. To consolidate his status, he feels moved at times to show others that he is in control, which is not always easy to accomplish. Many young women are strong, highly independent, and assertive, and a contest of wills between the two may develop, with arguments and fights in public over the most trivial issues. She is not a simple victim, and the roles in the relationship are not to be taken for granted but must be negotiated repeatedly. To prove his dominance unequivocally, he may attempt to "break her down" in front of her friends and his, "showing the world who's boss." If the young woman wants him badly enough, she will meekly go along with the performance for the implicit promise of his continued attentions, if not love. A more permanent relationship approximating the woman's dream of matrimony and domestic tranquillity is often what is at stake in her mind, though she may know better.

As the contest continues and the girl hangs on, she may seem to have been taken in by the boy's game, particularly by his convincing rap, his claims of commitment to her and her well-being. But in this contest anything is fair. The girl may play along, becoming manipulative and aggressive, or the boy may lie, cheat, or otherwise misrepresent himself to obtain or retain her favors. In many of the sexual encounters informants relate, one person is seen as the winner, the other as the loser. As one male informant said, "They trickin' them good. Either the woman is trickin' the man, or the man is trickin' the woman. Good! They got a trick. She's thinkin' it's [the relationship's] one thing; he playing another game, you know. He thinkin' she all right, and she doing somethin' else."

In the social atmosphere of the peer group, the quality of the boy's game emerges as a central issue, and whatever lingering ambivalence he feels about his commitment to acting as husband and provider may be resolved in favor of peer-group status. In pursuing his game, the young man often uses a supporting cast of other women, at times playing one off against the other. For example, he may orchestrate a situation in which he is seen with another woman. Or, secure in the knowledge that he has other women to fall back on, he might start a fight with his steady in order to upset her sense of complacency, thus creating dynamic tension in the relationship, which he uses to his own advantage. The young woman thus may begin to doubt her hold on the man, which can bring about a precipitous drop in her self-esteem.

The boy may feel proud because he thinks he is making a fool of the girl, and when he is confident of his dominance, he may "play" the young woman, "running his game," making her love him. He may brag that he is "playing her like a fiddle," meaning he is in full control of the situation. Though his plan sometimes backfires and he looks like the fool, his purpose is often to prove he "has the girl's nose open," that she is sick with love for him. He aims to maneuver her into a state of blissful emotionality, showing that she, not he, is the weak member of the relationship.

During this emotional turmoil the young girl may well become careless about birth control, which is seen by the community, especially the males, as being her responsibility. She may believe the boy's rap, becoming convinced that he means what he says about taking care of her, that her welfare is his primary concern. Moreover, she wants desperately to believe that if she becomes pregnant, he will marry her or at least be more obligated to her than to others he has been "messing with." Perhaps all he needs is a little nudge. The girl may think little about the job market and the boy's prospects. She may underestimate peer-group influences and the effect of other "ladies" that she knows or suspects are in his life. If she is in love, she may be sure that a child and the profound obligation a child implies will forge such a strong bond that all the other issues will go away. Her thinking is often clouded by the prospect of winning at the game of love. Becoming pregnant can be a way to fulfill the persistent dream of bliss.

For numerous women, when the man turns out to be unobtainable, just having his baby is enough. Sometimes a woman seeks out a popular and "fine," or physically attractive, young man in hopes that his good looks will grace her child, resulting in a "prize"—a beautiful baby. Moreover, becoming pregnant can become an important part of the competition for the attentions or even delayed affections of a young man—a profound, if socially shortsighted, way of making claims on him.

## PREGNANCY

Up to the point of pregnancy, given the norms of his peer group, the young man could simply be said to be messing around. Pregnancy suddenly introduces an element of reality into the relationship. Life-altering events have occurred, and the situation is usually perceived as serious. The girl is pregnant, and he could be held legally responsible for the child's long-term financial support. If the couple were unclear about their intentions before, things may now crystallize. She now considers him seriously as a mate. Priorities begin to emerge in the boy's mind. He has to decide whether to claim the child as his or to shun the woman who has been the object of his supposed affections.

To own up to a pregnancy is to go against the peer-group street ethic of hit and run. Other street values at risk of being flouted include the subordination of women and freedom from formal conjugal ties, and some young men are not interested in "taking care of somebody else" when it means having less for themselves. In this social context of persistent poverty, they have come to devalue the conventional marital relationship, viewing long-term ties with women a burden and children as even more of one. Moreover, a young man wants to "come as I want and go as I please," indulging important values of freedom and independence. Accordingly, from the perspective of the street peer group, any such male-female relationship should be on the man's terms. Thus, in understanding the boy's relationship to the girl, his attitudes toward his limited financial ability and his need for personal freedom should not be underestimated.

Another important attitude of the street group is that most girls have multiple sexual partners. Whether or not this claim is true in a particular case, a common working conception says it holds for young women in general. It is a view with which many young men approach females, initially assuming they are socially and morally deficient, though many are willing to adjust their view as they start to "deal" with the woman and to get to know her intimately. The double standard is at work, and for any amount of sexual activity women are more easily discredited than men.

To be sure, the fact that there is a fair amount of promiscuity among the young men and women creates doubts about paternity and socially complicates many relationships. In self-defense the young men often choose to deny fatherhood; few are willing to own up to a pregnancy they can reasonably question. Among their street-oriented peers, the young men gain ready support for this position; a man who is "tagged" with fatherhood has been caught in the "trick bag." The boy's first desire, though he may know better, is to attribute the pregnancy to someone else.

The boy may be genuinely confused and uncertain about his role in the pregnancy, feeling great ambivalence and apprehension over his impending fatherhood. If he admits paternity and does right by the girl, his peer group will likely label him a chump, a square, or a fool. If he does not, he faces few social sanctions and may even win points for his defiant stand, with his peers viewing him as fooling the mother and getting over her. But ambivalence may also play a role, for men who father children out of wedlock achieve a certain regard, as long as they are not "caught" and made to support a family financially on something other than their own terms. Hence the boy may give—and benefit from—mixed messages: one to the girl and perhaps the authorities, another to his peer group. To resolve his ambivalence and allay his apprehension, the boy will at this point perhaps attempt to discontinue or cool his relationship with the expectant mother, particularly as she begins to show clear signs of pregnancy.

At the insistence of her family and for her own peace of mind, the young woman wants badly to identify the father of her child. When the baby is born, she may, out of desperation, arbitrarily designate a likely young man as the father; at times it may be simply a lover who is gainfully employed. As I have mentioned, there may be genuine doubt about paternity. This atmosphere often produces charges and countercharges; the appointed young man usually either denies responsibility and eases himself out of the picture or accepts it and plays his new role of father part-time.

In the past, before welfare reform, the young woman sometimes had an incentive not to identify the father, even though she and the local community knew whose baby it was, for a check from the welfare office was much more dependable than the irregular support payments of a sporadically employed youth. With today's new welfare reality, there is much more incentive to publicly identify the father and try hard to hold him accountable. Moreover, the new welfare laws give sexually active young people pause and will likely work to decrease the long-term incidence of out-of-wedlock teenage pregnancy. In this new context sanctions are more strongly applied, if not on moral grounds, then for financial and legal considerations. In these circumstances the young man has greater incentive to do right by the young woman and to try out the role of husband and father, often acceding to the woman's view of the matter and working to establish a family.

But such young men often are only marginal members of the street-oriented peer groups, if they hang with these groups at all. Instead, they tend to emerge from decent, nurturing families with positive outlooks. The young man is likely to be further advantaged and "blessed" with what community members refer to as a "decent daddy" or with a close relationship with a caring old head who looked out for and helped raise him. Religious observance is often also an important factor in the lives of such young men, and locally they are viewed as decent people. In addition, these men usually are employed, have a positive sense of the future, and tend to enjoy a deep and abiding relationship with the young woman that often can withstand the trauma of youthful pregnancy.

Barring such a resolution, however, a street-oriented young man may rationalize his marriage as a "trap" into which the woman has lured him. This viewpoint may be seen as his attempt to make simultaneous claims on the values of the street group and those of conventional society. As one young man said in an interview,

> My wife done that to me. Before we got married, when we had our first baby, she thought, well, hey, if she had the baby, then she got me, you know. And that's the way she done me. [She] thought that's gon' trap me. That I'm all hers after she done have this baby. So, a lot of women, they think like that. Now, I was the type of guy, if I know it was my baby, I'm taking care of my baby. My ol' lady [wife], she knowed that. She knowed that anything that was mine, I'm taking care of mine. This is why she probably wouldn't mess around or nothing, 'cause she wanted to lock me up.

In general, however, persuading the youth to become an "honest man" is not simple. It is often a very complicated social affair that involves cajoling, social pressure, and at times physical threats.

An important factor in determining the boy's behavior is the presence of the girl's father in her home. When a couple first begin to date, some fathers will "sit the boy down" and have a ritual talk; single mothers may play this role as well, sometimes more aggressively than fathers. Certain fathers with domineering dispositions will "as a man" make unmistakable claims on the dwelling, informing the boy, "This is my house, I pay the bills here," and asserting that all activities occurring under its roof are his (the father's) singular business. In such a household the home has a certain defense. At issue here essentially are male turf rights, a principle intuitively understood by the young suitor and the girl's father. The boy may feel a certain frustration owing to the need to balance his desire to run his game against his fear of the girl's father.

For the boy often can identify respectfully with the father, thinking about how he might behave if the shoe were on the other foot. Both "know something"—that is, they are aware that each has a position to defend. The boy knows in advance that he will have to answer to the girl's father and the family unit more generally. If the girl becomes pregnant, he will be less likely to leave her summarily. Furthermore, if the girl has brothers at home who are about her age or older, they too may influence his behavior. Such men, as well as uncles and male cousins, particularly if they have respect on the street, not only possess a degree of moral authority but also may offer the believable threat of violence. Concerning the traditional father's role and his responsibility to protect his daughters, the Reverend Mosby, a seventy-five-year-old minister, had this to say:

If a boy got a girl pregnant in my day, he married her. That's what I had to do. She was my best girl, so I didn't have no problem with that. When she became pregnant, I just went on and got married. It wasn't no problem. Her father said, "What you gonna do about it? Are you gonna do the honorable thing or what? I wanta know." You gotta tell him something. "Put yourself in a man's shoes. I expect you to act like a man." You ain't gonna tell Daddy you wasn't going to marry his little girl. But Daddy's not around [today] now when daughter gets pregnant. The daddy say, "Look, if you don't marry my daughter, you're gonna have to deal with me." But if Mama gonna say, "You gonna have to deal with me," you don't have no problem with it. It doesn't put any fear into you. I can take care of her [the boy might think]. But he doesn't know whether he can take care of Daddy or not. 'Cause Daddy ain't gonna play fair, you know what I mean? Mama might play fair. Daddy ain't gonna play fair—Daddy gonna get the shotgun. Daddy tells him right in the front, "Now, I want you to take care of my little girl. You're dating her, and I'm not gonna let any other boy come here." He's trying to give you a message: "Now, if you mess up, I expect you to clean up."

When you were courting, you hadda go meet the family. And Daddy and Mama looked you over, and if they approved, then you could come to the house, calling on their daughter. Today, the girl is out there courting, and the mama don't know nothing about it. She don't even know the boy. And she ain't got time—she's so busy courting herself, she ain't got time to find out who her daughter's seeing. And then sometimes—going to the bar with her daughter. Especially if she's had a baby at seventeen and eighteen, there's not too much difference in the age, right?

I see some of the mamas and daughters wandering in the bar. There's no way in the world a child of mine could drink. When I was going to the bar—I never went [to] them that much—but when I was going to the bar, I couldn't go in the bar with her. Because I had to have that respect.

And as one young man said in an interview,

The boys kinda watch theyself more [when a father is present]. Yeah, there's a lot of that going on. The daddy, they'll clown [act out violence] about them young girls. They'll hurt somebody about they daughters. Other relatives, too. They'll all get into it. The boy know they don't want him messing over they sister. That guy will probably take care of that girl better than the average one out there in the street.

In such circumstances, not only does the boy think twice about running his game, but also the girl thinks twice about allowing him to do so.

A strongly related important defense against youthful pregnancy is the "decent" inner-city family unit. Two parents, together with the extended network of cousins, aunts, uncles, grandparents, nieces, and nephews, can form a durable team, a viable support group engaged to fight in a committed manner the problems confronting inner-city teenagers, including street violence, drugs, crime, pregnancy, and poverty. This unit, when it does endure, tends to be equipped with a survivor's mentality. Its weathering of a good many storms has given it wisdom and strength. As has been argued throughout this volume, the parents are generally known in the community as decent, but more than this, they tend to be strict on their children; they impose curfews and tight supervision, demanding to know their children's whereabouts at all times. Determined that their offspring will not become casualties of the inner-city environment, they scrutinize their children's associates, rejecting those who seem to be "no good" and encouraging others who seem on their way to "amount to something."

By contrast, in domestic situations where there is only one adult—

say, a woman with two or three teenage daughters—the dwelling may be viewed, superficially at least, as an unprotected nest. The local street boys may be attracted to the home as a challenge, just to test it out, to see if they can get over by charming or seducing the women who live there. In such a setting a man—the figure the boys are prepared to respect—is not there to keep them in line. Girls in this vulnerable situation may become pregnant earlier than those living in homes more closely resembling nuclear families. A young man made the following comments:

> I done seen where four girls grow up under their mama. The mama turn around and she got a job between 3 P.M. and 11 P.M. These little kids, now they grow up like this. Mama working three to eleven o'clock at night. They kinda raise theyself. What they know? By the time they get thirteen or fourteen, they trying everything under the sun. And they ain't got nobody to stop 'em. Mama gone. Can't nobody else tell 'em what to do. Hey, all of 'em pregnant by age sixteen. And they do it 'cause they wanta get out on they own. They can get they own baby, they get they own [welfare] check, they get they own apartment. They wanta get away from Mama.

## THE BABY CLUB

In the absence of a strong family unit, a close-knit group of "street girls" often fills a social, moral, and family void in the young girl's life. With the help of her peers and sometimes older siblings and the usually very limited supervision of parents, after a certain age she primarily raises herself. On the street she plays seemingly innocent games, but through play she becomes socialized into a peer group. Many of these neighborhood "street kids" are left to their own devices, staying out late at night, sometimes until one or two in the morning, even on school nights. By the age of ten or twelve, many are aware of their bodies and, according to some residents, are beginning to engage in sexual relations, with very little knowledge about their bodies and even less about the long-term consequences of their behavior.

The street kids become increasingly committed to their peer groups, surviving by their wits, being cool, and having fun. Some girls begin to have babies by age fifteen or sixteen, and soon others follow. Many of them see this behavior as rewarded, at least in the short run.

As the girl becomes more deeply involved, the group helps shape her dreams, social agenda, values, and aspirations. The hip group operates as an in crowd in the neighborhood, although decent people refer to its members as fast and slick and believe they have tried everything at an early age. Girls raised by strict parents are considered by this hip crowd to be lame or square and may suffer social ostracism or at least ridicule, thus segmenting the neighborhood even further. The street peer group becomes a powerful social magnet, drawing in girls only loosely connected to other sources of social and emotional support, particularly the weak and impoverished ghetto family typically headed by a single female.

When some of the girls get pregnant, it becomes important for others to have a baby, especially as their dream of a "good life," usually with an older man twenty-one or twenty-two, begins to unravel. They may settle for babies as a consolation prize, enhancing and rationalizing motherhood as they attempt to infuse their state with value. Some people speak of these girls as "sprouting babies," and having a baby may become an expected occurrence.

As the babies arrive, the peer group takes on an even more provocative feature: the early play and social groups develop into "baby clubs." The girls give one another social support, praising each other's babies. But they also use their babies to compete, on the premise that the baby is an extension of the mother and reflects directly on her. This competition, carried on at social gatherings such as birthday parties, weddings, church services, and spontaneous encounters of two or more people, often takes the form of comparing one baby to another. First the baby's features are noted, usually along the lines of "spoiledness," texture of hair, skin color, and grooming and dress, as well as general "cuteness." To enhance her chances at such competitions and status games, the young mother often feels the need to dress her baby in the latest and most expensive clothes that fit (rather than in a size larger, which the baby can grow into): a fifty-dollar sweater for a three-month-old or forty-dollar Reebok sneakers for a six-month-old. This status-oriented behavior provokes criticism from more mature people, including mothers and grand-mothers. As one forty-five-year-old grandmother said,

> Oh, they can't wait until check day [when welfare checks arrive] so they can go to the store. I listen at 'em, talking about what they gon' buy *this* time. [They say,] "Next time my check come, I'm gon' buy my baby this, I'm gon' buy my baby that." And that's exactly what they will do—expensive stores, too. The more expensive, the better; some will buy a baby an expensive outfit that the baby only gon' wear for a few months. I seen a girl go . . . went out, and she paid, I think she paid forty-five dollars for a outfit. I think the baby was about six weeks old. Now, how long was that child gon' wear that outfit? For that kind of money. They do these silly, silly things.

And as a twenty-three-year-old woman college graduate from the community (who did not become pregnant) said,

> Once there was a sale at the church at Thirteenth and Beau-fort. A friend of mine had some baby clothes for sale. They were some cute clothes, but they weren't new. They were seat suits, older things. The young girls would just pass them by. Now, the older women, the grandmothers, would come by and buy them for their grandchildren. But the girls, sixteen or seventeen, had to have a decked-out baby. No hand-me-downs. Some would pay up to forty dollars for a pair of Nike sneakers. They go to Carl's [a downtown children's boutique]. And the babies some-times are burning up in the clothes, but they dress them up anyway. The baby is like a doll in some ways. They [young mothers] sometimes do more to clothe the baby than to feed the baby.

But this seeming irresponsibility of the young mother evolves in a logical way. For a young woman who fails to secure a strong commitment from a man, a baby becomes a partial fulfillment of the good life. The baby club deflects criticism of the young mothers and gives them a certain status. "Looking good" negates the generalized notion that a teenage mother has messed up her life, and amid this deprivation nothing is more important than to show others you are doing all right.

In public gathering places the mothers lobby for compliments, smiles, and nods of approval and feel very good when they are forthcoming, since they signal affirmation and pride. On Sundays the new little dresses and suits come out and the cutest babies are passed around, and this attention serves as a social measure of the person. The young mothers who form such baby clubs develop an ideology counter to that of more conventional society, one that not only approves of but enhances their position. In effect, they work to create value and status by inverting that of the girls who do not become pregnant. The teenage mother derives status from her baby; hence her preoccupation with the impression that the baby makes and her willingness to spend inordinately large sums toward that end.

Having come to terms with the street culture, many of these young women feel an overwhelming desire to grow up, a passage best expressed by the ability to get out on their own. In terms of traditional inner-city experience, this means setting up one's own household, preferably with a good man through marriage and family. Sometimes a young woman attempts to accomplish this by purposely becoming pregnant, perhaps hoping the baby's father will marry her and help her realize her dream of domestic respectability. However, an undetermined, but some say growing, number of young women, unimpressed with the lot of young single men, want to establish households on their own, without the help or the burden of a man.

Sometimes a young woman, far from becoming victimized, will take charge of the situation and manipulate the man for her own ends, perhaps extracting money from him for "spending her time." At parties and social gatherings, such women may initiate the sexual relations, asserting some control over the situation from the start. Some men say that such a "new" woman is "just out to use you"; she becomes pregnant "for the [welfare] check, then she through with you." Consistent with such reports, in the economically hard-pressed local community it was for a long time socially acceptable for a young woman to have children out of wedlock—supported by a regular welfare check.

In this way, welfare and persistent poverty have affected the norms of the ghetto culture, such as the high value placed on children. "The check" has thus had an important impact on domestic relations between young men and women. In the past, the young woman could count not only on the public aid but also on a serious interest on the young man's part after the baby arrived. And, very often, the honest man was discouraged from marrying the young woman for fear of putting the check in jeopardy. In the Reverend Mosby's day the young man frequently took at least a fatherly interest in his child, and the girl's father and the rest of the extended family could at times be expected to encourage the boy to become an honest man, thus creating dynamic tension between the requirements of welfare on the one hand and pressure from the family to do right on the other. The welfare check, in some instances, has served to bond the young man with the woman, without the benefit of wedlock—in effect uniting them in the regular expectation of the welfare check. In the impoverished conditions of the inner city, when the check arrives, the young man may expect his share, even though he and the young woman do not reside under the same roof. If a new suitor emerges—and one frequently does—there are sometimes arguments, and even violence, over who has rights to the check, as various individuals voice their claims.

With the advent of welfare reform, more young women and men are inclined to pause, to be more circumspect in their sexual habits, in large part because the check is no longer to be counted on. Babies may become less significant symbols of status, but they will continue to be important symbols of passage to adulthood, of being a grown woman, and of being a man. Most young mothers and fathers, I believe, do not have babies just for the check, but in structurally impoverished areas, the regular cash the check provides is not unimportant. In the past it perhaps was a question less of whether the girl was going to have children than of when, for she often saw herself as having little to lose and much to gain by becoming pregnant, and this remains true in a social sense. In the new climate of welfare reform, however, there is more of an impetus for young men and women to take greater responsibility for their personal lives and, in turn, to have fewer babies out of wedlock. But the jury is still out on this.

## THE GOOD MAN AND THE NOTHIN'

In their small, intimate groups, the women discuss their afternoon soap operas, men, children, and social life, and they welcome new members to the generally affirmative and supportive gatherings. Although they may criticize men's actions, especially their lack of commitment, at the same time they often accept such behavior, viewing it as characteristic of men in their environment. Nonetheless, the women draw distinctions between "the nothin' " and the "good man." The nothin' is a "a man who is out to use every women he can for himself. He's somethin' like a pimp. Don't care 'bout nobody but himself." One older single mother, who now considers herself wiser, said,

> I know the difference now between a nothin' and a good man. I can see. I can smell him. I can just tell a nothin' from the real thing. I can just look at a guy sometimes, you know, the way he dresses. You know, the way he carries himself. The way he acts, the way he talks. I can tell the bullshitter. Like, you know, "What's up, baby?" You know. "What's you want to do?" A nice guy wouldn't say, "What's you want to do?" A nice guy wouldn't say, "What's up, baby? What's goin' on?" Actin' all familiar, tryin' to give me that line. Saying, "You want a joint? You wan' some 'caine?" Hollerin' in the street, you know. I can tell 'em. I can just smell 'em.

In this social climate the good man, who would aspire to play the role of the decent daddy of old, is considerate of his mate and provides for her and her children, but at the same time he runs the risk of being seen as a pussy by the women as well as by his peer group.

This inversion in the idea of the good man underscores the ambivalent position of girls squeezed between their middle-class dreams and the ghetto reality. As one woman said with a laugh, "There are so many sides to the bad man. We see that, especially in this community. We see more bad men than we do good. I see them [inner-city girls] running over that man if he's a wimp, ha-ha."

Family support is often available to the young pregnant woman, though members of her family are likely to remind her now and then that she is messed up. She looks forward to the day when she is "straight" again—when she has given birth to the baby and has regained her figure. Her comments to girls who are not pregnant tend to center wistfully on better days. If her boyfriend stops seeing her regularly, she may attribute this to the family's negative remarks about him, but also to her pregnancy, saying time and time again, "When I get straight, he'll be sorry; he'll be jealous then." She knows that her pregnant state is devalued by her family as well as by her single peers, who are free to date and otherwise consort with men, and she may long for the day when she can do so again.

When the baby arrives, however, the girl finds that her social activities continue to be significantly curtailed. She is often surprised by how much time and effort being a mother takes. In realizing her new identity, she may very consciously assume the demeanor of a grown woman, emphasizing her freedom in social relations and her independence. During the period of adjustment to the new status, she has to set her mother straight about telling her what to do. Other family members also go through a learning process, getting used to the girl's new status, which she tries on in fits and starts. In fact, she is working at growing up.

Frustrated by the baby's continuing needs, especially as she becomes physically straight again, the girl may develop an intense desire to get back into the dating game. Accordingly, she may foist her child care responsibilities onto her mother and sisters, who initially are eager to help. In time, however, they tire, and even extremely supportive relations can become strained. In an effort to see her daughter get back to normal, the grandmother, typically in her mid-thirties or early forties, may simply informally adopt the baby as another one of her own, in some cases completely usurping the role of mother. In this way the young parent's mother may minimize the deviance the daughter displayed by getting pregnant, while taking genuine pride in her new grandchild.

## OF MEN AND WOMEN, MOTHERS AND SONS

The relationship between the young man and woman undergoes a basic change during pregnancy; once the baby is born, it draws on other social forces, most notably their families. The role of the girl's family has been discussed. The boy's family is important in a different way. There is often a special bond between a mother and her grown son that competes with the claims of his girlfriend. The way this situation is resolved has considerable consequences for the family and its relationship to the social structure of the community. In teenage pregnancy among the poor, the boy's mother often plays a significant role, while that of his father, if he is present at all, is understated. Depending on the woman's personality, her practical experience in such matters, and the girl's family situation, the mother's role may be subtle or explicit. At times she becomes deeply involved with the young woman, forming a female bond with her that is truly motherly, involving guidance, protection, and control.

From the moment the boy's mother finds out a young woman is pregnant by her son, the question of whether she knows the girl is important. If the young woman means something to her son, she is likely to know her and her family or at least to have heard something about her from her son. On learning of the pregnancy, the mother might react with anything from disbelief that her son could be responsible to certainty, even before seeing the child, that he is indeed the father. If she knows the girl's character, she is in a position to judge for herself. Here her relationship with the girl before "all this" happened comes into play, for if she likes her, there is a good chance she will side with her. She may even go so far as to engage in playful collusion against her son, a man, to get him to do right by the girl. We must remember that in this economically circumscribed social context, particularly from a woman's point of view, many men are known not to do right by their women and children. To visit certain inner-city streets is to see a proliferation of small children and women whose fathers and husbands are largely absent. These considerations help explain the significance of the mother's role in determining how successful the girl will be in getting the boy to take some responsibility for the child.

The mother may feel constrained, at least initially, because she is unsure her son actually fathered the child. She may be careful about showing her doubt, however, thinking that when the baby arrives she will be able to tell in a minute if her son is the father. Thus, during the pregnancy, she nervously waits, wondering whether her son will be blamed for a pregnancy not of his doing or whether she will really be a grandmother. In fact, both the boy's and the girl's relatives often constitute an extended family-in-waiting, socially organized around the idea that the truth will be told when the baby arrives. Unless the parties are very sure, marriage—if agreed to at all—may be held off until after the birth.

When the baby arrives, plans may be carried out, but often on condition that the child passes inspection. The presumed father generally lies low in the weeks after the baby's birth. He is apt to visit the baby's mother in the hospital only once, if at all. In an effort to make a paternal connection, some girls name the baby after the father, but by itself this strategy is seldom effective. In cases of doubtful paternity, the boy's mother, sisters, aunts, or other female relatives or close family friends may form visiting committees to see the baby, though sometimes the child is brought to them. This inspection is often surreptitious, made without the acknowledgment of the girl or her family. The visitors may go to the girl's house in shifts, with a sister dropping in now, the mother another time, and a friend still another. Social pleasantries notwithstanding, the object is always the same: to see if the baby belongs to the boy. Typically, after such visits the women will compare notes, commenting on the baby's features and on whom the child favors or resembles. Some will blurt out, "Ain't no way that John's baby." People may disagree and a dispute ensue. In the community the paternity of the father becomes a hot topic. The viewpoints have much to do with who the girl is, whether she is a good girl, and whether she has been accepted by the boy's family. If the she is well integrated into the family, doubts about the paternity may slowly be put to rest, with nothing more said about the subject.

The word carrying the most weight in this situation is often that of the boy's mother, as is shown in this account by a young man:

> I had a lady telling me that she had to check out a baby that was supposed to be her grandbaby. She said she had a young girl that was trying to put a baby on her son, so she said she fixing to take the baby and see what blood type the baby is to match it with her son to see if he the daddy. 'Cause she said she know he wasn't the daddy. And she told the girl that, but the girl was steady, trying to stick the baby on her son. She had checked out the baby's father and everything. She knowed that the blood type wasn't gon' match or nothing. So the young girl just left 'em alone.

If the child clearly resembles the alleged father physically, there may be strong pressure for the boy to claim the child and assume his responsibilities. This may take a year or more, since the resemblance may initially be less apparent. But when others begin to make comments such as "Lil' Tommy look like Maurice just spit him out [is his spitting image]," the boy's mother may informally adopt the child into her extended family and signal others to do the same. She may see the child regularly and develop a special relationship with its mother. Because of her social acknowledgment of her son's paternity, the boy himself is bound to accept the child. Even if he does not claim the child legally, in the face of the evidence he will often acknowledge "having something to do with him." As one informant said, "If the baby look just like him, he should admit to himself that that's his. Some guys have to wait till the baby grow up a little to see if the baby gon' look like him 'fore they finally realize that was his'n. Because yours should look like you, you know, should have your features and image."

Here the young man informally acknowledging paternity may feel some pressure to take care of his own. But owing to his limited employment and general lack of money, he feels that he "can only do what he can" for his child. Many young men enact the role of father part-time. A self-conscious young man may be spied on the street carrying a box of Pampers, the name used generically for all disposable diapers, or cans of Similac—baby formula—on the way to see his child and its mother. As the child ages, a bond may develop, and the young man may take a boy for a haircut or shopping for shoes or clothes. He may give the woman token amounts of money. Such gestures of support suggest a father providing for his child. In fact, however, they often come only sporadically and—an important point—in exchange for the woman's favors, social or sexual. Such support may thus depend upon the largesse of the man and may function as a means of controlling the woman.

If the woman "gets papers" on the man, or legalizes his relationship to the child, she may sue for regular support—what people call "going downtown on him." If her case is successful, the young man's personal involvement in making child support payments may be eliminated: the money may simply be deducted from his salary, if he has one. Sometimes the woman's incentive for getting papers may emerge when the young man lands a good job, particularly one with a major institution that includes family benefits. While sporadically employed, the youth may have had no problem with papers, but when he finds a steady job, he may be served with a summons. In some cases, especially if they have two or three children out of wedlock by different women, young men lose the incentive to work, for much of their pay will go to someone else. After the mother of his four children got papers on him and he began to see less and less of his pay, one of my informants quit his job and returned to the street corner and began to hustle drugs.

Under some conditions the male peer group will pressure a member to admit paternity. The key here is that the group members have no doubts in their own minds as to the baby's father. When it is clear that the baby resembles the young man, the others may strongly urge him to claim it and help the mother financially. If he fails to acknowledge the baby, group members may do it themselves by publicly associating him with the child, at times teasing him about his failure "to take care of what's his." As one young man said,

My partner's [friend's] girlfriend came up pregnant. And she say it's his, but he not sure. He waitin' on the baby, waitin' to see if the baby look like him. I tell him, "Man, if that baby look like you, then it was yours! Ha-ha." He just kinda like just waitin'. He ain't claimin' naw, saying the baby ain't his. I keep tellin' him, "If that baby come out looking just like you, then it gon' be yours, partner." And there on the corner all of 'em will tell him, "Man, that's yo' baby." They'll tell him.

Although the peer group may urge its members to take care of their babies, they stop short of urging them to marry the mothers. In general, young men are assumed not to care about raising a family or being part of one, but this is contradicted by many of these men's strong family values. So many of them are unable to support a family that they hesitate to form one that is bound to fail, in their minds. Much of the lack of support for marriage is due to poor employment prospects, but it may also have to do with general distrust of women to whom the men are not related by blood. As my informant continued,

They don't even trust her that they were the only one she was dealin' [having sex] with. That's a lot of it. But the boys just be gettin' away from it [the value of a family] a whole lot. They don't want to get tied down by talkin' about playin' house, ha-ha, what they call it nowadays, ha-ha. Yeah, ha-ha, they sayin' they ain't playin' house.

In a great number of cases, peer group or no, the boy will send the girl on her way even if she is carrying a baby he knows is his. He often lacks a deep feeling for a woman and children as a family unit and does not want to put up with married life, which he sees as giving a woman some say in how he spends his time. This emphasis on "freedom" is generated and supported in large part by the peer group itself. Even if a man agrees to marriage, it is usually considered to be only a trial. After a few months many young husbands have had enough.

This desire for freedom, which the peer group so successfully nurtures, is deeply ingrained in the boys. It is, in fact, nothing less than the desire to reestablish the situation in their mothers' homes. A son is generally well bonded to his mother, something she tends to encourage from birth. It may be that sons, particularly the eldest, are groomed to function as surrogate husbands because of the high rate of family dissolution among poor blacks.

Many young boys want what they consider an optimal situation. In the words of peer-group members, "they want it all": a main squeeze—a steady and reliable female partner who will mimic the role their mothers played, a woman who will cook, clean, and generally serve them and who will ask few questions about the ladies they may be seeing and have even less to say about their male friends. The boy has grown accustomed to home-cooked meals and the secure company of his birth family, in which his father was largely absent and could not tell him what to do. He was his own boss, essentially raising himself with the help of his street peers and perhaps any adult (possibly an old head) who would listen but not interfere. For many, such a life is too much to give up in exchange for the "problems of being tied down to one lady, kids, bills, and all that." The young man's home situation with his mother thus competes effectively with the household he envisions with a woman his peer group is fully prepared to discredit.

Now that he is grown, the young man may want what he had while growing up, plus a number of ladies on the side. At the same time he wants his male friends, whom he must impress in ways perhaps inconsistent with being a good family man. Since the young men from the start have little faith in marriage, small things can inspire them to retreat to their mothers or whatever families they left behind. Some spend their time going back and forth between two families; if their marriages seem not be working, they may ditch them and their wives, though perhaps keeping up with the children. At all times they must show others that they run the family, that they "wear the pants." This is the cause of many domestic fights in the ghetto. When there is a question of authority, the domestic situation may run into serious trouble, often leading the young man to abandon the idea of marriage or of dealing with only one woman. To "hook up" with a woman, to marry her, is to give her something to say about "what you're doing, or where you're going, or where you've been." Many young men find such constraint unacceptable.

In many instances the young man does not mind putting up with the children, given his generally small role in child rearing, but he does mind tolerating the woman, whom he sees as a threat to his freedom. As one man commented about marriage,

> Naw, they [young men] getting away from that 'cause they want to be free. Now, see, I ended up getting married. I got a whole lot of boys ducking that. Unless this is managed, it ain't no good. My wife cleans, takes care of the house. You got a lot of guys, they don't want to be cleanin' no house, and do the things you got to do in the house. You need a girl there to do it. If you get one, she'll slow you down. The guys don't want it.

Unless a man can so handle his wife that she will put few constraints on him, he may reason that he had better stay away from marriage. But with a growing sense of being independent of men, financially and otherwise, fewer women may allow themselves to be treated in this manner.

As jobs become scarce for young black men, their success as breadwinners and traditional husbands declines. The notion is that with money comes control of the domestic situation. Without money or jobs, many men are unable to play house to their satisfaction. It is much easier and more fun to stay home and "take care of Mama," some say, when taking care consists of "giving her some change for room and board," eating good food, and being able "to come as I want and to go as I please." Given the present state of the economy, such an assessment of their domestic outlook appears in many respects adaptive.

## SEX, POVERTY, AND FAMILY LIFE

In conclusion, the basic factors at work here are youth, ignorance, the culture's receptiveness to babies, and the young man's attempt to prove his manhood through sexual conquests that often result in pregnancy. These factors are exacerbated by persistent urban poverty. In the present hard times a primary concern of many inner-city residents is to get along as best they can. In the poorest communities the primary financial sources are low-paying jobs, crime—including drugs—and public assistance. Some of the most desperate people devise a variety of confidence games to separate others from their money.

A number of men, married and single, incorporate their sexual lives into their more generalized efforts at economic survival, or simply making ends meet. Many will seek to "pull" a woman with children on welfare, since she usually has a special need for male company, time on her hands, and a steady income. As they work to establish their relationships, these men play a game not unlike the one young males use to get over sexually. There is simply a clearer economic motive in many of these cases. When the woman receives her check from the welfare department or money from other sources, she may find herself giving up part of it to ensure male company.

The economic noose restricting ghetto life encourages men and women alike to try to extract maximum personal benefit from sexual relationships. The dreams of a middle-class lifestyle nurtured by young inner-city women are thwarted by the harsh socioeconomic realities of the ghetto. Young men without job prospects cling to the support offered by their peer groups and their mothers and shy away from lasting relationships with girlfriends. Girls as well as boys scramble to take what they can from each other, trusting only their own ability to trick the other into giving them something that will establish their version of the good life—the best life they can put together in their environment.

We should remember that the people we are talking about are very young—they range in age mainly from fifteen years to their early twenties. Their bodies are grown, but they are emotionally immature. These girls and boys often have no very clear notion of the long-term consequences of their behavior, and they have few trustworthy role models to instruct them.

Although middle-class youths and poor youths may have much in common sexually, their level of practical education differs. The ignorance of inner-city girls about their bodies astonishes the middle-class observer. Many have only a vague notion about birth control until after they have their first child—and sometimes not even then. Parents in this culture are extremely reticent about discussing sex and birth control with their children. Many mothers are ashamed to talk about it or feel they are in no position to do so, since they behaved the same way as their daughters when they were young. Education thus emerges as a community health problem, but most girls come in contact with community health services only when they become pregnant—sometimes many months into their pregnancies.

A baby could in cold economic terms be considered an asset, which is without doubt an important factor behind exploitative sex and out-of-wedlock babies, though this seems to be changing. Public assistance was one of the few reliable sources of money, low-income jobs are another, and, for many people, drugs are yet another. The most desperate people thus feed on one another. Babies and sex were once more commonly used for income than they are now; women continue to receive money from welfare for having babies, and men sometimes act as prostitutes to pry the money from them.

The lack of gainful employment today not only keeps the entire community in a pit of poverty but also deprives young men of the traditional American way of proving their manhood—by supporting a family. They must thus prove themselves in other ways. Casual sex with as many women as possible, impregnating one or more, and getting them to have his baby brings a boy the ultimate in esteem from his peers and makes him a man. Casual sex is therefore fraught with social significance for the boy who has little or no hope of achieving financial stability and hence cannot see himself taking care of a family.

The meshing of these forces can be clearly seen. Trapped in poverty, ignorant of the long-term consequences of their behavior but aware of the immediate benefits, adolescents engage in a mating game. The girl has her dream of a family and a home, of a good man who will provide for her and her children. The boy, knowing he cannot be that family man, because he has few job prospects, yet needing to have sex to achieve manhood in the eyes of his peer group, pretends to be the decent and good man and so persuades the girl to give him sex and perhaps a baby. He may then abandon her, and she realizes he was not the good man, after all, but rather a nothin' out to exploit her. The boy has gotten what he wanted, but the girl learns that she has gotten something, too. The baby may bring her a certain amount of praise, (in the past) a steady welfare check, and a measure of independence. Her family often helps out as best they can. As she becomes older and wiser, she can use her income to turn the tables, attracting her original man or other men.

In this inner-city culture people generally get married for love and to have something. But this mind-set presupposes a job, the work ethic, and, perhaps most of all, a persistent sense of hope for an economic future. When these social factors are present, the more wretched elements of the ethnographic portrait presented here begin to lose their force, slowly becoming neutralized. For many of those who are caught in the web of persistent urban poverty and become unwed mothers and fathers, however, there is little hope for a good job and even less for a future of conventional family life.

# FIVE

# The Decent Daddy

H E code of the streets and the world it reflects have taken shape in the context of the existing structures and traditions in the black community in the United States. Some of these traditions go back to the time of slavery and have served to keep the community together for many generations. Elements of the code, which works to organize problematic public areas, can be traced back to the Roman era, to the shogun warriors, and particularly to the old American South and West[1] or even to biblical times: "An eye for an eye, a tooth for a tooth." And in drug-infested and impoverished pockets of American cities today, where many residents lack faith in the law, people, but especially youths, often take responsibility for their own safety and security, letting the next person know they are prepared to defend themselves physically, if necessary. The code poses visible threats to those traditions, but at the same time two of its key elements reflect those same traditions—decency and violence.

The unprecedented improvements that the manufacturing era brought to standards of living for urban working-class people were perceived by blacks as an opportunity to make an assault on the caste-like system of race relations in the United States. Leaders in the black community were convinced that the situation of blacks was being compromised because of individual behavior. White prejudice would say that black people are somehow not proper enough, clean enough, decent enough. Black men and women who were successful in some way were encouraged to lead the community, presenting themselves as "race men" and "race women."[2] One of their missions in life was to put the black community's best foot forward, to disabuse whites of their often negative views of black people by encouraging proper and decent behavior. In the black community they took on the role of old heads; they functioned as elders and mentors for young people, while teaching everyone by word and by example to behave in ways that would reflect well on the race.

This chapter is about the decent daddy; the next, about the inner-city grandmother. Both types have been important role models ever since the days of slavery. Both remain important today—their presence obvious throughout this book—but their roles are changing.[3]

## THE DECENT DADDY

The decent daddy is a certain kind of man, with certain responsibilities and privileges: to work, to support his family, to rule his household, to protect his daughters, and to raise his sons to be like him, as well as to encourage other young people to demonstrate these qualities, too. Today, he may be a factory worker, a common laborer, a parking-lot attendant, a taxi driver, or even a local pharmacist, a doctor, lawyer, or professor, striving hard to be a good husband and father. He tends to carry the weight of the race on his shoulders and represents his community to outsiders. He is highly principled and moral and tries to embody what to him are the best features of the wider society. Mr. Bland, a black taxi driver from rural South Carolina, reports,

> [He was] a wonderful person. Strong. Wise. [In the Deep South] blacks and whites would seek him out for advice. They'd talk about planting, livestock, anything. And they'd even talk

about life. He had their respect. He had everybody's respect.
And when you watched him engage the white folks, laughing
and talking with them, you could almost forget that he was a
black man. He'd take 'em to his little shed, and they'd stay in
there talkin' for a while, and then they'd come on out. I'm telling
you, this man saw people as people, as human beings. To him,
bad didn't know no color, though he was certainly aware of the
place of the black man.

But more often than not, for him it was the individual person.
If you treated him and his right, then he'd treat you right. Didn't
matter what color you were. Respect got his respect. And too,
he'd always give the next person the benefit of the doubt, but
he'd give you enough rope to hang yourself, now. Then he
wouldn't fool with you no more. He'd drop you quick. You don't
never want to cross him; naw, you don't wanta do that. He could
just look at you and make you feel like [nothing]. What you give,
you gon' get from him.

He'd take us [boys] fishing. Show'd us how to fish and all. But
during those times, we'd all learn about a lot more than just
fishing. We learned about life, how to treat people. See, too,
when you [as a child] ask him a question, he might not answer
for a long time. I'm telling you. But when he would, it was always
something powerful. He just knew stuff. He knew all about life.
He was so wise.

This role has persisted throughout periods of sharecropping, segregation, industrialization, and beyond. The decent daddy not only
raised his own children this way, he would gather young boys on
street corners and persuade them to follow his lead. A large part of
his agenda was the defeat of racial apartheid—caste—in the wider
society. Being proper and good enough—that is, assimilating the values of the wider, dominant system—would, he was convinced, lead
to acceptance in that system. A critical mass of the members of the
black community supported this view, which was reinforced by institutions such as the church.

Furthermore, the decent daddy had something tangible to offer—
jobs. Although discrimination in the workplace has always been a

serious and often demoralizing problem for black people, there were jobs, even if often menial, to be gotten, and he had the connections to help young people find them. Some men worked two and three jobs to earn a decent living and take care of their families. During the 1960s and 1970s, as the system opened up and a black middle class began to develop, their children often had opportunities for social mobility. Today the decent daddy's role of sponsorship is being challenged by deindustrialization and the loss of those jobs in a racially conscious society in which black men's talents and contributions are not always appreciated. The decent daddy is also engaged in a kind of public relations war, working to distinguish himself from what he considers to be the worst features of his community. As a result, much of his own behavior is geared to counterbalancing the street element, if not to defending himself and his own from the street. He tries hard to uphold the dominant society's standards, but his efforts are often not readily apparent to that society, which is liable to confuse him with the street element.

Yet, in the inner-city black community, though there are relatively few of him, the decent daddy is still the embodiment of grit and backbone. Moreover, he stands for propriety, righteousness, religion, and manhood, and is considered a blessed man. The well-being of his family is his testament. Socially conservative, independent, strong, God-fearing, he believes in the work ethic. He is in charge of his family and has the respect of his woman and children; in exchange, he provides for them. He tries to supply them not only with food, clothing, shelter, and other material things but with spiritual nurturance as well. Furthermore, he enjoys the respect of his community, for these qualities are on public display in the neighborhood and earn him ready deference from neighbors, friends, and casual acquaintances. When he approaches the corner tavern—as he does on occasion—the greeting from people on the corner is a respectful "How's your family?" Typically, a decent daddy is known by everyone—by the hoodlums, by the boys who rip and run and game the girls into having their babies and then don't own up, and by the most violent people in the community.

A man's success at this task is profoundly linked to his financial wherewithal—the steady job that is the hallmark of American manhood. Believing in the sanctity of hard work, the decent daddy often works two jobs in order to have more than enough money to support his family's lifestyle. But in a world where marriage and monogamy have gone somewhat out of style, he requires something that he can show in return. He often wants to be the undisputed head of the household, or at least to present himself as such. Accordingly, he wants to make the major decisions concerning the family, and in company the woman should not speak out of turn or talk too much and make him look small. The woman must know her place, which is taking care of the house and preparing food to his satisfaction. Violations of such rules reflect poorly on him, suggesting disrespect in front of his friends. Many decent women negotiate an arrangement like this in order to obtain a worthy partner, a hardworking man, and a good provider and protector.

Such a man tends to have little patience with men who fail to meet their responsibilities as fathers or husbands. Intolerant of excuses that blame discrimination or the lack of jobs, he holds individuals responsible, not the system, and sees resorting to "aid," or welfare, as showing a lack of gumption. He admits that racism is a problem, but he also knows that it can be a lame excuse for not applying oneself to the task at hand. He believes that in this world you make your own bed and that you can succeed if you try. With such presuppositions he approaches the young men he finds unemployed on the streets today. He truly finds it difficult to sympathize with those who cannot find work, let alone with those who do not want to work, and who through their stance insult those who do. Don Moses, the gypsy taxi driver quoted earlier in this volume, related the following incident:

> My personal relationship with most of the kids growing up [in my neighborhood] is very good for the simple reason there's something about children when they're little and you've treated them right all the way up—right meaning you took the time to take them places, took the time to maybe take them to the gym, took the time to just say a few words to them if you saw them do something wrong. I'm proud to say that the kids really do respect me. So much so that a month ago I was up on the block— I seldom go up there anymore to stop and stay and do my little

hustle (my little honest hustle). It's not that I fear the place or anything like that. It's just that I don't like the mentality of the kids up there. I don't like to be in that atmosphere and see it every day. It agonizes me. It tears at the very fabric of my heart to see the young kids that went to school—you know, I raised my children in the area—to see them doin' drugs. Some of them I hardly recognize; they look like people twice their age. It hurts me. That's the major reason why I don't really go in the area.

One night this little girl—she was so sweet, and there she was right there soliciting. I put her in the car, sat [her] down, and I said, "Don't you know who I am?" She said, "Well, what's that got to do with it? You're a man, aren't you?" So I told her, "Did I say anything to you to make you think that you could solicit me and I would accept your solicitation?" She said, "No, but you're still a man, aren't you? I deal with men older than you." She was just crude, you know. I said, "Do you remember the sweet little girl that used to be in third grade with my daughter?" She said, "Yeah." I talked to that girl about an hour. I ended up giving her five dollars. She said she was hungry, and I said I hoped that went for food. When I finished talking to her, she started crying. I mean, she cried. She sobbed. She bawled. She just cried and told me how sorry she was. I noticed one thing, though. I look back on that and I see, you know, she was giving me the real tough "I don't care, this is how I am now, I don't care how I was back then" until I gave her the five dollars. As soon as I gave her the five dollars, she started crying, crying and sobbing, told me that she knows that's for real. And she's sorry that she's there and she loved me. She said, "I really love you. Me and my older sister used to pretend that you were our father. You were the father that we always wanted because you didn't drink; we never saw you drunk. We never saw you staggering down the street. We never saw you messing with anybody. We never saw you soliciting at the girls or anything like that. I'm so sorry I said that to you." She was just bawling her heart out. However, I used to see her almost every day. I haven't seen her since. I'm just hoping she went into drug rehab and got herself together. There's been a few. I admit that of all the ones that

I've talked to, I can think of seven or eight that [got themselves together]—two of them I took to a rehabilitation center.

In many respects Mr. Moses is the epitome of the decent daddy, playing the role not only in his own household but also in the neighborhood, providing especially strong support to the local children and, in doing so, playing the part of old head. In Mr. Moses's day role models were available, people who set powerful examples of the work ethic and personal responsibility. Today more and more young men are emerging from socially disorganized home situations, have strongly embraced "the street," and are faced with a high-tech workplace, for which they are usually not qualified, or with the menial-service sector, in which the pay is so low that they are unable to make a living. Many of these young men have had limited or no personal experience with a decent daddy and have little to model themselves on. Hence they are not at all hesitant to play the role poorly, because they have not been exposed to the original model and thus tend to have a rather narrow perspective on it.

Yet, ironically, many of these young men do know enough about the role to miss it. From their experiences on the streets and in the homes of uncles and friends, they know the outlines of the role—the form if not the substance. The boys hear old heads tell stories that glorify the role, but they are familiar with few details about the person. In my discussions with various young men, very often without fathers in their homes, a "Mr. Johnson" of folklore emerges as the embodiment of the decent daddy they can relate to. The Mr. Johnson they can recall was a strong man who would "laugh and talk, but he didn't play." He was very stern about the rules of his house and left little doubt that he ran the household. Typically, he worked for the Budd Company (a manufacturer) or one of the other now defunct factories in the Philadelphia area, and often had a part-time legal hustle on the side. He had plenty of money as well as the respect of his friends and neighbors. He drove a Buick 225 or a Ford Crown Victoria and kept it immaculate. He would go to the corner now and then, but he always maintained his position of respect with the other men. When arriving, they would say, "Hi, *Mr.* Johnson, how's your family?" And he would answer, "Fine, how's yours?" He was not one to stand for nonsense or to suffer fools gladly. He would attend church regularly, but sometimes he would miss the service, and Mrs. Johnson would answer for him to the minister: "Aw, that man's working. He's always working." To his children, he was a taskmaster, always telling his boys and girls "what's good for you" and to "make something out of yourself." He was strict and sometimes had his children address him as "sir"—or say, "Yes, sir" and "No, sir." When boys came to court his daughters, he wanted to know everything about them, but he demanded that they respect his household and take off their hats inside his house. And he would insist that the boys behave responsibly, especially with regard to the family.

Many of the young men I interviewed, who are today anywhere from twenty to thirty years old, betray a certain amount of anger mixed with sadness when they speak of their own father. And some have shed tears, for they believe that they would have turned out better if they had "had such a daddy." Lacking actual contact with such a model, though, many of the young men who think they are enacting the role of the decent daddy are doing so imperfectly at best. When they talk about playing house, they are thinking as much of controlling the household as of supporting and protecting it. One of their worst fears is being dissed by anyone, particularly their women. Given their poor employment prospects, they are in serious danger of being dissed by the women in their lives.

As noted in the preceding chapter, for a young man to play house effectively he needs enough resources to make the woman love him without his resorting to abuse. According to the lore of the street, he must be able to support his lady before she will let him spend her time. In addition, he must be able to afford to have her nails done, have her hair tracked, and supply her with gold adornments and whatever else she requires. Such requirements place great pressure on the young man to make money any way he can, legally or illegally.

When the young men determine that they are unable to play house, they often drop out of the game. They fail to follow through on their responsibilities, do not marry the mothers of their children, and often become, at best, part-time fathers and partners. At the same time they can become exercised over women who challenge their image as the man in control. Such young men want the control, respect, and deference due the decent daddy, and they often feel that as people playing their version of this role, they are entitled to them. Furthermore, they are liable to develop short fuses, becoming especially sensitive to slights and more than ready to defend their claim to respect at any moment. The most frustrated may become abusive toward their women.

Homes where a decent daddy is present are often seen by the community as protected nests. A certain moral aura surrounds them, frequently with the full support of the women involved. The decent daddy wants his daughters' male suitors to share his orientation, and he has the authority to reject those who do not pass muster. He is trying to build something, and the young men often, though not always, respect that.

As a result of his typically low-key, if not reserved or unspectacular, role the decent daddy has in recent years grown somewhat invisible in the eyes of the wider society. His image in the media competes with the images of drug dealers, hoodlums, and others who work the underground economy—in other words, those groups and individuals on whom the media base their image of the inner-city community. But decent daddies are important for the moral integrity of the community. If they are not supported with education and job opportunities, the drug dealers and the street-oriented are free to set the standards.

## MARTIN DAVIS: A DECENT DADDY

Martin Davis is a young man of about twenty-five who has a steady job as a furniture mover for a secondhand store downtown. Martin grew up in the inner-city community of West Philadelphia and has been going with a young woman named Joleen for a number of years. Six years ago, when Martin first met Joleen, she already had a son, Terry, by a man named Maurice, who took his parenting obligations lightly. Maurice, known as a big-time drug dealer, always had plenty of "nice" things to give to Joleen. They made a striking couple as they appeared at the various houses and joints of the community.

When Joleen became pregnant with Terry, Maurice had less and less time for her, particularly once she began to show. When the baby arrived, he placed even more distance between himself and her.

Martin had known Joleen for many years but always considered himself too square to "get with" her, and so he admired her from a distance. But when he saw that things were not going so well between her and Maurice, he saw his chance and they started going out. After they had been seeing each other for about a year, Martin and Joleen had Tommy. Unlike Maurice, earlier, Martin visited Joleen regularly, helping support her financially and physically taking care of the boys. Martin especially enjoyed roughhousing with the children and taking them on outings. They were not living together—Martin's moral code would not allow him to do that—but he spent as much time as he could with his "family." To many in the neighborhood, the two went as husband and wife, but equally important, he went as the father of both boys. That he loved them deeply showed in his behavior toward them and their mother. During much of this time Martin saw little reason to marry Joleen. He was happy, his sons were happy, and their arrangement raised few eyebrows.

It is important to note that Martin comes from a long line of decent families. From the rural hills of North Carolina to Philadelphia, most of his people have had the benefit of wedlock and family-sustaining working-class jobs. One of his aunts is pastor of a church attended predominantly by people in some way related to each other. In Martin's family, kinship ties are strong and encompass men as well as women. As a result, when he was growing up, Martin had his share of male role models, including his father and a number of uncles, who played ball with him and counseled him in the ways of the world. Yet when Joleen became pregnant no sanctions were invoked.

After several years of this informal arrangement with Joleen, Martin's sense of family began to assert itself. At the same time Maurice (Terry's father) was beginning to show renewed interest in Joleen, and this sent chills of anxiety through Martin. He began to feel that since he loved Joleen and was prepared to be responsible for her and her children, he ought to marry her. The notions of decency and responsibility with which he had been raised became entwined with his love for Joleen, and he decided that the proper expression of this feeling was marriage.

When Martin announced his decision to his friends, however, it was met with scorn as well as support. The young men with whom he socialized saw marriage as a loss of freedom and derided him for wanting to "put his head in the noose." They didn't believe he could meet the responsibilities of being a husband; they also thought he was putting himself in a position in which a woman might exploit him. But his family was supportive. His aunt, the pastor, received the couple in the chambers of her church, counseled them briefly on marriage, and then gave her blessing. In the end Martin chose his family's support over his friends' objections and married Joleen.

Martin had the benefit of exposure to traditional men and women who had served effectively as caregivers and role models. In impoverished inner-city areas such relatively advantaged young men are unusual. Yet, as I have seen in my research, it is common for young men at some point in life to attempt to become family men, particularly if they believe they are in love and have a certain level of independence, financial wherewithal, and the support of their families. Many want desperately to play this domestic role but fail to establish and maintain intact families. Some give up because they are unable to play house—to provide financially for women and children in a way that will result in adequate deference and respect from all concerned. Without a job, a man may lose respect as well as his say in what goes on in the home. When men do get married and are unable to establish domestic control, physical abuse sometimes follows. There can be a cascade effect in which the abused wife then abuses the children.

## MR. CHARLES THOMAS: A DECENT DADDY

"Charles Thomas" is in many respects the epitome of the decent daddy. Now sixty-seven, born and raised in the South, he came to Philadelphia as a young man. He had relatives in the city and eventually assimilated into the community, where he married and raised a family. His is the image of the strong black man—he worked for many years as a federal police officer, carried a gun, and ruled his household. At the same time he is a deeply religious man, a lifelong churchgoer with a strong belief in family, the Bible, and the Golden Rule. However, there is within him a line that, if crossed, will cause him to become violent, although he doesn't easily reach that point. Mr. Thomas's son, Mike, was stabbed to death on a dark street, and Mr. Thomas still grieves over this loss. In fact, the violent death of his son has "ruined" his family, causing his wife to have a nervous breakdown and his daughters to carry with them in their everyday lives a good deal of anger. As a hard man with strong notions of the place of women vis-à-vis men, he is reminiscent of the men of the Old South. His case illustrates many of the themes of this book, particularly the prevalence of street violence among youths and the tension between decent and street orientations.

> Here's a for instance. I'm sitting on the steps, young fellow comes up the steps, goes past me. I lean back, "Hey," and he come back, "How you doin'?" "I'm all right. How you doin'?" I said, "You can't go in there." Just like that. I did it a thousand times, not only to him. My daughter, she lookin'. I say, "You cannot go in there because, number one, she cannot have company this afternoon, because I'm not pleased with her homework lately. And number two, you pass by me without speakin'. And number three, I'm not particular about you bein' in that house anyway." "What's wrong with me, Mr. Thomas?" "There's nothing wrong with you. It's just that you're not the type I want in my house." You won't believe the defiance I met back there, which I knew I was gonna get. You won't believe the defiance. I said, "Let me tell you somethin'. I'm not on trial. The issue is closed. I don't have to give you permission to come in my house. That's my house; I'm the boss there. Please don't come back again."
>
> Now, the first time he came, I wasn't in. I heard. You can imagine how he acted. All in the kitchen. You don't come into my kitchen. So I was layin' for 'im anyway. I had heard—you

know. My wife, she said, "You and him ain't gonna hit it." I said, "Well, it's not so much me and him not gonna hit it. How did you and him hit it?" That shift gears on her right there. "How did you and him hit it?" I said. "Well, I didn't get you involved." "Well, you should have. You know I don't want that type in this house. You know what he's about. He's about smacking girls in the mouth. He's about pulling down the pants in his car." I said, "You know what he's about. I'm really surprised and disappointed you let 'im in here." "I knew you were gonna say that." I said, "I'll take care of it now. I'm sure he'll be back today because he feels comfortable."

So soon as he parked his car, I spotted 'im. He was a young fellow—twenty-three, twenty-four—and he had a nice car, a very nice car. But I'm not dumb. I'm sittin' on the steps, and he just matter-of-factly walked past. His mind was on my daughter in the house. This is where he was coming in at, and that was it. He didn't even speak to me. So I had to get right with him. And it was a pleasure. I was prepared for anything, incidentally, 'cause he was just that rough. He would think nothin' of knockin' the dad down. I heard about him from more than one source. Let me see—I knew his mother—very good friend—and his dad—very good friend. His mother, Willa, she's still livin'. They were decent people, went to church every Sunday. But this was towards the changing of the guard, if you know what I mean by that—entering the early part of the transition where he was losing out—fathers, you know. Between the army and—you know, it started then, in the forties. It started real gradual—not many people picked it up, but you could see.

So this was around 1980. I realized what type of person I'm dealing with. And I knew from the jump—I knew, as soon as the guys told me he was coming to my house, I knew it was going to be a problem. Matter of fact, a couple of guys came to stand around to make themselves available—that's how bad it was. A couple of my friends. Because he will knock a man down. They would say, "When you confront him, do you think we should be around, or what?" And I would nix it only because I was the type, if he raises his hands at me, I would have shot him.

Not that I was bad; I was just that type. That's me. Well, he soon got it together 'cause he could see me. See, he could see the guy he had to deal with who wouldn't hesitate to hurt 'im. He knew that. Then he'd tell some of his friends, "Well, you know—" "Oh, yeah, well, you know him, he's from Thirty-sixth Street, he'll hurt you anyway." You know, they'll say somethin' like that. "You ain't gonna just push him by. He might hurt you." That's what his friends would say to him.

But that's all gone now. You're gonna catch some hell now. Now, who knows? The only thing you can do is love her. See it's like this: "How you doin' today?" "Oh, pretty good, Dad." "What's up?" "Well . . ." "Looks like something's on your mind. How you doin' with the guys?" Go at her in a nice way. "Well, Dad, Fred and I, we're goin' to a movie tonight." There are so many things we could talk about—the way he walks, it goes on and on and on. There are so many things I could tell you.

One day I was driving the car. Sara was in the car—my daughter, teenager. My wife was in the front seat. I had picked her up from somewhere, her girlfriend's. This will show you now. I'm driving. "I gotta go to the bathroom" was the first thing come out of her mouth. Now, we're driving from a couple blocks north of Market to South Fifty-eighth Street near Whitney— we're talkin', what, sixteen blocks. We're talking maybe at the most I'll give you eight minutes, ten at the maximum. So my wife, Mary, says, "We're not stoppin' in none of these bars." Then she mention it again. Meanwhile, I'm still drivin' towards home. "I gotta go to the bathroom." I say, well, if she has to go that bad, I know somebody all around West Philly. I say to Mary, "If she has to go that bad, we're gonna have to stop." "Can't you hold it, Sara?" "I think I might spit up." So finally we got home. She went in the house. Mary got ready to get out of the car. I said, "Sit in the car a bit." She said, "What's what?" I said, "I hope you ain't buyin' all that bull." "Oh, there you go." That's what I gotta hear: "There you go again. Somethin' wrong." I said, "Somethin' very much wrong. Now, she just left her girl-friend's house. She's gotta go to the bathroom that bad? She wasn't even in the car a minute. She's fidgety. She don't look right to me, Mary." You know what, she was high. Reefer. She was fidgety. She showed all the signs of bein' high. Her eyes were glassy. I looked at her hard. Only I can look like this at my kids. She got the message, too. Now, that died down and I was berated of course by my wife. So now let's roll the years up ahead. You know what she said? "Mom, Dad, that day he picked us up at so-and-so's house, we was in there doin' some reefers. I was high as a kite in that car. Dad is scary." Now she's grown over that. And I looked over at Mary and I said to her, "You know what bother me about you?" I said, "The one thing bothers me about you, you could see a accident and yet you don't see one. I'm pretty disturbed at your attitude 'cause you do this all the time with these kids." And I said, "I'm not gonna be around forever." Oh, sure enough we broke up, but this was years, *years*, 'cause I made it a point not to leave home, oh no, till that baby was in his twenties. I deliberately did that. Oh no, I wasn't gonna do like my father did. At that time. 'Cause my mom left him when he was runnin' around. So anyway, I said, "But, you know, you disturb me. And I'm very much disturbed because you constantly see and you don't see. I point out stuff to you, and I know I'm on the money, I can't even get an amen out of you. That's why I'm disturbed. And I'm gonna figure some kind of way to deal with you. The boy's the same way. You and my sister, y'all make me sick sometimes." I berate her.

My sister tell me about her son, Jo-Jo. "Jo-Jo's in there takin' a nap. He's tired, Charles." I said, "I see Jo-Jo in the street. I know what Jo-Jo's tired about. Jo-Jo's tired of jumpin' on that pussy out there in the street and everything else." I see Jo-Jo. The only Jo-Jo she sees is the Jo-Jo who comes home and gives Mom that big hug and he's tired of practicing. That's the Jo-Jo she sees. My Mike, they're the same age—fifteen. As a matter of fact, I went into Mike's room, and he was layin' underneath the cover, and I could actually see him laughin' underneath the cover. I said, "You old rascal you. You are somethin' else. Ma don't know nothin'." I said, "I want you to knock that stuff off and start doin' a little more practicin', you understand me? Or I'm gonna break it up altogether." I said, "You understand me?"

"OK, Dad, I will." See, and she's constantly missin' the boat. Not only my sister but her, too. You see what I'm tryin' to say? So we have to discuss that kind of parent also.

In the old days the black man was strong. Even the white man would take note. I'm gonna take my family to church this morning, ain't nobody gonna stop me. And guess what? That white man knew that. That white man was smart. "Don't bother the old man, Elijah, today when he's takin' them kids to church." That's what he's gonna say. This guy here feared God and he revered God and he loved God. This was quite a guy.

## MICHAEL'S DEATH

Greene and Chelten in Germantown. This is the early seventies. Gang fighting was rampant then. It was the worst period of gang fighting in Philadelphia's history. [Frank] Rizzo was the mayor. The police department had a attitude more or less: let the Negroes kill each other. They'd take action when a white was inadvertently killed or somethin'. That's when they would mobilize the full resources of the community, the agencies, and the police department. So my son was caught—he was a track star at Germantown High School. He was everything that a dad could expect out of a kid. He was the type of kid that any dad would have been proud of—six feet one, sports star, counselor at fifteen, happy as a counselor of Catholic kids and public schoolchildren, extremely popular young fellow with black and white students who attended Germantown High School.

On October 18, 1974, he was on his way to a get-together with the track team, a party more or less, and he was caught by violence—the Greene Street gang—and was asked, "What gang are you from?" They were high off of drugs and wine and everything you could think about. You could say you weren't in no gang, but that didn't mean anything. It's the biggest gang in the world, the one where they say, "I ain't in no gang." So one of them held a gun on Mike, and one stabbed 'im. And he died on the street. My wife suffered a total breakdown. His sister suffered a breakdown. His brother had some problems that are still evident, and these problems are still evident to this day. We're talkin' from the seventies to the nineties these problems are ongoing, but the family has been destroyed. And the tragedy of this tragedy is the police was well aware of gang warfare. They seen these hoodlums walkin' down the street lookin' for somebody, but it was in a black neighborhood.

This was around 10 P.M. They definitely saw them. That's been established. I know they saw them. But to stop them and to search them and to question them, they would have found a couple knives and a couple guns. But they sit right on their ass in the patrol car seein' this with the same attitude that I told you when I first opened up this interview. The same attitude—bunch of niggers. Now, had that had been the same group—what it's important to understand—if you could have transposed this gang, if you could have put this gang in any white neighborhood, they would not have got one block. And that's why I'm very bitter to this day. You hear me? Not a block if it had been in a white neighborhood. They would have been stopped, searched, and arrested—and dispersed. Those with guns would have been locked up, knives would have been locked up, and the other ones would have been kicked in the ass and told to get out of here and never let me see you around here again. That's it, nothing else to talk about.

That's why I'm bitter. I lose a kid—it was well before his time or maybe it was his time; that's not the point—the point is that if this had been in a white neighborhood, these same hoodlums had been walking down a white neighborhood, they would have been immediately stopped by the same police that was sitting on their ass as a gang rampaging up and down the street. Anytime you see a gang of that caliber, you know there's trouble. That's it.

I talked to the district. I did all a poor man can do. I went on the news. On top of that, to add insult to injury, the judicial system is the same today as it was yesterday. See, these kids don't understand this. So my boy—five years, six years, or whatever. Innocent kid like him—five, six years. Now, all you gotta do is look at the case of the Puerto Rican [youth] who was recently attacked in the Northeast—policeman's son. The ones in my case, they ain't the only ones. The judge, District Attorney [Lynne] Abraham, she wanted them all so she could impress her constituencies up in the Northeast. Rizzo called her one tough cookie. There's no doubt in my mind that many of them kids in the penitentiary today should not be there. But they were all scooped up, even the ones that were not involved, just in the gang. They were there. They were given ten, fifteen, twenty years in the penitentiary for the rest of their life. And being that this policeman's son was doing a hell of a lot more than my Mike did—'cause he was involved to some extent; he was drinking beer that night and raising hell with the rest of 'em—the same judicial system today is the same one that prevailed in the seventies. I went to the police department and said, "You're gonna tell me—I got the names of everybody involved in the assassination of my son, I want 'em arrested." "Well, Mr. Thomas, we got the main two. We got the guy that had the gun and the guy that had the knife." The rest of 'em are walkin' the streets to this day. Now, look at the other case, they've got some kids doin' time in the penitentiary now—ten to twenty, twenty to forty—who were just there, shouldn't even be in jail.

If Mike had been a white boy from Northeast Catholic High School, I guarantee you at least ten people would have still been in the penitentiary. Without a doubt in my mind. 'Course I'd a killed every one of them if I could have caught 'em, don't misunderstand me. I had a different gang. My daughter prevented me from doin' it 'cause she said, "Dad, that was not the gang." My daughter Annie said, "Dad, that was not the gang." 'Cause I was ready to kill every one of 'em. Mike was worth that to me. I don't wanta come off as a law-abiding citizen. I went to the courtroom to kill 'em. 'Cause I was greedy, I wanted 'em both there. I had already got it in my mind I wasn't going to hit Herb Reed [a local journalist]. I was not going to hit any of the policemen. I was not going to hit any of the court officials. I had made up my mind I was goin' to blow both of 'em brains out. But see, I couldn't never get 'em together. Either one had trial, one didn't, or whatever. I wanted 'em both together. You wanta know who I am? This for Mike to chill 'em both out right on the spot. But to show you the judicial system in this country still prevails, still there now. Now, don't let a white kid get killed by a accident. Then you see the full brunt of law. He ain't gonna get killed no other way but a accident. Now and then it's pre-meditated, but most of the time it's like Mike. Just for instance they had caught a white boy and killed him just on general principle. That street corner would have been clear for the next five years. Trust me. I could go shopping on that street corner for the next five to six years without any problems.

This happened in Germantown. But I was living on Willows Street [in West Oak Lane] at the time. But after the assassination—one of the local columnists termed it an assassination; I don't know why he said that, but that was his terminology. I asked the judge when she sentenced this fellow. I said, "You're very lenient toward this man and his family. What about my family, sittin' there distraught? My wife—gone. Two daughters—gone. My sister—gone. What about them?" Oh, she says, "Well, Mr. Thomas, I still feel sorry for them." Judge's name was Tyson. "I feel very sorry for your family, but you understand these fellows are young and they make mistakes. You know, these fellows are young and they were drinking that night. They've got to live with this for the rest of their life." I said, "They sure will with you puttin' them in the street." "Well, Mr. Thomas, I don't appreciate your saying that." I said, "Well, I'm sayin' it because it's true. They'll be in the street in three or four years." That's how much my son means to the system. Today black-on-black crime is rampant. Last week we had—what?— seven homicides. In fact, someone could pull out a gun right here and now and shoot everybody in here.

My wife suffered a breakdown, a mental breakdown. Still today. Which is now the nineties. That was in the seventies. Twenty years. We're still hurting. Absolutely. Some serious problems there to this day. I couldn't stay with her. I love her, I take care of her, I do what I have to do for her, but in order for me to survive for the family, I did what I did. I rue the day. She's my friend. My daughters—same thing. They went through hell themselves. It's tough. His friends—terrible. Half of 'em—he was a leader, Mike was a leader of a bunch of young fellows—and half of them collapsed. They gave it up, including a couple white guys. They became drug addicts, drunkards. Mike was extremely strong. I'm not beeping his horn 'cause he was my boy. I'm only sorry now that I didn't let Channel 10 tape the funeral. I regret to this day I didn't let them tape that. They wanted to tape the funeral.

Some of 'em wanted revenge, and I talked to them. Even the young fellow who witnessed it, he who went through hell. I had to put my arms around him and protect him from them 'cause he didn't wanta testify. His father didn't want him to testify, of course. And I told him that he had a responsibility to Mike to testify. It was a question of character. He was a young kid, scared to death. He said, "I'm gonna testify if it kills me. Mike was out there for all of us. That's the way Mike was. I'm gonna testify no matter what my father says."

Mike was going to a party with a fellow he knew. They saw the gang comin' down the street. Mike thought, "They ain't gonna bother me, I ain't about this." The gang surrounded them, proceeded to attack them. One kid ran, they shot at him. They killed my boy, stabbed 'im. They said they wanted to get somebody. And, Lord, somebody they got. A local newspaper's editorial board said they were so moved by your letter, we're going after this case. They sent a reporter around—"We want him to dig in." That letter was so impressive. They said they wanted to get somebody. They got somebody who goes to church every Sunday. They got somebody who counsels at a Catholic school. They got somebody six feet one. They got somebody that looked out for the old drunks in the neighborhood. They said they wanted to get somebody, and they got somebody who fought for the disadvantaged—at his age. They got somebody who took care of the drunkards in the street. I swear it's the truth. The local newspapers said, "Mr. Thomas, the letter you wrote us is impressive." They wanted to get somebody—that was my headline—they got somebody. They got somebody who brought little pigeons home with broken legs. I swear I'm telling you the truth. They got somebody who would come home with disadvantaged children—in spite of the fact we were poor. My wife would call me: "That Mike got a couple of them drunks again." I said, "Go ahead and feed 'em." I said, "You know how he is. Go ahead and feed 'em." So they got somebody. Up the street they had a home for retarded derelicts, disadvantaged folks. Mike would go bring 'em down for supper. They got somebody, got somebody that was full of love, a brave young man. Could outrun any of 'em. Stayed there with that kid who was afraid. He was Jimmy.

He was living on Coulter Street. His mother sent him over to her mother's house in Germantown. And the very place she sent 'im to, where she thought she was doing the right thing and I disagreed with that violently—don't ever tell her, but to this day there's some bitterness. But she did it out of love and out of fear. One of the boys in the other gang, from the street we lived on, went over to that neighborhood. "Who stabbed Michael Thomas?" "I wasn't there." "Who stabbed 'im?" "I ain't gonna tell you." Shot 'im right in the head. They knew him quite well. He was an ass-kicker. Shot 'im in the head, went to jail for it. Mike was so well liked. Boys who never picked up a gun had guns in their hands. I had my hands full. I had to take off from work. I didn't work for three or four weeks.

I came in to lead 'em. I said, "No, I'll handle it my way." My older friends and I, we will kill 'em. If I could of caught 'em in that schoolyard they hang out, they'd of been gone. I drove by there every day. Strapped down. I didn't give a damn what policeman would see me. My brother come over to the house strapped down in front of the cop, to the hospital. "Let's go, Charles, we've got some work to do." Cop right there lookin' at us, didn't say nothin' to 'im. The one just died. He said, "Let's go. We've got to go out there and take care of the others." My sister, the same way. She knocked on the boy's door and tried to stab 'im, a woman he never been involved with in his life. My sister, to this day she's sufferin'. Called me this morning from Harrisburg about the killing. To this day.

When Mike died that night, that Friday night, before he died, all them drunks and derelicts he used to take care of got to gatherin' around the house. They knew somethin' was wrong. Some of them come in and talk, just sittin' on the steps, like a dog know its master's been killed. Mike was an extremely strong man, extremely strong—six feet one, reddish hair, quite a guy. So that's the way it is in this country.

I taught Mike to respect your property. He wasn't a perfect kid. But he knew your car, he would help. Cursin' in front of your wife was somethin' that wouldn't happen. Drinkin' wine in front of your wife just couldn't happen. He would put the bottle away. "How are you, Mrs. Anderson?" She would see he had wine; that ain't the point. No swearing, no smoking.

I worked two jobs. I was a police officer for the federal government. I did that for twenty years, and I did work on the side, too, what with eight children—five girls and three boys. People say, "Well, at least you got seven more. They don't understand." Judge Janice Ridley made a better woman out of my wife. Better woman. She's better to this day. In fact, the one who shot at Mike—see, I'm mad 'cause he didn't run; I'm bitter that Mike didn't run—but then again, after thinking about, if he'd a ran, he'd of left the other boy helpless. The other boy left Mike on the ground to die and he ran around ten blocks, and the guys were bitter. I had to keep them guys off poor Jimmy. I said, "He can't help it if he's afraid. Don't bother 'im." "Don't bother 'im? He left Mike out there to bleed to death!" All he had to do was just stop a car, motorist would have took him to the hospital. But he just kept running. Didn't stop till he got to Brandwine Street. To this day it has destroyed him. Now and then I go over to the place where he worked at. He come up to me, hair different: "Hi, Mr. Thomas, I'm still ashamed of myself. I left Mike out there to die. I was afraid." I said, "This is gonna feel that way." He said, "You've been a wonderful man. All these years you kept them guys off of me." The guys wanted to hurt 'im 'cause he left Mike.

All these years. He said, "All these years from the time I was sixteen—now I'm pushing forty—you kept those guys off of me. Mr. Thomas, you're quite a man." He said, "I let you down. I let Mike die on the street." I said, "Don't say that. You did what you had to do." He said, "But I was a coward. I could of stopped the police. I could have stopped anybody and said, 'There's a man here hurt. Let's take 'im to the hospital.' " He said, "I was afraid to death. I ran for my life." Didn't stop running till he got to our house. Now, we're talkin' about down Germantown Avenue, clear back into West Oak Lane, Mike layin' on the ground dying. The guys were bitter. He had to leave school. I did all I could. I took him to school. I got my friends to protect 'im. That went on for years. Then you can imagine how I felt to have him walk up to me last year. Goin' to get my car fixed at this certain place. "You remember me?" I said, "Yeah, I know you." He said, "How's the family, Mr. Thomas?" He said, "I'm still ashamed." I said, "Don't be that way. Mike wouldn't want you to." And I consoled 'im. "You've gotta come around and see the family. They'd love to see you." They hate his guts. But I told him that. I kissed him, I held 'im, I did what a man should do. He said, "Mr. Thomas, I ain't been nothin' since." I said, "Now spit this out." "Mike would have never left me out there. He could have ran and left me if he wanted to. He stood there with me. I said, 'Mike, let's run.' Mike said, 'They ain't gonna bother us.' "

But everywhere you go, you know, I see—every time I see a kid in sneaks walkin' on his toes, six feet one, at that age, fifteen and a half—never got to see sixteen—high cheekbones, athlete. . . . I told 'im, "Mike, whenever you see a gang comin', run." But he ain't that type. I was just talkin' to myself and I knew that. His brother will. His brother'll run. Mike wasn't that type. That's the way he is. I knew it. "Mike, your mom's quite concerned about you." He said, "Dad, I don't wanta go to Grandma's house." That's what hurt me so bad. He said, "Dad, I don't wanta go over there. They're gang-fightin' all over." I said, "Well, your mother, she's with you kids all the time, and she feels you'll be safer over there."

The gangs in our neighborhood knew 'im. The Star Gang knew 'im. They fought with the Mellor Street gang. They knew 'im, respected 'im. They were bitter at the guys who killed him. His mother didn't understand that. She's lived that over a thousand times. On the night he was killed, he asked my daughter Annie, "I don't wanta go there tonight. I wanta stay with my girlfriend." Oh, this kills me. This kills me all over again. She said, "Mike, I don't wanta see you go over there, but Mama'll give me hell if I don't take you over there. You've gotta go." Mike said, "I don't wanta go over there. Don't tell Mom. I wanta stay with my girlfriend tonight. Annie said, "No, Mike." Now, I do have one consolation. Had he a called me, "Dad"— 'cause what I say goes—"I don't wanta go to Germantown tonight." "Why, Mike?" "I wanta see Augusta. I've been practicing all week and this and that. I don't wanta go tonight, Dad." "Put your mother on the phone." "Hey, I know, you ain't never home, now you're gonna tell me what to do." I said, "That's right. He's not goin' over there tonight. He don't wanta go, and he's not goin'." That's what woulda happened. But he never called. He usually calls. He never called. He went. You can imagine how his sister felt when he said to her, "I don't wanta go," and she said, "You gotta go because of Mom." What a tragedy.

I took her to doctor after doctor. [But] in my heart, I'll never forgive her. I can't help it. I'll never forgive her. No animosity, but I'll never forgive her. Her mother lived over there. Her father had died. She already had one son livin' over there. He went to the army, but he was back and forth there. He went to Germantown High. Mike—she sent 'im into the hornets' nest. He was safer with us. Mellor Street loved him and revered him. And the Star Gang loved him: "That's Mike. Don't bother Mike." Never once did they bother Mike. They knew what Mike was about. But because the Star Gang would come over to fight Mellor Street, she was scared Mike would get caught up in the gunfire. But they would have never put their hands on 'im. And they proved it. When this happened, both gangs went over to Germantown. It was terrible. Some people got shot up. Nobody got killed. Some people definitely got shot up, no question about it. I'd a had a little party for 'em all. I just couldn't catch 'em. They knew I was out there. They knew it. Three or four of my friends were committed, I just couldn't catch 'em. They knew. "Mike's dad out there. We know he's out there. I ain't goin' out there." They knew I was over there standing on the corner. I went over there and stood on the corner.

You go up to Graterford, 90 percent in that penitentiary are black—Eighteenth, Seventeenth Street, you name it, in that penitentiary, five, ten, fifteen, twenty years. Now, if they hadda been give one-half of the support—that's the tragedy right there—that their white counterparts have gotten, see?

When I finally realized it wouldn't help my family none if I went to pieces, that is where I put the brakes on it. That's what saved me. I owed it to Mike. I still feel as though I owe him that. But he wouldn't want me to be sittin' in Graterford with his mother walkin' up and down the street with his clothes on, like she did. I don't even wanta go into that. His mother had a total breakdown. You gotta try to understand that pain. And his sister. Mainly it was self-realization, when I realized the trouble she was in and the family was in. Right now there's trouble.

The judicial system—they do not represent us. They're going all kind of different ways now because of the diversity of the economic situation in this country, the prejudice in this country, the political atmosphere in this country. There's a resurgence of the right now. Hard times are here. Difficult times are here. But as for me and my family, specially for me, fear the Lord, trust Him, and believe in Him, all the days of my life. Nothing is going to turn me around from that. As for me and my flock, we'll transcend all the political, transcend the economy, transcend the resurgence of the right-wing element in this country that's destroying this country; as for me and my flock, I will trust Him all the days of my life, come what may.

There was a groundswell of love for Mike. It brought tears to your eyes. Classes were suspended that day. The funeral—I went out of my way to divert a riot at the school. I'm still dealing with it. But what keeps me going, like I said, for me and my flock . . . Something within—there's something within, that spirit. That spirit that regardless of what may come that tells me to hold on. He's with me every step of the way. Now, some people laugh at it. Out there in them fields, our forefathers: "Come by here, Lord. Come by here. Somebody needs You." His daddy would tell him, "Son, you gotta get ready for church. It's prayin' time." That's what Daddy would tell us. But Daddy's gone today. That's why there's so much chaos and deterioration of the family structure. Somehow or other, we've gotta reach back and do what we've done ever since the beginning of time.

In conclusion, the roles of decent daddy and other old heads are becoming problematic in today's economic and social circumstances.[4] The alienation brought about by these circumstances goes way back in the history of black people in this country. It came to a head and grew visible to the wider community during the civil rights movement and the cultural nationalist movement that followed it. The image of decency associated with Martin Luther King Jr. was challenged by many young people. The Black Panthers and other groups (advocating "black is beautiful" and no more "turning the other cheek" to white racism) encouraged young people to be "black," and that image was often associated with the street. (The broader story of the resurgence of ethnic particularism throughout American society is a factor here, too.)

In the meanwhile, the wider white society proved to be as resistant to integration as ever. Being "proper enough, decent enough, clean enough" did not, with a few exceptions, lead to acceptance in that society. De facto segregation continued, resources for schools and public services in predominantly black neighborhoods declined, and poverty became more concentrated—and the street became more visible.

These factors have seriously undermined the role of the traditional old heads, who were associated in young black people's minds with the wider society. Their moral authority is weakened when being nice doesn't lead to material benefits: a good job for a young man, a good household for a young woman. The rise of "bad heads" (like certain rap artists) and the publicity they receive further challenges the position of the old heads. In the most distressed areas, young people still defer to old heads (like Tyree's grandmother) in public. But this deference can come close to being patronizing; in fact, drug dealers sometimes greet such a person with "You al' right, old head?" The implication is that the old head may want drugs.

Today's young people who reside in pockets of concentrated ghetto poverty, even the most decent, often have less experience with stable communities and families than their own parents or grandparents did. The old days of the manufacturing economy are more than a generation away. The more successful families and individuals have left the inner city for the wider community. There are more incentives for the strongest decent women to value careers and job potential over the role of grandmother, and the wider society attaches less value to the role. But more significant are the very serious challenges that beset the decent daddy and the grandmother of today's inner-city ghetto. As poverty becomes more deeply entrenched, as drugs proliferate, and as the level of violence rises, the community grows demoralized. It is in this social context that the grandmother is tested, particularly when her daughters, often in their teens and early twenties, have babies without the benefit of wedlock. Too frequently they succumb to the street, becoming addicted to crack cocaine, effectively losing their minds and leaving their children at times to fend for themselves. It is here that the grandmother is pressed into action to raise another generation. The pressures, trials, and tribulations she faces will be explored in the next chapter.

# The Black Inner-City
# Grandmother in Transition

FROM slavery onward, in the most trying of circumstances, the mother—and by extension, the grandmother—has been an extremely important source of
support for the black family.[1] Correspondingly, the
black grandmother holds a special place among her people, both in
folklore and in real life. Through the generations, many have characterized her as the anchor holding in place the family and indeed
the whole kinship structure. E. Franklin Frazier summed her role
up nicely:

> In her explanation of why the responsibility of "her chillen" falls
> upon her, this old woman [a seventy-seven-year-old ex-slave]
> expresses the characteristic attitude of the grandmother in her
> role as "oldest head" in the family. Where the maternal family
> organization assumes such importance as among a large section
> of the Negro population, the oldest woman is regarded as the
> head of the family. Some of these grandmothers will tell you of
> their courting, which sounded very much like that of the grand-
> daughters' today [1939]. Often, instead of having been a prelude
> to marriage, it culminated in motherhood and the responsibili-
> ties which it imposed. Even when they married, sometimes mar-

riage was of short duration, and the responsibility of rearing and supporting their children fell upon them. Thus is has been the grandmother who has held the generations together when fathers and even mothers abandoned their offspring.[2]

This chapter seeks both to paint an ethnographic picture of this traditional pillar of strength in the black community and to indicate the reasons, structural and personal, for the grandmother's resilience through changing forms of adversity, from slavery through the impoverishment of today's inner city. The lack of jobs brought about by the economic shift from a manufacturing to a service base and by the growth of the global economy—particularly widespread jobless-ness and the appearance of crack cocaine as a central feature of the ghetto underground economy—has greatly exacerbated the problems with which the grandmother has been called upon to do battle. How she has been able to manage and why her position is now more threat-ened than perhaps it has ever been sheds light on the very nature of the black community and what is necessary to sustain and nourish it. For although the network of grandmothers continues to form a com-munal safety net, that net is weakened and imperiled. Young women are still maturing into the traditional grandmother role, but their increasingly small numbers are making their obstacles proportion-ately greater.

## THE ROLE OF THE GRANDMOTHER: THEN AND NOW

In the days of slavery and then of sharecropping, when black men generally were unable to achieve economic independence, the black grandmother was often a heroic figure whose role required great sacrifice. The black man was frequently, but not always, emasculated, weakened, or simply neutralized by the social control efforts of the wider white society, and was thus reduced as a competitive force in a male-dominated society.[3] But the black woman was not usually per-ceived to be as much a threat to the hegemony of the white man as the black man was. According to folklore, such women were then allowed to develop into strong, independent, willful, wise, and omniscient matriarchs who were not afraid to compete with men when necessary.

With the advent of the industrial economy, black men became better able to support themselves and their women and children and began to function less ambiguously as head of the family.[4] Accordingly, over time the grandmother's traditional role was diminished but never completely dismantled. Even in the "good old" days of available jobs at decent wages, the grandmother was there in a crisis to pick up the slack when difficulties arose,[5] and at times she even competed with the man for dominance within the family (see Alice Walker's *The Color Purple* for a fictional treatment of the theme). Traditionally, her meager savings and her home were at the disposal of family members during temporary hard times.

Today, with the loss of well-paying manufacturing jobs and the introduction of drugs (particularly crack) and the violent drug culture into the ghetto, the black grandmother is once again being called upon to assume her traditional role.[6] As in the past the heroic grandmother comes to the aid of the family, taking responsibility for children abandoned by their own parents, asserting her still considerable moral authority for the good of the family, and often rearing the children herself under conditions of great hardship.

The grandmother's central role has become institutionalized in the black community and carries with it a great deal of prestige but also a great deal of stress.[7] However, because this role is imbued with such prestige and moral authority and is so firmly entrenched in the culture, many of those who assume it see it as highly rewarding and necessary, if not critical, for the survival of the black inner-city family.

A review of the literature on grandparenthood reveals that the existence of the institutionalized grandmother role is a major feature of black family life, particularly among the poor. Among inner-city blacks, because of this strong tradition, it appears to be a mandatory role with established rights, obligations, and duties,[8] and those who refuse it may be judged by many in the local black community as having abdicted a vital responsibility. Hence, when called upon, black grandmothers appear constrained to play out their role.

Traditionally, grandmothers have served as "kin keepers" for the extended family. This function seems much greater among poor blacks[9] and is deemphasized among the middle and upper classes.[10] Extensive kinship networks in general are more in evidence among poor black families[11] and tend to diffuse with upward mobility. Even so, women appear on the whole to be resilient, protective of home life and culture, and much more important to the working of the family than many men are wont to acknowledge. The stereotype of the meddling mother-in-law, which has become well established in general popular culture—for blacks, it finds comedic expression in the Sapphire figure and her mother in *Amos and Andy* or, more recently, in *The Jeffersons*—reflects this important, yet sometimes resented, position. However, such popular portrayals represent a very small part of the black female's actual familial role.[12]

Because the role of grandmother has such communal support— even public acknowledgment and expectation—unmarried teenage mothers of fifteen or sixteen easily turn to their own mothers for help, which is generally forthcoming.[13] In this social context, depending on the age of maturity of the new mother, the experienced grandmother may take over the care of the newborn, partly because she lacks full confidence in her daughter's ability to be a mother and an adult and partly to help keep her daughter from being as deviant as she would be otherwise, at times even helping her to resume her social life. In addition, the grandmother may take pleasure and pain in revisiting the role of a mother in a more than simply vicarious way. For these reasons a girl tends to achieve a new, if provisional, status in her mother's eyes once she becomes an unwed mother.[14] At the same time, through the trials and tribulations of motherhood, such girls often gain a new appreciation of their mother,[15] as well as of themselves.

Moreover, the community is prepared to make a conceptual distinction between a biological and a "real" mother. A common neighborhood saying goes that any women can have a baby, but it takes caring, love, and "mother wit" to be a real mother. Regardless of the circumstances, the birth of a baby is considered to be a truly blessed event. Accordingly, a profound female bonding takes place as the mother begins to pass her wisdom and experience down to the daughter. At social gatherings neighbors, relatives, and friends often augment this knowledge with their own fond remembrances and tales of maternity, attempting effectively to socialize the new mother into the preferred role of real mother. At the same time they try to prepare her to survive on her own terms, with or without a man. Given that families dissolve at a high rate among poor inner-city blacks and that women then prevail upon their extended family members and friends—often other females—for moral, emotional, practical, and financial support, the familial experience among the poorest may be described as matriarchal. Kinship ties, fictive or real, cemented through the grandmother, thus become the backbone of the inner-city extended family and, by implication, of young children in particular. The grandmother fills an important, perhaps the preeminent, domestic female role in the community.

The community consistently looks to the mother or grandmother to play or strongly support this mothering role, a duty handed down to her through tradition and by her own socialization. Typically, a young girl with a limited outlook and sense of options for the future is easily enlisted for this role. In conditions of persistent poverty, she may look forward to the rewarding roles of mother and, by extension, of grandmother. Young men sometimes come to expect such young women to bear their children and to make few claims on them in the process; at the very least, they view birth control as the woman's responsibility, as a matter of "taking care of herself." A common notion in the inner-city poor community is that bearing and raising children is the business of women and that men should be involved only marginally except in matters of discipline and finances, which are almost always in short supply.

Today the grandmother increasingly emerges as a hero who was waiting in the wings and has now been activated by the social and economic crises besetting the poor black family.[16] When more options become available to poor blacks, and the miseries of poverty, drugs, and violence recede, the heroic grandmother may once again retire to the wings, because her role is perceived to be less necessary, socially and economically. Hers, then, is a role that has been nurtured, supported, and legitimated over time, because of the ghetto family's chronic lack of resources, its subsequent vulnerability, and particularly the inability—or unwillingness, in many cases—of young men to fulfill their parental obligations and responsibilities.

In many cases vulnerable family members turn to their families and close friends when they are threatened by predators. The grandmother often provides the most reliable support. Given her traditional role, it is generally believed that she cares and that she will marshal family resources, call the authorities, and even mobilize the community for an organized protest against those plying the local drug trade. In any event, she will know what to do. These beliefs shape the conception that family members as well as community residents tend to have of her role. Today, in playing her positive community roles, some of these women actually lead marches down the street and picket crack houses. In a literal sense, they fight to preserve their neighborhood and especially the lives of its children.

This social context is important to an understanding of the grandmother's role, which, as we noted, has a long tradition but has at times been diminished. If it is resurgent now, that is largely because the social context—the dearth of able male breadwinners, the rise of crack-addicted daughters and male predators, and the general encroachment of the street culture into the fabric of the community—demands it. In her traditional role, the grandmother may really be viewed, romantically at least, as a selfless savior of the community. Her role may be compared to a lifeboat. If she is pressed into service, it is because the ship is sinking. And, to many residents, the inner-city ghetto community does seem to be sinking into ever more entrenched poverty and to be increasingly undermined by the realities of the street culture as the mainstream culture slips further away. The ideal traditional grandmother is generally viewed as decent, or a "real" grandmother, and thus close to mainstream society. The one who shirks her expected role is considered a nothing, but particularly if she is associated with the street. How far grandmothers deviate from the traditional role may be an indication of how far the social type is itself falling victim to persistent poverty and to present realities. It may also indicate the diminished ability of the community to produce citizens who can function adequately in the wider society.

Conceptually, two types of grandmothers may be discerned: the decent and the street-oriented. The decent one tends to be much better off financially. Accordingly, she is able to marshal various props of decency and to make claim on wider values like the work ethic, propriety, and church and to gain affirmation of a sort through these connections, which further serve to enhance their authority. She is very far from the street, and generally likes it that way. She tends to be somewhat suspicious of and careful with most anonymous black people she encounters for the first time; her doubts begin to dissipate only when she gets to know them better and determines they are more decent than street.

Along with church and religion, she espouses abstinence, and often she does not drink or smoke. She takes religion very seriously, and pictures of Jesus, Martin Luther King Jr., and sometimes John F. Kennedy grace her walls. An aura of decency hangs about her, and these emblems attest to her decency, as anyone who visits her quickly learns. The word "decency" is an important part of her vocabulary and conversation. In her presence everyone defers. She usually has a solid financial position. Whatever its sources—whether from a pension, Social Security, or welfare—she has an income and tends to manage her money well enough that she is known to have a "stash." This reputation enables her to exert some leverage over family members. Depending on how they behave, she metes out favors, giving them things, tangible and intangible. Her grown children may make more money than she does, but they tend to run through it more quickly. Carefully managing her money, she tends to be thrifty and wise and able to live within her means, so the little she has may seem like a lot and go a long way.

In addition, in times of family distress or real trouble, this grandmother is often able to assume the role of an activator.[17] Not only does she have resources of her own to commit to family needs; she has the moral authority to prod other members of the family to commit their own resources of time, money, and care to aid the family member in trouble or need. In one family I interviewed, when a daughter became addicted to crack, her siblings initially responded simply with expressions of "shame, shame" and little more. But their mother was able to prevail on them to help out materially and even to take in one of the daughter's children. And she "went to work" on the girl, counseling her strongly and offering "tough love."

Thanks to their normally better educational background, the decent people usually have more resources than the street-oriented people, and this goes for grandmothers as well. Such grandmothers are more able to obtain help from the system. They are the ones who can deal with the welfare agency and have their addicted daughter's benefit checks diverted to them so that the money actually goes to the children and not for drugs. They not only provide help themselves but know to whom to turn in order to get even more.

Racism, the changing economy, unemployment, and changing social values all affect the people in the community. But the grandmother, particularly if middle-aged or elderly, often takes an ideologically conservative view and tends to have little tolerance for structural explanations. Given her prior experience in the local community in the days of the manufacturing economy, in matters of idleness and unemployment she is ready to blame the victim, because she feels that there is work to be had for those who are willing to do it and that people can abstain from doing wrong if they want to. It is her belief that the various social problems plaguing the community stem more from personal irresponsibility than from any flaw in the wider system. At times she feels she is paying the price for the failures of family members. As one seventy-eight-year-old grandmother rather vehemently expressed herself,

> Well, I don't have too much sympathy about these drugs. Everything is drugs, drugs, if it wasn't for the drugs. As long as someone is not holding you down, prying your mouth open, and pourin' it down your throat, you don't have to take it. So you take it because you want to take it. And nobody else has beat the habit, so what makes you think you're stronger than the other fellow? You see what it has done to his life. Now, if you're forced into it, then you're a victim of circumstance.

Certain other women who wake up one day and find themselves in the grandmother's role are at best ambivalent about it. They are, however, constrained to try to enact it because of the forces of tradition and the present-day circumstances. What else can they do? Not to do something would be seriously to abdicate their responsibility to their kin. With very limited resources, they may experience bitterness and stress, at times resenting their daughters and grandchildren, yet they work to help their kin because that is their place, which they largely accept.

Still other women completely abdicate, or are indifferent to, their traditional responsibility with respect to their grandchildren and this role. Often, though not always, they are associated with the street. These street grandmothers are much more at the mercy of circumstances beyond their control. They tend to be deeply invested in the "rough" street culture. They are apt to drink, smoke, take drugs, cavort with men, and generally engage in behavior that discredits them in the eyes of others, who then say things like, "She's weak," or "She's not ready," readily measuring her with respect to the ideal traditional grandmother role—which is loving and decent. The label "weak" or "not ready" may simply be describing the inability to define oneself according to the role. Even those who shirk the grandmother role know that they have deviated from a norm. Some feel enormous guilt, which often prods them to attempt to play this positive role as best they can in spite of their personal circumstances. Hence the traditional grandmother role has become something of a standard, a conceptual touchstone of the value system into which many young girls are initiated and actively grow.

All of this has resulted in a core cadre of black women in poor inner-city neighborhoods who are fountains of strength, reservoirs of resilience. In these communities they play out this strong decent role, becoming rock-solid figures others have learned to depend on and even to mythologize. When the family is intact, this woman is often the person other family members praise and look to for authority and direction; she gives advice and others take it. If the family is broken, she keeps the pieces at least loosely together. She may have few material resources, but she has enormous moral authority and spiritual strength.

On the average, a woman becomes a grandmother at about the age of thirty-seven; some do so at thirty-three or thirty-four, though some are, of course, elderly. Typically single, she may have a steady boyfriend or sporadic male company. Thus some semblance of nuclear family life is apparent, but there may be no formal domestic ties. Her home is a social center, a kind of nest for the family, where her grown children regularly come and go. Generally, her daughters are still living with her when they begin to have babies, further complicating the home's social activity. The woman herself may be employed but often in a low-level service or clerical occupation, such as that of nurse's aide, while the daughters may be working at a fastfood restaurant. By pooling their resources, they cope, but barely. Concerned about helping out the family, the grandmother buys clothes and toys for the kids, takes responsibility for child care, and when necessary gives moral support to the mothers. In addition, the grandmother draws social sustenance from her female friends, her church, and her neighborhood. At local coffee and liquor gatherings, they sometimes exchange the latest gossip about others in the neighborhood and share accounts of their own family problems. They discuss who's going with whom, who's working, and whose child is "on the pipe" (attested to by a clear loss of weight). In the course of such talk, important social and moral lessons are drawn, and children are carefully instructed in the rules of right and wrong. Children who grow up in this kind of household learn the rules and values of communal family support and are strongly encouraged to be "good" and "sweet." Rooted in this tradition, if they successfully negotiate the hazards of the neighborhood street culture, they have a chance to achieve social stability in the ghetto culture.

## THE INTRODUCTION OF CRACK

One of the worst hazards is crack. Once a member of the family "hits the pipe," a process begins that destabilizes an already weak unit and sets the stage for the grandmother to assume her heroic role. It starts when the daughter gets in with the "wrong crowd" or, as the grandmothers say, the "rough" or the "street crowd." She begins to run around at all hours of the day and night, hangs out in the wrong places, goes to bars; that is, she succumbs to the fast life. If she has children, she has less and less time for them. Ironically, the grandmother often unintentionally aids and abets her daughter's fall into this life by babysitting for the children and helping out financially and in other ways, thus giving the daughter the freedom to pursue a good time. As the daughter becomes increasingly drug dependent, she becomes a "different person," and the grandmother who was giving support becomes aware, sometimes rather precipitately, that she has two or three young children to raise. Then she realizes that the amount of responsibility she has casually been taking for her daughter's children has mushroomed and suddenly become onerous. Money often becomes a critical problem, as her daughter begs, demands, and cajoles her for it. Ambivalently, the grandmother may give in. But in time she finds that she is the only one giving—and receiving little in return. This recognition of the daughter's crack problem appears to overwhelm all but the strongest grandmothers, but for these it may serve to crystallize the whole situation. A series of events then occurs that "puts things on her mind."

This is when the crisis comes to a head. During this period, for instance, the mother, the daughter, and the daughter's siblings have many fights over what role is to be played by whom. They try to get the daughter into line. They talk to her as though the drug problem is something she got into on her own and can get out of on her own; they go through a period of denial that the girl is really an addict. Meanwhile, the girl herself is changing. She neglects her appearance, her personal hygiene, and her health. She becomes increasingly irritable and frustrated. She takes less and less care of her children and may even begin to abuse them. Family members can clearly see this and finally can ignore it no longer. They begin to talk about it, and the girl starts to lose respect in the family. As she becomes cut off from the family, she gravitates ever more completely to the street. The neighbors begin to talk about her. Her reputation becomes sullied, and she is increasingly discredited as a full person in the community. People often whisper about her addiction to crack. In the local community being on the pipe is a mark of profound deviance, and those who hear about it may react with surprise—depending on the kind of girl she was known to be before "all of this." To end up on the street is to have fallen from putative decency and to be headed nowhere socially.

Crack addicts are known to be capable of doing anything to obtain the drug. Women will engage in all forms of prostitution; some formerly outstanding and decent girls will offer complete strangers a "blow job" for as little as two dollars. Once they are on the pipe, decency and norms of propriety are far from their mind.

At a certain point the mothers of these women are often forced to disown their daughters, even to put them out. Saying things like "She ain't doin' nothin'," such a grandmother asserts that her daughter is not functional as a real mother, that she is abdicating her critical mother's role. It is a very damning assessment. In effect, such a grandmother is working to neutralize her affinity to her daughter and thus her maternal responsibilities to her. This is one of the ways in which she begins to sever the connections, culturally making way for herself to take over the child care responsibilities of her daughter. She does it with a vengeance, coming to grips with her gradual assumption of this new role.

The grandmother's goal in seizing control of the household is to ensure the survival of the family. In contrast to her daughter, she takes a long view of the family and has the moral authority to remind various members of their obligations with regard to generations past and present. An extremely important link, she can rally the others to deal with the crisis even if they are skeptical of the efficacy or even the wisdom of intervention.

Unemployment, the prevalence of crack, and the increasingly complex social scene all make the grandmother's job more difficult. If her daughter gets on crack, it is never simple for the grandmother to take over the role of mother. Usually, she has served as a part-time mother, but the assumption of full-time child care responsibilities makes her resentful, bitter, and frustrated, especially if she has to physically battle her daughter. Moreover, she feels she has already raised her own children and should not have to take responsibility for raising another generation. Frustration may saddle her with a sense of failure. In this situation tension easily builds and may spill over into fights, violence, and, on occasion, even murder.

It is important to note that the grandmother does not always perform the work of primary caretaker by herself. Rather, she calls on others in her immediate and extended family for help, especially grown siblings of a wayward daughter who until now have been sitting on the sidelines watching and wringing their hands. In this regard, she serves as an activator, a facilitator, whose main concern is the welfare of the children. To be sure, she does much of the labor-intensive work involved here, but often with the help and moral support of her other children and possibly some of her more extended kin. She and these family members, when they are encouraged, work to reinforce one another, and neighbors will often do what they can.

When the grandmother is able to withstand the tension this situation creates, a strong religious component is apt to be present. Stepping in for her daughters becomes her duty to God. To take care of the children—to serve more fully as their primary caretaker—is to fulfill a religious obligation to Him. It is often this set of convictions that enables her to carry on, to muster the sometimes superhuman strength required to act in the face of profound adversity—of seeing her own child ravaged by drugs, of waging the sometimes knock-down, drag-out fights she has with her about authority over the children or the spending of money.

In these circumstances the grandmother frequently spiritualizes her situation, taking the whole predicament as a "test" from God that she must pass, for "God knows the answer if you don't." In meeting the test, she seeks to take care of the children as best she can. Through this interpretation, she feels less of a burden than she otherwise would. She feels that if she prevails, she will be glorifying God. This is where she gets the strength to deal with the moral adversity: "I'm not perfect, but I'm trying to be Christ-like." Crack is a test. The devil is constantly working on you, but the Lord works in strange ways. God is love, wisdom, eternal life. Taking care of your grandchildren is part of all this, even if your daughter is going to hell. You may not be able to save your daughter, but you can save your grandchildren.

The following first-person account of one decent grandmother, transcribed from a tape-recorded conversation, illuminates both the strength of will of these women and the increasingly dire circumstances with which they must do battle. "Betty Washington" exemplifies many of the traits of the typical inner-city black grandmother, including a strong sense of commitment to family, especially the children, a desire to live an orderly, respectable life despite the personal and social problems that surround her, and a sustaining faith in God.

## BETTY'S STORY

I'll be forty in August, and I was born here in Philadelphia, North Philly. When the drugs came in around the corner, everything just went crazy, you know, completely crazy. And even though I lost my house in a fire, I wouldn't want to go back there either. It was really bad there. My oldest daughter, that's where she really had her problems at. It was a mixed neighborhood, Puerto Rican. When I had my first daughter, I was eighteen. I have two girls. One will be twenty-one in July, and the oldest one's just turned twenty-two.

I went to Catholic school. Back then it was only twenty dollars. I was born Catholic, raised Catholic. I would have liked to have finished it, but at the time money was tight, and I couldn't. Then I went to public high school, but I didn't graduate. Being that you came from Catholic school, you learnt more in a Catholic school, then you went to a public school, it was hard to get the teachers to understand that work that they were giving you, you already knew. You know, the counselors, they didn't really listen to you. So I was really, like, bored. The best thing I had was geometry. The other classes that I had, the work was too easy. And I wouldn't go to some classes. I'd go to the library, I would sneak over to different churches, stuff like that, and being that this counselor wouldn't listen to me what I was sayin', I was just hangin' out. After that, I started goin' to night school, different programs, stuff like that. I was educatin' myself basically.

When I got pregnant with my first daughter, I was married. I had both my children while I was married, but I haven't been married twenty years. I got divorced. What happened? Well, it was the time the Black Muslims came in. We had a business, everything was goin' fine, he got involved with the Black Muslims. After he got involved with the Black Muslims, he wanted me to convert. I wouldn't do it. Everything just went haywire. Like they told him, "She won't convert, you don't need her." So he was basically going along with everything they said, and it got that he wouldn't do for me, he wouldn't do for the kids. I wasn't goin' to fight with him; you go your way, I'll go my way. That's essentially what it was. I had a lot of problems with the Catholic Church. They want you to go to their courts and whatnot. But by that time the man was already seein' somebody. He was already involved and had kids and everything, so it didn't make sense for me to go through that. The marriage was gone, you know. I didn't see no sense in it. They didn't actually excommunicate me from the church, but I got a lot of static when it came time to send my kids to Catholic school. There was a lot of trouble with the pay rate. If you was Catholic, you didn't have to pay as much in tuition. So there was a lot of static, but it was necessary, so it didn't faze me. I had a tough time in the divorce, you know, but I did raise my kids Catholic. They only thing is they just didn't go to Catholic school. The oldest one was in there, but they took her out. She was just that bad. They took her out in first grade. But I couldn't afford tuition for them anyway.

I raised my daughters on my own pretty much, with the help of my mom. It was not a problem until they got older 'cause she was so attached to them. There was a lot of problems there. I had a boyfriend. That didn't work out either. We had a lot of problems raising Angela. It's hard raising a child and you get a mother interferin', you know. We were younger then. I say she was younger too and set in her ways. So when I started having problems with my daughters, she couldn't see it, because she wasn't there every day, you know, and then after everything came to a head and everything got out of hand, she took 'em. *Then* she was able to see what I was talkin' about.

They would run away a lot. They were twelve and eleven. After we had the fire, it was real emotional. I was tryin' to get everything situated with the insurance. I had a lot of problems, you know. I got ripped off with my insurance and the contractors and everything. The house never did get fixed up. And things just wasn't as they were. I hadda go out and work. I had to start doin' things that they wasn't used to. They was used to bein' with me, and then I had to start goin' out findin' a job, lookin' for a job, leavin' them with different people. And it just caused a lot of problems with them, and they couldn't adjust. Sometimes they would stay at home, sometimes they'd stay with a neighbor, sometimes they'd stay with my mom. At the time when they really needed me, I couldn't really be there for them. So it was hard. Goin' back to the district attorney, goin' back to the court. It was difficult.

*Angela's Problems Become Chronic*

And their whole behavior just changed. Angela was twelve years old. She started doin' drugs.[18] Well, at the time it was marijuana. It was the neighborhood. They got kind of wild. They were gettin' more freedom, much more freedom. There was a lot of peer pressure. She used to start doin' things that were so out of place for her. And I guess I was a little strict on her, you know, on account of it was just me. I had to be the mother and the father. And once I started lettin' 'em get out there, they just changed. Well, she has always been a bad, problem child. She got kicked out of first grade. And then the neighborhood started deterioratin' and there was a lot of peer pressure, and she's not the type of person that could stand on her own. She listens to everybody on the outside, no matter what you say.

So everything just started goin' haywire. I had her in counseling for a long time; that didn't work. You know, the counselor couldn't help her much 'cause she was what you call a habitual liar. Her whole attitude just changed. She wanted to fight. She started pullin' knives on me. And this is a young girl. I tried but . . . She started when she was twelve, and I was at work. There was always some guy, somebody. You know, she's always liked the older men, always having the older men. She was close to her father even though she was two when he left. I can't say she doesn't remember. She was two when he left; after then there was no communication whatsoever. I always say for her wantin' to be with older men, she looking for her father, you know.

I know I brought her up right; I know I did everything right for her. I might not have been *the best*, 'cause I had problems myself. I couldn't do everything, but I did the best I could, but she's—I don't know—she's just a bad seed. My other daughter was a A student. She was one of the first kids they took out of the regular public school and sent to white neighborhoods, takin' the bus. She was good. But then she got on drugs. She was supposed to go to the School for the Performing Arts. She could have went to Cheyney College. She could have done anything she wanted.

But Angela, she just a bad child. She didn't care what you do to her if you punish her, how much you talk to her, how much you cry, scream, whatever. She didn't care. Like I say, to me it was a lot of peer pressure. A lot of what she did had to do with bein' that we were livin' in a Puerto Rican neighborhood. Most of the problems I had were with Puerto Rican guys. I had to go out to these people and fight 'em: "Leave my daughter alone." She almost got shot by the cops 'cause she was livin' around the corner in an abandoned house with a whole bunch of those guys. And it was a shock too because I didn't think that she was social-izin' with them. The way I had brought her up, it was out of place, completely out of place. The first time I actually had to leave my job and come home because she had ran away was because of marijuana. She was just stoned. She was doin' weird stuff. First I thought it was attention; she wanted a lot of atten-tion. But she really had a problem.

It came to it that she had to be put away. I had to actually put her in a home, and I regret the day I did that because instead of her gettin' better, everything got worse in there. It just got worse. But at the time there was nothin' else I could do. I had myself to think about. I had the youngest one to think about. And this child, she wanted to fight. She pulled knives on me, she said people were gonna blow the house up. This is the type of child that she was. I got her back after about a year. She was doin' the same thing, still wantin' to fight and whatnot. And I didn't think that DHS [Department of Human Services] was really helpin' as much as they could have been.

When she went on crack, her whole attitude changed: "I just don't give a damn" attitude. And she was so—how can I say it?—she had no scruples about it, none whatsoever. After I got her back—she was nineteen—she stayed here for a while, but at the time I didn't really, really notice she was doin' crack. I knew she smoked marijuana. We started goin' to the same school. I was goin' for the computers, and she was goin' for nurse's aide. And she did good, A's and whatnot, but she didn't complete it. And I still didn't really know, because at the time she was staying with my mother again and she was back and forth here. And she got pregnant. And she as always startin' fightin', and I couldn't deal with that, so I had to put her out while she was pregnant. The landlord's daughter lives upstairs. That caused a lot of problems 'cause the landlord would find out what was goin' on. She wanted to bring boys in, she didn't want to do nothin', she wanted to fight all the time, so I had to ask her to leave. And I really didn't connect it to the crack. I knew she was doin' somethin', but I just didn't know she was doin' that. And then after she had the baby, I still didn't know. They didn't really tell me too much. She didn't stay in the hospital too long. I was thinkin' they let her go, but actually she left the hospital.

*Betty Becomes a Grandmother*

Then that's when she said, "You're still my momma." I stayed over with her for a week, and she would go out, and she would not come back. Eventually, she went fourteen days and she didn't come back, so I wound up bringin' the baby back here with me. And that's when I realized she was on the crack. She was not behavin' like a mother. But she's always been the type of person who eventually lets you know what she's doin'. And she come home, she told me she was doin' what not. And by then I had already knew. By me takin' the baby back to the clinic and everythin', the doctors told me. I didn't understand what was goin' on with the baby, the withdrawal symptoms and what not. I had already made up my mind, if she wasn't goin' to take care of the baby, if she wasn't goin' to do right, then I would take him. But I tried to give her a chance to take care of her own baby, but that didn't work out. I had to stay here. She wasn't ever here. Jamaicans would come lookin' for her wantin' me to give 'em back their money that she took. I'd give her money to go get Pampers and milk, and she'd take that. I sent her to the Laundromat. Someone else would bring the clothes back, she's gone with the money.

What I did was I went with her to court because she knew I was goin' to find out eventually. She went to get custody of her baby, but she didn't have any place to stay. And the address she used, she couldn't stay there, because these people was involved in drugs, you know. And we got joint custody. I figured when we had joint custody, everything would work out. That didn't work out. So I had to get full custody. By the time he was ten months, I had full custody.

This is the type of thing this child has always been in. She's always gettin' beat up. She always gettin' raped and whatnot. She never want to press charges, which I didn't understand at the time that this is the way she was livin'. She was livin' doin' these things to take care of her habit. Actually, I didn't know that at the time. I didn't understand it. And things just got out of hand, and I couldn't deal with it, you know, fightin', men comin' here lookin' for her. And things just wasn't working out. I had the landlord to deal with. I got to have some place to stay. I had to tell her to go. It was like I had to watch over my back, I had to watch everything, I had to hide everything, my food, my silverware. I had to do those kinds of things. And I couldn't live like that. She was takin' things out. Nobody here but me, her, and the baby. I go get something and it's gone. It didn't make sense to me, you know. I couldn't sleep. There was just no peace for me, no peace at all. So I had to say, "I love you, but you got to go. There is nothin' else I can do for you." I tried to get her in rehab; she wouldn't go.

Even right now, I'm still goin' to counseling. I've been goin' to the center ever since I had trouble with my kids, and that's since about 1980. I still go, talk to the counselors. I go to grand-parents' support group. I'm not ashamed, you know. If I need help, I'm going to get it, just talkin' to somebody, the hot line, stuff like that. I do those things. I worry about her a lot, but there's nothing else I can do for her. She got to start doin' things for herself. It's hard. It's a good support group. You find out you're not by yourself. There's a lot of people like that.

Now I have the little baby. She's thirteen months now. I got custody of the oldest boy. I went to court. That's a lot of money goin' back and forth to court. You know, I had to do that; then the father, he decided he wants to get upset because I won't let him see them when he wants to see them. You know, he had a set time to come and see 'em. He never showed up, but he took me to court. I had to wind up payin' the money, altogether about seven hundred dollars, and still to this day we have four court orders for him to come and see his son on Sunday from one to three; he has not once showed up, not once, not one time.

When you have a crack baby, it's always some problem. It can be physical. You don't really understand the babies, what the babies want from you, you know, the crying, the anger. The babies get hyper, you know, they get really upset, and that's a lot to deal with, a lot to deal with. So you take them back and forth to the clinic. And there's always somethin' wrong with these children. What really happened with this baby, the little boy, he wound up with some kind of infection. I knew she [Angela] had herpes, but I didn't know she had syphilis. The baby got sick, and they thought he had meningitis. Well, if I didn't have custody of him, there was no way that I could have had him treated without the mother. Where was I supposed to find her at? Where was I supposed to look for her at? And I didn't know at the time, but I found out two months later she had syphilis, second stage, secondary syphilis. And that's hard, that's really hard.

She fades in and out of my life. If she's not at the hospital right now, I couldn't tell you where she is. She just had another baby, only weighed two pounds, it's still in the hospital. Right now, the little baby, I'm trying to get custody of her. I filed a petition to get custody of her. What they're telling me now is you've got to have an address for the father and the mother. I don't have the address. I don't know where they are. They say I have to go find 'em. Where am I supposed to look for them at? I know nothin' about the father. I don't know where to find the mother unless she's in the hospital. She might be there two days; then she's gone. To get custody of her, you have to get involved with DHS. It's so different from last year because once she got tested for cocaine and they knew she didn't have a place to stay, the baby was automatically turned over to DHS. All she had to do was agree to let me have her, which she did. Like I say, I have her now for thirteen months. The new baby, I don't know what they're goin' to do with, I really don't. She still don't have a place to stay. She still test cocaine. What the social worker tells me now is "Just because she's doin' cocaine doesn't mean you can take the baby from her," which is so different from last year, you know.

### From the World of Work to the World of Welfare

But you have to step in and take the responsibility. You have no other choice. I don't want to see him in a foster home, and I would hate to see right now for them to be split up like that. But it's hard. Yeah, everything is in God's hands. He show you what you have to do and what you don't have to do. The only problem I have is that there's no man in my life. I don't have time for those things no more. Everything is those children. Everything is a circle around those kids. You have to have a place to stay, you have to get food, you have to do these things. So it's hard.

I haven't worked since I got the oldest boy. I live off aid. You have a court order where the father pays the court. No matter how much he pays, you only goin' to get fifty dollars of it. He does that, but he's just not involved with the babies. He's a security guard.

You're takin' care of those babies from the time they come

home from the hospital. You know, the mother's doin' nothin' for 'em. You're doin' everything for that baby. If I let her take that baby out of here and take him to a crack house, I'm responsible 'cause I know what's goin' on. So it was a lot of conflict. I couldn't let her take the baby. I had to watch him. This is somethin' I had to do. There's nothin' else you can do except let the baby go be put in a foster home, and I'm not about to let that happen. So I did it for the first. I didn't never expect to have another one, you know. With the first one they see that you mean business, that you goin' to do what you say you goin' to do. But that don't faze them, that don't faze them.

My mom's been real good. She's been real good about helping me with the first one and then the second one, but this time she's like "If you do that, you won't never come out of it. I don't think you should go ahead and keep on takin' her babies for her." Which I can understand in a way, you know, because I don't have the space for 'em. I'm lookin' for a place now. I really don't have the room for 'em. And these babies take up a lot of time, you know; they take up a lot of your time. The youngest one is in this program for slowly developed children. Her teacher comes now on Tuesdays and Thursdays, comes down and teaches her. You know, you go to the clinic every week, the special baby clinic, the neurology clinic. The first thing they say in the hospital is it has to do with cocaine because she was exposed to cocaine. And that's hard. And I hate that labelin' them children like that, but it's the truth.

I don't feel so much angry. I feel as though even if she was to get herself straightened out, it would be hard for me to give them children up, you know, 'cause I feel as though they've been neglected, something's been taken away from them. The mother has been taken away from them. They don't know her, and if you just take these kids and give them back to her, that's goin' to be hard on the children. How are you goin' to explain? You know, the children don't understand what's goin' on. The know their grandmother right now is the mother, and it would be hard for 'em. They don't have no contact with her, don't see her. That's goin' to be hard on them, and I couldn't do that. I would rather raise them 'til they get of age, you know. Right now, there's nothin' much I can say to them. I can't say, "Well, this is your mother," 'cause I don't see her. She's supposed to come see 'em, and she never shows up. So I feel for the children more than I feel for the mother right now. I really do.

There's no sense gettin' upset. This is what you have to do. If you didn't see any sense in it, you wouldn't be doin' it. That's the way I look at it. These kids are special. They're special kids because they have been exposed to crack. So it's a lot of time, a lot of patience, and a lot of love. You've got to give it to 'em. So I enjoy it. I really do. I do it. I get tired sometimes. Sometimes I get frustrated, but I don't dwell on it, you know. I don't dwell on it. Right now the most important thing is these children. That's most important. Yeah, some people say that God is testing them and good things is goin' to come out of it.

Right now financially it's hard. I really need a place, I need a place of my own. Livin' in this apartment is not good for the kids. It's a problem all the time, problems with the neighbors, problems with the landlord. They come and use my phone when I'm not here. I have to keep it locked in my bedroom, and then I can't hear it. At the time I took this place, it was just me, and I was workin'. I thought once I earn some money, I'll get out of here. Once I got the grandbabies, all that stopped, you know. Life is hard, it's really hard. It's always somethin', always, always somethin'.

### Life of a Black Grandmother in the 1990s

And even though I don't see their mother, when we do hear from her, it's so much confusion and turmoil. I get so upset with her. I wish she'd just go and stay away, just stay away completely. It got to the point where I wouldn't even stay in here, because she would come here and she'd want to fight, you know, arm fight. I was often worn out. So now I get up and I go every day. You know, you say things for their own benefit; they don't want to hear that. And the main thing is these kids are in my custody. *I'm* takin' care of these kids. *I've* got to do what's best for the children, not you. Regardless of whether you're their mother or not, I don't want to hear that. You're not doin' anything for them, and I can't let her take these children knowin' the lifestyle she lives, you know. That's the main thing right there. I can't do that. They could wind up anywhere. So this is what I had to stipulate. Like the judge told me, "You're responsible for these children. The mother or the father comes for 'em, they are not to have 'em." That's the number one rule. That's what I have to live by. And my rules are, I'm goin' to do what I have to do. If I wanna go out, I go out. I'm not goin' to stop what I'm doin' to let you come and go when you please. You know, I can't do that. And most of the time when I wait for her, she never shows up anyway. It didn't make sense for me to sit here all the time just waitin' and waitin' and waitin'. She never shows up.

Just like the father, you know. I sit every Sunday, and he never comes. I got so I'm not doin' that any more. Let the court say what they wanta say. It doesn't make sense, you know, to get this child all geared up to go, even without sayin' anything to him, to get them all ready to go to see his father, he never shows up. So I stopped. I just stopped. It's too much. This boy is three years old, and he hasn't made a effort to show up. This is Robert. And Carla's the youngest one. T. J. is my youngest daughter's boy, but he's not in my custody.

Carla's not really in my custody; she [was] just turned over to me by DHS. I have to get like what they call a confirmation of custody, and that's like $200, $350. Unless I know the address for the father and the mother, they won't go ahead and file a petition. I don't know what I'm goin' to do there. I really don't know. I don't know where the girl is. She's livin' in an abandoned house somewhere, where I don't know. I have no address for her, you know, none at all. I was up at the hospital on Monday. I had an appointment with the social worker, talkin' to her, and she was askin' me, "What are you goin' to do? She needs help." The only thing I could tell her was, I can't come up there every day, because I don't have the carfare and I have a list of houses I'm supposed to be lookin' at. I'm trying to do that every day.

## Mothers, Crack, the Law, and God's Test

They really need to pass a law—in fact, I thought they had did this—any mother that has a baby that was exposed to crack, they was supposed to put 'em in jail. They haven't done that. And I think that instead of waitin' thirty days after they get out of the hospital to have their tubes tied, they should do it while they've got them in the hospital right then and there, tie their tubes. Until they do something, these women are goin' to keep on havin' these babies. They goin' to keep right on doin' it. And it's rough on grandparents 'cause you know the grandparents are the ones who are goin' to take these children. A lot of them are goin' to do it. Some of them, they just won't do it. But a lot of them are goin' to do it, you know, 'cause it's bad puttin' these kids in foster homes. You hear so much bad things about foster care. All the things that goin' on, a lot of bad and whatnot. So it's rough, so you take 'em. You take 'em and you raise 'em.

I don't go to church that much. Somebody might invite me to a church, I might go. Most of the times, like I said, I do a lot of talking, friends. I have a lot of support from friends, my mom. I still go to counseling, and I talk things out. I pray a lot too. You know, you pray a lot . . . and just hope for the best and hope that you're doing the right thing. It's hard. You now, every day it's always somethin'. And then when you get to thinkin' everything goes all right and you're feelin' good and whatnot, something happens. So you just take it one thing at a time. I feel like I'm bein' tested 'cause there's a lot goin' on right now that I really don't have no control over. So it's hard.

## Can Adult Daughters Return to the Nest?

My youngest daughter, she want to stay here. She was leavin' T. J. here on a regular basis, but I stopped that 'cause he was upset bein' away from his mother. I was keepin' him while she was workin', and when she stopped workin' she started smokin' more marijuana. She has this old man, he was doin' drugs unbelievable. He had a roofin' business, and he was doin' good, bringin' the money home, and she was savin' it. But now they got thrown out of their apartment. It was his mother's company, but he was runnin' it for her, so he just messed up all the way round. If it was just her, I would be glad to let her come back here. But with the two of them, I couldn't afford for my rent to get raised. It just wouldn't work out. She's at that lazy point right now, a little lazy right now. And I just couldn't see it. She hasn't seen her father in twenty years, and all of a sudden he pops out of nowhere. Now she want to go and live off of him. So I don't know what she's goin' to do. She's kind of upset with me right now, but I can't have her here when I'm plannin' on takin' my baby.

She smokes marijuana. When you come and tell me you're doin' somethin', OK, fine. She's not doin' it to the point where I got to tell her, "Don't do that around your baby." But when you come and tell me you're doin' this heavily, 'cause you got so many problems, and I can't talk to you and try to make you see what you're doin' wrong, then, you know, what's the point? If you come and ask me to give you advice and I tell you how I feel about it and yet it upsets you, well then, what else can I say? You don't need to do it. I'm not goin' to tell you not to do it, because you're goin' to do it anyway. But that's what's happenin' with her. She gettin' worse with it. But she's not a dumb child. She could have gone to college, gave it up for this nigger to get strung out on drugs. He don't mean her no good. And when I was tryin' to tell her this, she didn't want to hear it. Now that I don't have nothing to say about it and she gets upset, I say, "Why, I did everything I could do." All I can do is pray for her. And she was good to me, she was really good to me, but in the last three months she's just . . . She's smokin' that stuff, and people got to understand that that stuff messes you up, really messes you up, so she's not herself. So all I can do is pray for you. I'll talk to you. If you want to talk to me, come talk to me and I'll tell you how I feel, but don't press the issue. I don't do that anymore. I think she's kind of upset with me because I won't let her come back here and stay with us. It's really no room. We can't afford to have our rent go up. I'm trying to get out of here myself. I'm not goin' to deal with the boyfriend, you know. You come by yourself, you and the baby, fine, but the boyfriend can't come. Especially someone who's doing drugs like he's doin'. I said no. I didn't put up with that with your sister, I'm not goin' to put up with your boyfriend, you know what I mean?

I can always tell when she's high, always. Like I say, my children have never really been able to hide anything from me, and they will—I can say that much—they will tell you. Even when I don't see Angela, whatever is goin' on in her life, when I do hear from her she tells me everything. I may not want to hear it, but she tells me everything that's goin' on in her life—whether she's been in jail, how many times she got beat up, what, who, everything. So that's one thing I can say.

*The Final Reality: Betty Accepts Her Heroic Role*

She says to me, "If I tell 'em I'm goin' to straighten myself up, would you let me have my kids back?" If I saw it, it would be a completely different thing, but just by comin' and tellin' me, uh-uh, because I would know better. I've heard it so many times: "Ma, I'm goin' to do this. Ma, I'm goin' to do that." And it never got done. Never. And there's always the hope. You know, I pray for you. I'm looking forward to seein' it happenin'. It just never does. It never does. It just goes in one ear and out the other ear. She called my aunt Esther. It was Angela's birthday. See, I know my kids so well. It was her birthday. I had called the hospital. They hadn't heard from her in about three days. It's not like she's goin' there every day to see the baby, which I already knew she wasn't goin' to be doin'. And it was her birthday. She called about nine-thirty. I knew who it was. She called cryin'. She and her boyfriend got in a great big fight. I didn't want to hear it. I did not like to talk to her. I did not. I let my aunt talk to her because I'm out, I'm havin' a good time, I was enjoyin' myself. I didn't want to be bothered, 'cause then that would just bring me down. You know, if I had to come home, stay up all night worryin' if this girl is goin' get killed or whatnot. I let my aunt talk to her. Like my aunt was sayin', you've got to not let yourself get upset. 'Cause soon as I hear her name—they say, "Angela's on the phone"—I just get all "What's going on?" And that's no good. That is no good, no good at all.

Betty feels keenly the pressures of her situation—internally from her family and externally from the street and institutional bureaucracy—but she is determined to endure in spite of them because she feels her responsibility is to future generations. Despite her own responsible behavior, however, her situation is becoming more and more difficult—possibly even untenable—because of her daughter's actions. Betty's daughter persists, for complicated reasons of her own, in bringing into the world children she is completely unable to care for. Angela has gotten caught up in the drug culture that has undermined the inner-city black community, in part as an indirect result of deindustrialization and the consequent loss of blue-collar jobs.[19] As was noted above, young men with few prospects of legitimate jobs often turn to the underground economy, particularly the drug trade. Getting women hooked on crack is one way for them to develop a customer base—and also a "supply" of easily manipulated women. And when Angela falls into this social trap, her entire social network is affected.

At the same time, the details of Betty's struggle reveal how complex her problems are. In order to receive welfare support, Betty was forced to quit her job as a nurse's aide, even though she enjoyed working. There is also the issue of caring for the children, especially the crack-addicted baby, who required special attention. The lack of good, affordable day care in conjunction with the rules of welfare eligibility left Betty with only one responsible course of action: to leave her job in the private sector in order, in effect, to become employed by the state to raise her grandchildren.

## CONCLUSION AND IMPLICATIONS

The difference between what is happening in poor black urban communities now and what happened in the past is accounted for by the economic and social changes that have swept urban America. Blacks have always been apart from the dominant society, and they have always been segregated and beset by the problems that come with segregation. The past thirty years have brought a greater inclusion of blacks in American society and a sharing of its fruits, but these developments have most often helped those blacks who were ready to take advantage of them—the middle classes, the educated people. The poor, who lack the skills, the education, and the outlook to take advantage of these new opportunities, have been not beneficiaries but more often victims of the changes.[20]

All this has implications for the way poor black families operate.[21] There has been a rise in the underground economy, which offers the most desperate people an alternative to the regular economy, which often does not support their basic human needs. But at the same time that the underground economy holds out an alternative, it has a socially deleterious effect on the rest of the community, undermining it in a very basic way. Those who are involved in the underground economy exploit the weakest members of the community, and so even the decent people among the black lower classes sometimes become ensnared in their schemes. Inner-city residents, particularly young men, want many of the things that middle-class white people have— nice cars, nice clothes—but because the wider system is so bankrupt in their minds, it becomes very important for some of the most alienated to combine these items with a marked unconventionality of dress and behavior. A counterculture thus emerges, with the purpose of making a cultural statement against a dominate society that many young inner-city blacks feel disrespects them. In effect, these young people are saying, "While I want what the white people have in terms of money and privilege, I don't want those pin-striped suits. I don't want to look like that. I want to do my own thing. I want to be my own person." Flashy jewelry is very far away from the pin-striped suit. So are the untied shoelaces and the coveralls with their suspenders hanging down at the sides that characterize that latest style of urban hip. In contrast, for the white kids who mimic them, these styles may just be a lark that they can easily give up when they realize it is time to become serious about life.

Probably the most worrisome development of all is the emergence and proliferation of what I would call the crack culture, which is to be distinguished from the ordinary underground economy and drug culture. Crack is special and leaves in its wake great numbers of casualties. Seen only indirectly by most other people, victims of crack in inner-city poor communities suffer acutely.

The primary victim of the present situation is the poor black family, which is experiencing a profound crisis. The crisis spreads as the young are drawn to the underground economy. The metaphor of a raging fire or a cancer comes to mind. Crack leads to illness, death, the proliferation of homeless children, crack babies, teenage pregnancy, violence, high rates of incarceration, and other social problems.

As was indicated above, in the inner-city community there is a social distinction between decency and the street; people with a positive sense of the future are associated with decency, and those headed nowhere socially are associated with the street. In the community the street has a kind of magical magnetic quality; it attracts those who are not well anchored to more conventional social forms. It is a seductive thing, and those of the community who would be decent must resist its lure. Those who fail to do so fall socially or are "out there in the streets." To prevail is to have resisted the street and to have done so in a manner considered praiseworthy by many who see themselves as decent. In this respect, decency and the street represent polarities around which social identity may be worked out and formed.

This is the context in which the grandmother must be seen. Her traditional role as an anchor, cornerstone, or even lifeboat of the black ghetto family emerges and crystallizes in this context. She becomes heroic, saving or assisting people who are receptive in some way, and she cannot be fully understood independently of it. The role is not that fundamentally different from the one she played in the past. Without her, the breakdown and disorganization would have even more dire consequences for community life.

Standing firmly against the counterculture, the black grandmother believes in the wider system, emphasizing a strong commitment to decency and propriety. She dismisses structural explanations for the various social ills besetting the community, convinced that if you just act right, you will be rewarded; if you are civil and decent, you can make it. She stands at the spot where personal responsibility begins to mesh with the structural problems. The grandmother who successfully plays her role tries to transmit her orientation to the young. But to prevail she must battle the increasingly pervasive street culture, and even the strongest of these indefatigable women sometimes despair of what the future holds for those they are trying desperately to save. The grandmother's resilience through the generations has been extraordinary, but she is now apt to feel tired and demoralized by the negative social forces tearing at her community. Her considerable personal resources are being stretched to the limit, if not beyond it. As they age, grandmothers become less able to control volatile adolescents, especially as the street lures them. Although generally loved and respected even when disobeyed, they may come to seem irrelevant, particularly to their grandsons.

At the same time that these traditional grandmothers are losing clout and energy, few of them are being replaced. Crack, unemployment, and other social problems that follow in the wake of deindustrialization tend to dispel the human capital of such grandmothers, so fewer women have the capacity to undertake the role. It is unlikely that Angela will ever follow in her mother's footsteps. As the grandmothers become less effective, the multiplier effects grow, and the most impoverished pockets of the black inner-city community move closer to disintegration.

# SEVEN

# John Turner's Story

YOUNG men who lack a truly decent daddy, or effective father figure, both as a role model and as a viable presence in their lives, are often hard-pressed to organize their lives in accordance with his standards, standards handed down from generation to generation through the myths and realities that have accumulated in inner-city homes, schools, street corners, and other staging grounds of urban America. The young man who is profiled in this chapter had a mental image of the upstanding man and father figure he often longed for and even wished to be. His attempts to enact the role were continually compromised, however, by the lack of an effective model, but also by the unrelenting pull of the street.

I met John Turner a week before Thanksgiving more than a decade ago. It was about two-thirty in the afternoon, and I was in a carryout restaurant I regularly patronized. I had seen this young black man behind the counter, in the kitchen, sweeping the floor, and busing tables, but I had not given him much thought. On this day he stopped me, excused himself politely, and asked if he might have a word with me. I was surprised, but I said, "Sure. What do you want to talk about?"

"I'm in trouble, deep trouble," he opened. "Whoa," I said, "let me catch up with you. What kind of trouble?" As he shared what was on his mind, I saw that his story involved many of the general issues with which I was concerned, and I asked his permission to tape the conversation. He consented.

John is a high school graduate, a former halfback on the football team who has done some boxing. He is about five feet nine inches tall and weighs about 165 pounds; he is built like the prize high school football running back that he was. He likes to dress in navy or dark green Fila athletic suits, designer jeans, T-shirts, and expensive white sneakers. In this uniform, he cuts a striking figure on the streets. John was twenty-one when I met him, and already the father of four children: three sons by three different women and a daughter by the mother of one of his sons. He now has two more, by a woman who used him only to get pregnant and now will not allow him to see the children. John accepts this arrangement, saving his energy to keep up as best he can with his other four children. In conversation, he shows no compunction about having had these children or about his relationship with their mothers. In fact, he expresses pride at having been so sexually active—not to mention manly, for having been able to produce children.

John lived with his mother, a sixteen-year-old epileptic brother, and a seventeen-year-old sister, who attended community college. John's father, a sporadically employed automobile mechanic, would occasionally come home drunk, abuse John's mother, and "fight with everybody." There were arguments over money, other women, and John's father's freedom to come and go as he pleased. When these fights took place, John would become depressed and leave the house, wanting to escape all the quarreling. Today John continues to see his father but says he doesn't have much respect for him as a man. "He left seven years ago, and he don't have much to do with us. [But] that's between my mom and dad. That's them. He coulda done better by us, but really, that's them. I'm grown now, and I try to help my mom as much as I can, 'cause I'm all she got. I'm her oldest son. My brother is just a baby; he's got epilepsy. And my sister, she's a woman, and she can only be so strong."

At the time of our first conversation, John Turner was in deep trouble with the law. He was scheduled to appear for a court hearing on charges that he had violated probation. He was very upset about this situation and was considering running away to Mobile, Alabama, where many of his relatives lived. He said he would almost rather leave town than face the judge again, because he was sure the judge would send him to prison for five years. I tried to advise him of the possible consequences of not appearing before the judge, saying he would be a fugitive from justice and so would probably be hunted by the authorities. I also pointed out that in any case he would probably *feel* hunted, possibly for the rest of his life.

I pressed him to continue with his story, and he began with an account of the events leading up to his predicament. About two years earlier he was seeing Audrey, a young woman who lived with her mother outside his own neighborhood in West Philadelphia, in the territory controlled by a rival group of boys. Now, John understood the code of the street very well. In West Philadelphia he had made a name for himself running his own neighborhood with the help of his own boys,[1] although at the time I met him he claimed he had left that life behind. As proof of his gang activities, he proudly showed me an ugly gash on his leg from a gunshot wound, a four-inch knife scar on the back of his neck, and numerous scars on his hands and knuckles, all of them indicating incidents of street violence to which he had been a willing or unwilling party. He wore scars as trophies, badges attesting to his daring and his well-honed street-survival skills. He spoke of occasions when he had fought three and four men at a time, and won.

John understood full well the risks of venturing into the enemy territory that was Audrey's neighborhood.[2] He had been involved with her for about six months. At that point Audrey was being harassed by some of the boys and girls in her neighborhood. For several days they had been bothering her, sitting and standing outside her house, teasing her and calling her names. This had been happening repeatedly over the past months, at times for no apparent reason. Upset, she would call John and complain, and he would feel, as a man, compelled to respond. Sometimes he would go to her.

At about eight o'clock on the night in question, Audrey called John and reported harassment by the local youths. John told her not to worry, that he would come over and see about it. Because the young men of the neighborhood had fought with him before, John knew there was a good chance for trouble that night. But a man like John does not run from trouble; he meets it head-on, for much is at stake. John wanted a measure of protection; he "did not want to be hurt again or killed by these guys." So before leaving his home, he put his mother's Derringer pistol in his pocket. "I did not want to hurt anybody," he said, "but just wanted to scare them—if I had to."

At about nine o'clock, on the way to Audrey's house, John spied a commotion on the street: police cars with flashing lights, policemen and residents standing around. It looked like a crime scene. On foot, almost a block away, he began to tense up. He was packing a gun, and he knew he had to do something with it because he expected to be stopped and checked out by the police. He tossed the pistol under a parked car and tried to walk on in a nonchalant manner. The police, just as he expected, asked him for identification and where he was headed. John cooperated, dutifully giving them his identification and telling them that he was headed to Audrey's house. But then a woman who had seen John throw something away suddenly said, "Officer, that young man threw something under that car back there."

This set the policemen in motion. They searched under the car and found the pistol. "Is this yours?" they asked him, holding the pistol.

"Yeah," he owned up. "It's mine."

John tried to explain to the police why he was carrying the pistol, but from their behavior, they seemed to know the score already. Many young men walk the street armed, most often not to harm someone else but to protect themselves. He told the police that he feared he would be attacked by a group in the local neighborhood, young men who had stabbed him before. He showed the policemen the scar on his neck. He explained that he was not out to hurt anybody but just to scare certain people if necessary. John figured that if he cooperated, if he was a man about it and told the truth, then maybe they'd let him go. But he also felt he had little choice. Since the pistol belonged to his mother, he thought they could trace it to him anyway (though the pistol proved to be unregistered). "So I told the truth," John said.


## ARRESTED AND SENTENCED

The police arrested John for illegal possession of a firearm, even though they told him that they understood why he was carrying it and that they believed he was telling the truth. John says they were impressed by his cooperation and politeness and had determined he wasn't the person they were looking for. But because he had broken the law by carrying an unregistered firearm, they said, "We have to arrest you." At his court hearing, the policemen actually appeared and spoke on John's behalf, saying to the judge, "He's a good young man. He did what he was told and didn't act smart." John viewed the court proceeding this way:

> I went to court by myself, with the public defender. They didn't even tell me that I had to get a public defender. When I went there, the public defender was there. He was lookin' for me. When the case came and he seen me get up, he said, "Oh, you Mr. Turner." He rushed me, rushed me through. I didn't know anything about this. This was my first time ever being locked up. I don't have a juvenile record. It was just like taking somebody out of college and throwing them in jail and expecting for them to know what to do. I didn't know what to do, man. I didn't know I had to get a public defender. I didn't know these procedures to go through. I never been on probation. I never had to report to nobody. This is new to me, man. I could see it if I was an everyday criminal doing this as a everyday thing, but you just can't take somebody off the street and label them and put them in an environment that they don't even know anything about.
>
> Understand what I'm saying? And you know what? I woulda did better working by myself. He [the public defender] just came

at me with some bullshit. And he didn't do me no good but made things worse for me. He tried to get me to lie to the judge. When I told him I wanted to plead guilty, he said, "They ain't got nothing against you; they can't say it [the gun] was yours; tell him it wasn't yours." I said to him, "Man, I'm not going in there lying. 'Cause if he find out I'm lying, I might get worse treatment than I'm getting now." So I told the truth. My grandmother always told me, "Tell the truth and shame the devil." Know what? I shoulda told a lie! 'Cause then I wouldn't had no probation. They couldn't pinned it on me, 'cause they didn't have no proof, but nowadays, you tell the truth, it's just as worse as if you had hung yourself. And I told the truth.

And later I found out that my mom bought the gun in Virginia and didn't register it, so really they couldn't a traced it back to nobody. They [the police] asked for the receipt for the gun, but my mom said, "Let them go on and keep the gun." They gave me a green sheet for me to come back and get the gun. My mom brought the receipt with the numbers on it and everything. My mom has it at home now. My mom say, "I think it's best for them to keep the gun. Then there won't be no more trouble."

During the hearing John protested the sentence, saying that he had three children to support. According to John, the judge replied, "What am I to do? Lots of criminals have children." This statement angered John, who then replied, raising his voice, "You're wrong, Judge. I'm not a criminal! I'm not a criminal!"

The judge gave John five years' probation, a $1,500 fine, and assigned him a probation officer, a black woman about twenty-seven years of age. John says that because he was unemployed, he was unable to pay his fine on time, but the probation officer and the court were unsympathetic; they held him accountable. Concerned about the fine, John's mother, who at the time worked at a pharmaceutical firm based in the Philadelphia area, became involved and was able to get him hired at her company as a lab technician handling urine samples. "It was the best job I ever had in my life," he said. "I was making $16,000 a year, which is pretty good for a young black man."

As he began working and bringing home a steady income, John

was able to purchase an automobile, date young women, and become a popular person in his own peer group. But his relationship with his probation officer began to sour, and she would give him bad reports for not meeting his probationary obligations. Her primary complaint seems to have been that he was entirely too careless about these obligations. John claims they had something of an informal relationship—that is, if he could not appear at her office, he would call. She would also call him to set up meetings at his home, but when she arrived, he might be outside in front of the house—and at times she would miss him altogether. He said she would put this into her report along with something like "John Turner was found in the street." John also commented a number of times on her good looks and how he would have liked to make her the object of his affections. These issues, it appears, worked to complicate his relationship with the probation officer.

One evening, about a year after his initial encounter with the law, John was stopped for a traffic violation. The policeman ran a computer check and found there was a detainer on him; he was wanted by the police, evidently because he had not paid his fine and had not worked the details out with his probation officer. The police arrested him, took him to jail, and booked him. By John's account, he remained in jail for about two weeks, and during that time his family was never notified. This was around Thanksgiving, which John says was "very sad" around his house, since he wasn't there.

Finally, John had a hearing before the judge who had originally sentenced him. Among other things, the judge asked him if he was currently employed, and he wanted to know the name of his employer and how long he had been employed. John complied, giving the name of the pharmaceutical company. The judge responded, "Then you must make a good salary. Your fine is $1,300, and you must spend thirteen weekends in jail." John was shocked, not just at the judge's statement but at the probation officer's attitude and behavior; she did not speak up for him during the whole proceeding.

John's employer told him he must quit his job "temporarily," until his legal difficulties were resolved. After John had finished completing the successive weekends in jail, there was no job waiting for him. He then looked for a new job, without success, for many weeks. The places where he inquired told him they needed no help or that they would call him—which they never did. As his best efforts repeatedly proved unsuccessful, he became increasingly demoralized.

## PROBLEMS AT WORK

Finally, John found a minimum-wage job as a busboy at an Italian restaurant. His duties included busing tables, mopping floors, peeling potatoes, and general prep work. He said he was paid about $100 per week. His work shift varied, but he often worked seven days a week, usually from 3 P.M. to 9 P.M. or so. His pay was reportedly irregular; his employer at times paid him part of his pay on Monday then some more on Friday, or else he gave him $50 on Friday and then another $50 on Monday. John sometimes had to argue with his boss for his pay. Also, he reported, he had to endure the insults of his Italian co-workers. John said, "These people right off the boat have no respect for blacks. They would call me nigger right on the job. They were always messing with me. Now, the boss was a good man. He liked me, and we got along, but the rest of 'em didn't give a care about me."

John admits with some pride to having a short temper and being used to settling disputes physically. He felt that a person who is wrong must be made to answer for the injustice. Once he invited a young white restaurant employee who was riding him to go outside to settle it in the parking lot. When they went to the lot, John began to talk; and when this did not work, he punched the other employee in the face. The next day, reportedly, when John arrived for work, the boss very reluctantly told him not to take off his coat, because he was fired. A few days later the boss called him back to the job, mainly because he was such a good worker.

John felt that in general the people at the restaurant were prejudiced against him. This perception made his work there very stressful, for he wanted to lash out at people he saw as his adversaries, but he also felt pressure to keep his job. At the time he was contributing to the support of his mother, his sister, his epileptic brother, his girlfriend, and his children. In addition, he needed money to pay the installments of his fine, which he claims he was not always able to do on time, and this led to other difficulties with his probation officer. Feeling trapped in his job, John didn't know what to do; he simply endured.

Because of his problems paying his fine, John told me, he had to go before the judge again, a judge who had the reputation, even among the police, of "hanging young black males." John was all but certain that the judge would send him away for five years. In an earlier encounter he had seen the judge and the public defender laugh at him: "They don't mean me no good."

By the time I met John Turner, he was quite sour on the system, believing it could never deliver him a fair trial. Still, he felt a strong commitment to his immediate family and a great need to play the role of the daddy of the family. He feared that a jail term would leave them without the financial and moral protection only he could offer, and therefore they would be vulnerable to the forces of the street; this concern made him very anxious. With the prospect of a jail term looming, he said, repeatedly, "I got to help out at home as much as I can. My mom, she don't have a boyfriend, she don't have a fiancé. I'm all she's got. I'm her oldest male child, and she depends on me. I'm her backbone. . . . Now, I don't mind going to jail. I mean, I can take it. I'm a man. I'm not scared of jail. It's my family. They need me. I make just $400 a month, and I use it to help make ends meet for my family. I bring home every penny I can. I can't go to jail. But I just don't know what to do now."

## A DAY IN COURT

Moved and intrigued by John's story and wanting to render whatever assistance I could, I offered to contact an attorney for him; at the same time, I advised him that if he fled he would only complicate his situation. I then got in touch with an attorney I knew, Leonard Segal, a partner in a prestigious law firm in Center City Philadelphia, and told him about John and requested his help. I gave Segal John's telephone number, and he called John. After hearing John's account, Segal told John, "Don't you worry about a thing. You're not going anywhere. I'll take the case."

Then John asked, "How much is it gon' cost me?"

"Absolutely nothing," Segal replied.

Though somewhat skeptical, John savored the prospect of legal assistance from a prestigious firm instead of having to rely on a public defender. In John's world, public defenders are common but have a very poor record at getting young black men justice, and he was reluctant to trust one with his case. Moreover, he had earlier over-heard the judge and a public defender making fun of him.

The case came before Segal on short notice, and he had a schedule conflict that kept him out of town on the day of the hearing. He called John and said he would send a friend in his place. He told John that he should look out for a female public defender Segal knew and that this person would represent John. Sensing John's skepticism, he tried to reassure him that he himself would monitor the situation and be on the case, but John was clearly worried and nervous. For the story of John's life thus far seemed to be about people building him up and then letting him down, and he fully expected to be let down again.

Early on the day of the hearing, John telephoned me with this discouraging news. In addition, he told me Segal had asked him if he had any money, concluding that this meant Segal would want to be paid after all. I assured him that this was not the understanding I had with Segal and that Segal probably wanted to know if he had money to pay the fine, if necessary. John seemed to relax upon hearing that explanation. However, he needed my support and was obviously worried that even I might not show up at the hearing as I had promised. I reassured him, "Don't worry. I'll be there. Listen, no matter what happens, I'll stay on the case, even if you have to go away" (his euphemism for going to jail).

When I arrived at City Hall that morning and approached the courtroom, I encountered John, his mother, and others standing around outside. John's mother, about forty-five years old, looked tired and much older than her years this morning. Clad in a dark green dress, she wore dark red lipstick, and her fingernails were freshly painted to match. She smelled of a strong perfume. I could see John's eyes brighten as he moved toward me. He smiled. "Hey, Eli," he said and shook my hand. I returned the greeting. John was dressed in an old army jacket, a gangster cap, and boots. I wondered why he had not come to court dressed more formally, and a few days later I asked him about this. He replied, "The judge might've thought I had some money or something, so I just wanted to cool it."

As I approached, John introduced me to his mother, "Hey, Mom, this is the professor."

She looked at me with a tentative half smile and extended her hand. "Hi, Eli," she said. "Thank you so much for what you're doing for John. His father has not done right by these kids, and I'm all alone. Thank you so much for helping us out." She acted somewhat familiar with me, behaving as though she had known me for a long time, and this put me more at ease. She genuinely appreciated my efforts.

After a while, I asked John about the public defender. "He's in there," said John, motioning toward the courtroom door. Having expected a woman because of Leonard Segal's instructions, I was surprised to find that John's counsel was a man. As I walked into the courtroom, John followed and pointed out a thirty-five-year-old white man dressed in a dark gray pin-striped suit who was sitting in the front of the courtroom. The proceedings had not yet begun, and apparently many other cases were to be heard. Soon the lawyer rose and started toward us.

Dressed in a brown tweed jacket with a tie, I introduced myself: "I'm Professor Elijah Anderson of the University of Pennsylvania, and I'm here on behalf of John Turner."

"Hi, I'm George Bramson, and I'm with Leonard Segal's law firm. I arrived at the office this morning and saw this piece of paper that said, 'Get over to City Hall and see about John Turner.' So I'm here."

Pleased to see the lawyer there, I told him, "I'm very much concerned that we do all we can for John." But Bramson gave the impression that he felt he had better things to do than spend his morning defending John Turner. His body language said as much. He kept looking at his watch, and he mentioned a deposition he had to take at 10:30. It was now nearly 9:30. I became concerned that he might not have time to see John's case through this morning.

As Bramson and I talked, the others left for seats nearer the front of the room. The scene was somewhat chaotic, with many people entering and leaving the room. We spoke about the courtroom and what sorts of people were here. There must have been about forty people in the large room, mainly black and Hispanic young men and their families. Most of the persons handling these people were white and male. To be sure, there were black officers and court workers, but they were in the minority. I got the impression, as well, that Bramson was more than ready to assume that John's predicament was entirely his own fault. He didn't say so, but he strongly implied that John was irresponsible and that he expected me to fully agree with him. I kept my own feelings to myself, for I felt John's case had been compromised enough; the last thing I wanted to do was to alienate his attorney.

Bramson said, "It seems that John doesn't listen to people, and he's failed a number of times to fulfill his probationary obligations." My view of John was more sympathetic, although I understood Bramson's position and partly agreed. In my opinion, John was a confused young black man in trouble, whose circumstances were complicated by his ignorance, by his limited finances, by who he was, and by the implications of all this. A young person who lacked significant guidance, he had tried to adapt to life on the street according to its code. While not entirely blameless, he needed a chance, which I felt was better late in coming than never. At this stage of his life, he was like a fly stuck on flypaper, and the more he struggled to get off, the more stuck he became. But the lawyer's view seemed hardened.

Finally, I said, "Do you think the judge will lock him up?"

"Well, I don't know. A lot of it's up to his probation officer," he said, nodding toward a woman in the front of the room.

I looked at her and asked Bramson, "Have you tried to talk with her?"

"Yeah, and she's really against him."

"Think it'll do any good if I speak with her?"

"You can try, see what happens."

I walked over to her and introduced myself. She offered a surprisingly friendly smile and extended her hand, which I shook. "I'm here on behalf of John Turner, and I'm trying to do all I can for him. Can we talk?"

But with the mention of John's name, her expression changed completely. She coolly shook her head and abruptly returned to her paper, effectively shutting down my campaign. Barely glancing up, she said, "It's out of my hands now. It's up to the judge." She didn't look up again.

I then walked back to Bramson. He said, "Well, you know, a lot depends on her. My plan is simply to argue for a continuance so that when Leonard Segal returns, he can take it from there." I was left feeling uncertain, wondering what would happen and fearing the worst. We waited.

At 9:45 the judge had yet to arrive. It was announced that he would be delayed and that another judge would sit in his place. Bramson was cheered by this, for the new judge might not be as arbitrary as the original one. As we waited for the cases before ours to be concluded, Bramson mentioned that there was a good chance we would be able to get a continuance, if not some resolution of the matter.

Without much else to do, I looked around and took in the scene. The large courtroom was abuzz with people. Sitting off to the side of the room, our party read newspapers, drank coffee, and made quiet small talk. This was a bonding experience, as we all seemed to be rooting for another chance for John. Finally, at 10:30, the acting judge called out, "John Turner," and signaled for John and his lawyer to approach the bench. I asked Bramson if I should approach the bench with them. He said, "No, but give me your title again. I'll use you as a character reference in my appeal." Bramson, John, and his mother then approached the bench. From the other side of the room, John's probation officer rose and moved toward the bench.

Bramson presented John's case to the judge, asking for a continuance of the case until such time as Leonard Segal could take it. The judge looked over at the probation officer and said, "And what do you think of that, Ms. Johnson?"

"No!" she replied. "No, your honor. This is his fifth time messing up. No." Actually, it was his third time before the judge, but she was adamant.

The judge concurred. "We'll have to wait for Judge Hoffman. He'll be in later in the morning."

Those gathered before the judge then dispersed. Bramson approached me, saying, "Holy cow! You may as well get ready to spend the whole morning here." He was perturbed, but he felt he had to be there since his boss had directed him to do so. He left to make some phone calls to rearrange his schedule, and I went to make my own phone calls. Then we waited, watching other cases come and go. Finally, Judge Hoffman arrived and immediately showed why he had a reputation as a judge whose conduct on the bench was highly unconventional. Just before John's case came up, he called a man who was sick at home and he made a big show of accusing him of being absent because of the upcoming Thanksgiving holiday. Spectators in the courtroom laughed. Bramson himself chuckled, but also shook his head in apparent disapproval of such behavior on the part of a judge.

The judge then called John Turner's name. Again, Bramson, John, and his mother rose and walked to the bench. The probation officer joined them. Judge Hoffman's performance this time was completely unexpected. He appeared to be very respectful to John's mother. "What a lovely mother you have, Mr. Turner," he said, nodding. Bramson began his appeal, but the judge said it was unnecessary. "Young man," he said to John, "I'm going to give you a new probation officer." The probation officer's face seemed to drop. "Now, I want you to report to your probation officer weekly and pay your fine on time. You must pay $100 per month. Now, if you don't do this, you're going to have to see me again. I don't want that to happen. You do as you are told, and everything will be fine."

This behavior was in sharp contrast to what we had been led to expect from John's reports of this judge. I suspect, however, that if John had had a public defender, the judge would have handled the case less sympathetically.[3] All of us present felt very relieved at the outcome. It was a real victory for us all, but especially for John. We retired to the corridor, and the lawyer began to lecture John, repeating what the judge had said. He told John he must be sure to pay his fine on time and should try to develop an understanding with his probation officer and be more responsible in his day-to-day life. John listened attentively and nodded in agreement, seemingly genuinely repentant. He promised to meet his responsibilities. His mother was very happy about the outcome and thanked me profusely. We all thanked Bramson, said our goodbyes, and dispersed.

## FINDING A UNION JOB

John returned to work at the carryout restaurant, and his employer welcomed him back. In many ways John had impressed his boss as a good worker, reliable, punctual, and honest. To keep up with John, I would occasionally visit the carryout and see him there, mopping floors, busing tables, or preparing food. He would give me the latest on his situation, telling me about his desire to do better in life and saying how grateful he was that I had helped him out in his time of greatest need. I was moved when he told me he had prayed and thanked God that I had come into his life and helped. He said, "I didn't think people did that anymore."

As time passed, John appeared to be getting along fine, although he seemed always to be working. His fine payment was $100 per month, and his salary was about $400. From this money, his mother expected some support, which John said he was very proud to provide. He also contributed to the support of his children in the form of irregular small payments to their mothers. That two of these women were on welfare and one was living with her parents made his financial burden less onerous. Audrey, who had recently given birth to a premature baby girl, was now living at his mom's house.

John's restaurant job included no benefits of any kind, and this concerned John a great deal. He worried about what would happen if one of his children was involved in an accident or came down with a serious illness. This possibility seemed to encourage John to try to better himself. The fact that he had children and women, particularly Audrey, in his life compelled him to be more mindful of whatever he did in life. In our conversations John would express his dreams of the good life and what he wanted to accomplish. As he made an effort to support his children financially, he began to see himself as a responsible, decent father. He thought his greatest obstacle was a lack of money to "do something"—get married, buy a car, or rent an apartment. So he began actively looking for a better job. Again he searched, and again it was difficult. For a few months he searched seriously, but to no avail. In time he concluded, "It's hard out here for a young black man. I'm telling you, it is hard." Repeatedly, prospective employers would let him submit an application, but they never called him.[4]

At the same time, John was facing increasing tensions with his fellow employees. He complained that they would sometimes pick on him and taunt him. "They know I can't fight back," he said, "I need this job and they know it. They know I won't hit back, and we argue a lot." He continued to get along well with his boss, however. The proprietor of the restaurant said, "Yeah, John is a good worker. He's all right. He's just young, and he has something of a temper. But he's a good worker. He always comes on time. He listens to me. I like him. He's a good boy."[5]

Seeing that John was having such a difficult time, I thought I would try to help him find a better employment situation. I then contacted Curtis Hardy, a sixty-year-old black union steward at a local hospital whom I had known for about five years. Curtis is married and has three grown children, two of whom have graduated from college. He is a proud man who likes to think of himself as someone who has paid his dues and has worked very hard for what he has. He arrived in Philadelphia from North Carolina some twenty-five years ago and now lives in Germantown. Having risen to the job of union steward, he feels a real sense of accomplishment. The work ethic and traditional values that are mainstays of the decent daddy are extremely important to him.

Knowing that Curtis was such a decent man and would probably lend a helping hand to others in need, I approached him about a job for John. I simply told him that I knew a young black man who badly needed a job, and described John's problems and difficulties finding work. Curtis was hesitant, yet quite candid about why. He said, "Eli, I been burned too many times now. This boy will probably just mess me up." But I persisted, trying to make a case for John as a young man deserving a chance. I mentioned that John was trying to support four children, that he was physically strong and a reliable and diligent worker, and that the new job might prove to be a real turning point in his life. He would be earning $8.50 instead of $3.50 per hour, and he would gain a kind of job security he had never had before, not to mention excellent health benefits.

After a while Curtis, though still skeptical, relented and said, "All right, tell him to go to the union hall on Tuesday and look for Joe Harris. Say that I sent him." I was elated and thanked Curtis, who said, "Now, you tell that boy not to mess me up, Eli."

Despite my elation I noted Curtis's hesitation and his concern about being messed up. Men like Curtis have usually worked very hard to get to positions of authority and prestige. So they tend to be very careful about associating too closely with people who might threaten their positions. To Curtis, John represents the street. Everything about him—his youth and immaturity, his inclination to settle disputes by violence, his peculiar version of responsibility—is hard for Curtis to swallow. He does not consider it a way to conduct one's life. He has raised his own children to be responsible, law-abiding, and decent. During his life in Philadelphia he has tried to determine which people to watch and whom to trust, and he has kept his children away from people like John. They get nice girls into trouble and get nice boys to join gangs.

The request from me, a professor and a friend, to help John makes for a certain amount of dissonance in Curtis's life, because he feels an obligation to me and he would like to demonstrate his power by obtaining employment for John.

Curtis says much by saying only, "Tell that boy not to mess me up!" Black people like Curtis who consider sponsoring someone like John Turner may be concerned on several levels. Because of their understanding of the history of racial prejudice in our society, they may sense that their hold on their own position is somewhat tenuous. They have often had to wage a vigorous campaign for the trust of employers and fellow workers. For them to sponsor someone for a job, they must be able to view him or her as fully trustworthy. Furthermore, a common feeling is that a black person who is judged incompetent on the job may easily make other black people look bad. Curtis, as a union steward, was not seriously afraid of losing his job.

But he was concerned about being messed up, about looking bad, particularly to relatively powerful whites. In response to these insecurities, black men like Curtis are usually extremely careful when recommending other blacks for jobs. Clearly, this is a decision he would rather not have to make. But he decides to help John out, to take a chance.

## TRUST AND INSECURITY

Thrilled at the prospect of getting a good job, John was eager to go to the union hall, even though it was across town and he lacked transportation. Using public transportation, he went and was punctual. He spoke with Harris, as Curtis had instructed, and was quickly signed up. It was now a matter of waiting two weeks before he would be hired, and he would definitely be hired. Curtis had said so, and John had faith in my word.

But about a week later I went by the restaurant where John worked and asked for him. His co-workers said, "He's in jail."

I was shocked. "What happened?" I asked incredulously.

"Oh, he beat up his girlfriend," one man told me.

John had been calling his employer, trying to get bail money, but to no avail. I didn't know what to think. After a few days I phoned John's home in hopes of getting information about him. To my surprise John himself answered the phone. I said, "John! I heard you were in jail. What happened?" He explained,

> Well, see, this girl, the mother of my one son Teddy. See, I drove my girlfriend's car by her house with my other son [by another woman] with me. I parked the car down the street from her house and everything [so as not to let her see the car, knowing this would make her angry]. So I took John Jr. [his son] up to the house to see his brother, and we talked for a while. But when I got ready to leave, she and her girlfriend followed me to the car. I got in the car and put my son in. Then she threw a brick through the window. Glass was flying everywhere. My lit-

tle son coulda got cut by it. So I got out of the car and went around and slapped the shit out of her. She knew better than that. I didn't really beat her, I just slapped her. Then she went home and told her mama that I beat her up in front of her girlfriend. So then her mama got all hot and called the cops, and they came and got me.

They locked me up for four days, Eli. It's a trip, Eli, you got to see that place. We got to talk about it. There were like sixteen guys in one cell, all black guys. It's a shame. I ain't no criminal. I didn't belong there. It's terrible. I think I got this bad cold from being in there. [He was currently suffering from the flu.] But then my mother talked with her mother, told her what really happened, and then her mother understood. So she talked her daughter into dropping the charges. So they let me out. But I'm out now, Eli. I'll tell you about it. Oh, Eli, the hospital called me. And I'm supposed to start work on Monday.

I congratulated him on the prospect of his new job, although I was beginning to have second thoughts about John and all I was trying to do for him. Within a week John was hired as a janitor at the hospital. He was an enthusiastic worker. Curtis told me he liked him and began taking him under his wing, showing him the ropes and introducing him to the work culture. John told me that when Curtis first met him he had lectured and warned him: "Now, whatever you do, don't mess me up. Good jobs are hard to come by, and you know this is a good job. You must keep your nose clean, do as you're told, come to work on time and everything will be all right. You'll be on probation for the first thirty days, and if everything checks out, you'll be in the union. You'll be set. Do what your supervisor says, but the main thing is to do your work. If you have any problem whatsoever, come and see me. Your professor's got a lot of faith in you, boy. He thinks a lot of you. Now, don't go and mess him up. Don't mess him up."

After two weeks at his new job, John was a big success. When I asked Curtis for a report, it was glowing: "Yeah, he doing all right. He's a good worker, works a lot [of] overtime. He's always on time, does as he's told. Uh-huh, he's a good worker." After five weeks he had a stellar work record, of which he was very proud. He passed his period of probation and was admitted to the union. Getting into the union was an important milestone in his life. It had some sort of mystical appeal for him; he had never been a member of a union, and he associated it with real power, independence, benefits, and job security.

## MORE TROUBLE

I didn't see John for almost three weeks after that, and I assumed things were going well in his life. But then, on a Friday night at ten o'clock, I received a telephone call from him. I was immediately concerned because he normally was at work from four in the afternoon until midnight. "Hey, John, what's up?" I asked.

"I'm in trouble."

"What happened?"

"They tryin' to put me in jail."

"Who? What?" I asked, trying to catch up with him.

"I got home a couple days ago, and my mother hands me this paper saying I have to report at three-thirty that day at the courthouse, so I did."

"What's the charge?" I asked.

"I didn't pay my fine. The judge [Hoffman] wouldn't listen to me. And my probation officer acted like he didn't know me," John replied.

"Well, have you been making your meetings with your probation officer?" I continued.

"Yeah, I been making every meeting, once a week."

I suggested we get together and talk at the Broadway Restaurant. Located on Fifty-second Street (a main business artery through the West Philadelphia ghetto), the Broadway was a well-known restaurant that specialized in reasonably priced home-cooked soul food. Open from early morning to midnight, the place attracted all kinds of black people, including families, single men and women, and young adults. Equipped with a quality jukebox, it was a popular hangout and staging area from the afternoon to late into the evening. A party was always going on. John and I had eaten there before.

We met out front a little after 10 P.M. John showed up with Lionel, his half brother whom he had found out about from his father two years earlier. We walked inside, sat down in one of the booths, and ordered our food. John was very depressed. He seemed not to understand the gravity of the charges against him. He repeated the story about his mother presenting him with the court order, the way the judge had treated him unsympathetically, the way his new probation officer (a thirty-year-old black man with whom he thought he had a good relationship) would not speak up for him to the judge.

" 'Cause I didn't pay my fine, the judge gave me eleven to twenty-three months in jail," said John. "I begged him not to do it, that I would try to come up with the money some way. Then he came down to six months in jail. He said that by not paying the fine that I was playing with the court. I told him that I was trying to take care of my family and my kids. I told him I just didn't have the money. So he told me six months and gave me two days to report for incarceration. He said the best thing I could do now was to come back with some money, and if I do that, then I might not have to go to jail. Man, I don't want to go to jail." His brother and I commiserated with him.

"Have you been making any payments on your fine?" I asked.

"Yeah, I paid $50, but me and my probation officer made a deal. He told me that I could pay what I could pay, and they couldn't send me away as long as I didn't have the money to pay," said John.

"But, John, you're making $8.50 an hour, you work at least forty hours a week plus overtime. You mean you couldn't pay more of your fine?" I was incredulous.

"Well, I'm trying to help my mother out. I'm trying to give money to my kids, and I been putting some money away in case something happens. My kids . . . I'm saving money for their college education."

"Well, John," I said, "if you don't pay your fine, you could go to jail. And if you're in jail, you won't be around to help your kids out. These people [the courts] mean business. They're serious."

John simply held his head in his hands and looked tired and sad.

Lionel backed me up, saying, "Man, why didn't you pay your fine? I don't want to see you go away. But there ain't no justice downtown, not for no black man. You got to do what they say. You shoulda paid it."

Looking dejected and forlorn, John finally said, "I took him [the judge] $200, and I told him I would try to get the other $1,100. It's the money for my kids' college education, but I'll take it out of the bank. And he told me that if I pay my fine, then maybe I won't have to go to jail. So I'm gon' get the money. Eli, I don't want to go to jail. I got a real chance now. The best job I ever had, and I don't wanta blow it."

We finished our food and continued talking for a couple of hours. It was resolved that John would withdraw the money he had been saving and use it to pay his fine. We left the restaurant, and I drove Lionel and John to their homes.

Note the manner in which money is spent by a person in John's circumstances. First of all, there never seems to be enough; when present, it seems to disappear quickly. With money, John becomes an important figure to friends and family members. He helped his mother with her household bills. He took his girlfriend out to eat in nice restaurants, bought shoes and clothes for his children, lent money to friends, simply ran through a significant amount, and saved some. The more money John made, the more places he had to spend it. At the same time he tried to put away a portion—as much as he thought he could afford. Instead of paying his fine, John had deposited this portion of his money in a local credit union; he had accumulated at least $1,300 there. Defending his behavior, he said he wanted to have money in case something happened to his children. "If John Jr. hurts himself and has to go to the hospital, I want to be able to pay them *cash* money." When I asked about his medical benefits at work, he said, "They just began after I got into the union."

John, as I mentioned before, has considered himself the man of the house ever since his father left home, seven years before I met him. In taking over his father's role, John presents himself as very responsible. He feels obligated to help his mother and siblings and to give his mother a portion of his pay. When he has more, she gets more. A similar principle operates where his children are concerned.

To meet his obligations to them, he takes cash to his various girl-friends, the mothers of his children. When he buys shoes for his children, he is taking an action with symbolic meaning; in a small way he is fulfilling his role as a decent father and provider.

The next day John went to City Hall to pay $1,000 toward his fine. His understanding was that if he brought the money down, he would not have to go to jail. In reality, though, the judge had only said he would consider his case with new information. There was no guarantee, but a paid fine was to be considered a positive development. However, after paying the money, John was locked up and placed in jail for six months. He called me that evening and said, "I'm in jail. I need a lawyer." He said the judge told him that he now needed a private attorney to file a petition for early parole, and that he, the judge, would then consider it.

## THE PROBATION OFFICER

As I thought of John's predicament, I wondered about his relationship with his probation officer. Shouldn't the latter have been monitoring the situation more closely? Their relationship appeared to be somewhat informal, if not arbitrary. The probation officer seemed, at least initially, to be supportive. John could call him, and they could talk. And John said he met him at all the appointed times. But when the problem of not having paid the money arose before the judge, the probation officer became very firm and formal. John said that at the hearing the probation officer ignored him and "acted like he didn't know me."

Could it be that the probation officer was simply trying to protect himself because of his sense that such informality with a client might compromise his job? On the one hand, this informality was positive and considerate, in keeping with the more humane goals of probation, and it allowed him to press John on the matter of his fine. On the other hand, it could be deemed irregular and thus result in disciplinary action against the probation officer. People like John—low-income, urban black males in trouble—generally have very low status in the minds of those staffing the system. Black probation officers, in particular, may feel that it is important to distance themselves from such individuals, from whom they are only a class removed. Equally important, he knew where such people fit into the culture of the local court system. When confronted by this system, the probation officer was likely to look out for himself first.

The probation officer did wish to assist John. But he found this difficult and alternated between formality and informality. In a telephone conversation he indicated his desire to help John. After learning who I was, he was very interested and helpful. He gave me information on the deal between John and the judge and attempted to collude with me against the judge. Knowing that I was working to help John keep his job, he told me, "I want you to know this. When John Turner was released to make arrangements with his employer for his stay in jail, he didn't tell them he was being incarcerated. He told them he was going to have an operation and was going to be out for two weeks. So you shouldn't go back and tell his employer that he's in jail." He ended by saying, "If there is anything else I can do, let me know."

I took him up on this offer and sought a second interview after John was released from jail. This interview supports and expands the foregoing analysis:

> When I first met John Turner, he lied to me. He told me he was in to see me a week earlier and that we had discussed something. I caught him in a lie. He turned me off right then and there. From then on, I did not feel like going out of my way for him, and I will and do go out of my way for some others. I supervise 150 people, and he is only one case. I told him that if he didn't pay his fine, that he was going to be incarcerated. No, I didn't hold hands with him and try to walk him through the system. There are guys I will do that for—they're older, they're the ones who respond. The younger guys are arrogant, and they think the world owes them something. The older ones know better, and I feel better about helping them.
>
> And the thing is, this guy knew that he was wrong. He knew about this judge's reputation. He even told me about the judge; he said the judge is crazy. So he knew better. He's a self-directive

person—arrogant and manipulative. He thinks it's all his show. He felt he was justified in carrying the weapon, since he'd been attacked by those guys, and that he shouldn't have to pay the fine. He wanted to get by, that's all. He had a lot of opportunities to pay. I mean he could have paid something, ten dollars—something symbolic. But he didn't pay anything. And when you see him, he's wearing gold chains and nice clothes, so he can't say he didn't have the money. Since he came before the judge all those times and still had not paid his fine, the judge just got fed up. He felt John Turner was not taking him seriously, especially when he came up with thirteen hundred dollars overnight. When he locked him up, the judge felt he had the last laugh.

Toward the end, though, we became friends. We talked more, and once I walked his girlfriend to the train to show her how to get out of town. We talked, and he wanted to have dinner, but I said no. I didn't think we should stretch it out. But we reached an understanding. He knew he was going to jail. To people like him, though, jail is no big deal. They go to jail, sit around and play cards; they don't mind so much. They're not afraid of jail, and that worries me. Going to jail for them is not the same as it is for me or for you. I got a nephew in prison right now, and he tells me about the life there. Alcoholics sitting around getting high in jail; they make their own stuff right in jail. He wanted me to bring him drugs. Can you believe that? I still live in the black community. I want to get away from all the riffraff, but I'm just not able to afford one of those big mortgages, ha-ha.

I've got seventeen nephews and nieces, because I got so many brothers and sisters. And I try to look out for them. But frankly, I'm afraid of some of these younger guys, what they'll do to people like me and you. They don't care, don't worry about jail. They'll take you out of here [kill you].

## SOCIALIZATION

After three months of incarceration John, with the help of another private attorney I found for him, was allowed to leave jail on a work-release program, and he returned to his job at the hospital. In this program John was expected to report to his job at night but to return to jail after work. John fulfilled his obligations dutifully, though not always cheerfully. He complained about the way the guards would abuse him and other inmates, at times using them as personal slaves and making them clean the place. He also complained about the physical conditions, the peeling paint and asbestos over his bed, and the dankness of his cell. But he served his time.

Over the next year, I periodically talked to Curtis to find out how John was doing on the job. For the most part his reports were strongly positive, saying that John was doing fine, coming to work on time, and doing his job. But at a certain point, according to John, Curtis and the other men were giving him a hard time. This was interesting, because so many of the men who worked as janitors were solid, working-class black men who were generally imbued with the work ethic, went to church, and prided themselves on their decent family lives. On further investigation I found out that many of them were reacting to John's intrusion into their group. John was someone these men found threatening for many of the reasons Curtis had initially expressed. In a real sense, John threatened their values as family men who had worked very hard to obtain whatever measure of privilege they had, and they saw him as something of an interloper, an outsider.

John was considerably younger than the other men, who regarded him as someone who needed to be socialized—"brought along" and perhaps shown the error of his ways. They had misgivings about John's many women, his out-of-wedlock babies, and his somewhat cavalier attitude toward taking care of them, as well as about his spending part of his time in jail. To deal with this, some of the men dubbed John "the halfway man." He still had dues to pay, as far as they were concerned.

On the street a man like John might take a certain pride in having babies, in being good with his hands (able to fight), or even in having jail time under his belt. According to the code of the street, these characteristics provide solid claims to manhood. But in terms of decent values such behavior is deemed irresponsible and even threatening. Men who consider themselves decent and responsible either avoid the John Turners of the world or attempt to reform them. So the men John worked with would joke with and about him, and they would make fun of his attachments to his women and children, in an attempt to shame him or to remind him that they disapproved of his past behavior. They hoped to bring him along to a better, more respectable way of doing things, but they often acted in ways that were emotionally painful to John.

Curtis, for instance, even though he was trying to be the old head and help John, began to join the others in their teasing. On one occasion the men were standing around before work when a group of women walked by. The men made appreciative murmurs about the women among themselves. Within earshot of the other men, Curtis, alluding to John's out-of-wedlock children, said to John, "Son, you better keep that thing in your pants! You can't take care of the ones you got now." The men had a good laugh at John's expense, and John felt that Curtis had "put his business in the street." Such ribbing, even when good-natured, quickly became tiring and offensive to John.

At the same time the street was beckoning. John wanted to make more money. He had already been a gang member, so he knew how to operate on the street. And he wanted to show the guys at work that he didn't have to put up with their taunts. So one day he abruptly quit. He gave no formal notice; he simply failed to show up for work. I learned about this only after two months, when I bumped into Curtis. I spoke with him and some of the other men about their experiences with John, and the above-mentioned story came out. They did not admit to their part in so many words (they claimed he didn't want to work), but in conversation it emerged that they had been ribbing him, attempting to socialize him to their way of doing things but at the same time trying to defend their own values.

In addition, the mothers of John's children had begun making demands on him. When he acquired a steady income and good benefits, several of them tried to legalize their claims on him; they "went downtown and got papers on him." The prospect of losing part of his pay helped sour him on his job, but that was hardly reason enough to cause him to give up such a good job. Another important factor was the fact that his mother, to whom he was strongly tied, had left Philadelphia for the South, and he needed to be with her.

## DRUG DEALING

About a year later I ran into John on the street. We shook hands, and he said how happy he was to see me and that we had to get together because he had so much to tell me about what had been happening with him. So we met at a restaurant and started catching up with each other. He spoke about how he had had to split: his mother had to have an operation and he needed to be with her. But within the first ten minutes of the conversation, he offered, "Eli, you've always been like an older friend to me, and I got a lot of respect for you. And I ain't going to lie to you. Eli, I used to sell drugs."

This was shocking to me but not altogether unbelievable. My next question was "Well, when did you quit?"

"Two weeks ago," he replied.

I said, "Oh." I was rather taken aback and began to wonder what was going on with him. I concealed my shock and did not want to appear offended, because this would have caused him to become reticent about his past, which I really wanted to know about. I encouraged him to tell me more. He continued,

> The biggest thing now is caps [crack]—five-dollar caps— right. You got a lot of young guys coming out of high school— seventeen, eighteen years old—standing on the corner sellin' the caps. And they're fighting for each other's corner. They're killin' people for five dollars, man. A lot of the stuff [violence] is over bad drug deals and turf. They got a lot of people that don't sell caps, but they put imitation stuff in the vials, you know, cheatin' people. Like up on Fifty-fifth Street, a guy just got killed over three caps. He had to be about eighteen—a guy named Rah-Rah. This is happening all the time. It's like an epidemic.
>
> And another guy I know, Emanuel Davis. He got killed. Now, he was selling caps, cheating people, and he was "big time." He

got shot in the heart. I knew him comin' up. Well, you know, back in the day I was in the gang, he was in a different gang. They said—the inside scoop on the story was that they [rival drug dealers] were tryin' to stick him up for his merchandise. As far as ladywise, it seems funny, but I used to go to school with a lot of beautiful ladies that I see now—you know how you see a lady when you're coming up that's hard to get with. Now you got five dollars, they'll suck your cock, lick your butt—for five dollars. For crumbs. I don't know what it is. But this drug is heavy. There are a lot of intelligent people strung out on this stuff, man. And it's the people you least suspect. You see, like up where I'm at [North Philly], there's a lot of white guys coming near Eighth and Girard. They come through—a lot of guys with good jobs, nice cars. They put this dope before their families.

To me, if you ask me, the key thing that can mess up a person's life is this cocaine, the pipe. It's dangerous. They call it Captain Kirk—beam me up, Scotty. The glass dick—that's what they call it. It's wild, man. I see a lot of friends of mine that was makin' it, selling it, man, doin' good. I come back from Georgia now, a lot of friends of mine sell it. Guys that I knew in the gangs when I was coming up. It seems like a lot of people just started out sellin' it. Then they started out messing with it. Like my cousin, man. It hurts me to see her every day. See, she used to be a lady that gets up, on the go, take care of her business. But now she'll lay in bed all day until somebody come by with a blast [a hit of crack]. Now she's laying in bed all day. And it seems like everybody's on welfare now. People who used to be working. And it seems like ninety out of a hundred people that's on welfare is on drugs. I'm tellin' you.

And to get the drugs, they'll sell anything. They're selling food stamps. You know the Korean stores. They buy cheap food stamps off them. They sell their food stamps. Their kids go without food, out here hungry. I see them, man. And this shit affects the kids more than anything. And no one's lookin' into it. No one's lookin' into it, Eli. Like I had this cocaine girl named Sheila—right?—come into our neighborhood with her seven-year-old son. You know how when you come into the black neighborhood and you're white, everybody cheat you. Well, she shows up and she spent six hundred dollars on drugs. Smoked it up right in front of me and her little son. Now, after that she couldn't go home. She couldn't go home. She came over to my house. So the predicament that she's in made me feel kind of sorry for her, right? Sheila came over there with no food, her son was running around. She spent all her money to get high. I'm telling you, I felt sorry for her. I gave her money for some food. The thing about it, when you're sittin' around with those kind of people when you've got money, you're a king. When you've got white cocaine, you're a king in this world. You're a king.

I'll be truthful with you, Eli, I used to sell that stuff. A couple of things went bad before Christmas, and I needed easy, quick money. I can tell you, man, but I couldn't tell everybody 'cause, I mean, even though I have respect for you bein' a doctor, I have respect for you bein' a older friend, and I never lied to you. What started hurting me, though, was that twelve girls one day came to my house for caps. They ain't got money. But I had bad luck. I was just down on my luck. 'Cause it wasn't in my heart to really be a drug dealer. See, to be a good dealer, it has to be in your heart. And your heart has to be in it. My heart wasn't in it. That was not me, Eli. And see, when you selling drugs, anybody come by to wash your car, go to the store for me. They treat me like a king. Man, I got all kinds of stuff, jackets, stuff that I always wanted. But I've always been a working man, see. And, it takes a certain breed of person to sell these drugs. If you have any dignity about yourself [you can't do it well].

All kinds of people just started coming to my house any time of night, looking for me, looking for drugs. All different times of night. I mean, all day long. Two in the morning. This is early. Three in the morning. They come at five, six, seven in the morning. And they come with the TVs, their VCRs and stuff. One lady sold all her food stamps, just to get high. And when I found out about it, I felt sorry for her. She sold 'em to one of the guys I had workin' for me. When I found out, I was mad. That hurt me. Then, on the next day, I found out where she lived at. And I gave her stamps back or at least half of them back to her—for her kids. It's sad. It makes you cry in your heart. Pretty girls, too. Pretty women, man. You see some of these ladies, and you would say, "Whew!" It's just, there's no limit to what they would do for the drug.

You know when I first started out selling this stuff, I used to go to the spots. I'd sit in there, observing the scene. You know, the drug house. Eli, if you could see what they do. They take a hit off that stuff, and they start rollin' around on the floor. Oh, man, trash everywhere. Matches everywhere. Everywhere. They don't clean nothin' up. They don't do nothing. Their biggest meal is Oodles of Noodles. That's all they eat. These pipers don't eat. The pipe is so strong that it just takes control of them. You got to be strong to stay away from that. You just can't be a follower. See, I always was a leader. And now my whole family's strung out on this stuff. That's why I know so much about it. I felt so bad that I stopped when they come to me. That hurt me to my heart. My cousin come by my house and say, "John, let me work for you. Give me a package." You give 'em something, they don't bring your money back. Then it's on you to make it up. If you don't make it up, you're in trouble. It just got to be bad business. Too much bad stuff.

So I just stopped. Some people got pissed off. But I just stopped. A lot of people started steppin' up to me, like, "You can't sell on my turf, you're not in this neighborhood." And when I got the message, I stopped. It was like a gang thing. A gang neighborhood thing. I had my own spot [turf], but see, I was doin' big money. I was doin' it down South Philly. But see, I don't know nothin' about selling it over there. I don't know how to turn it up and all that, give it straight. And they was likin' it. See, if I lived here and you lived up here and all the customers have come up there but this man down here givin' straight cocaine—whew! See, they all start comin' to me. I saw death. I knew I had to get out of the life.

But I was making good money. The best nights I would have would be Thursday and Friday—$1,500, $1,600 a night. That's with, you know, paying the people. I would walk away—I paid $400 for a half ounce—I would walk away with $800, $900 in the clear. But I seen a lot things coming, man. People trying to plot on stickin' me up. I was carrying too much money on me. People could see that. And you can't really trust nobody. They would stake out my house. I had to carry a gun everywhere I went—a 9 millimeter. Now, that's going backward. So I know what it is. I've been there. That was somethin' that was interesting. A lot of guys buying, shooting up.

Let me tell you something, I'm not selling coke. I never liked coke. Even when I was little [starting out], my brother was selling it: he'd say shit like, "Go ahead, take a snort." Put that stuff up my nose. I couldn't stand it. No. The only thing in my life is smoking reefer. And I don't smoke reefer no more either. When I was doing that, you know, I couldn't even go to the gym. It's a fucked-up life, man. A fucked-up life. I would just sit back and watch how these people act. I mean, the women don't even wear panties. They take their clothes off so quick. Comin' on like, "Hey, brother, can I get in your ear for a minute? Man, we can go in the back room and I'll take care of you for what you want." Now, if she do this man and his money run out, the next guy comin' in with money, she might say, "Hey, brother, for a hit . . ." I mean, that is the worst thing. She gave up her body. I know girls, man, they give up their life for a shot of motherfuckin' cocaine.

This girl I know, she's a nice girl. Her name is Cher. Pretty girl. Pretty, well built. She moved into the neighborhood, and then—next thing I know, a couple weeks I come around there and she's hittin' the pipe. Now she's sleepin' with all kinds of guys. And this girl was rough [very attractive]. I mean, this was a girl you could take home and say, "Mom, look what I found." Now she's fuckin' anyone. Just for a hit. When I first met her, I couldn't get next to her. Now anybody can have her. I don't want her now. Uh-uh. She was beautiful. You can always tell a piper, a lady piper. Their hair be all messed up. They always got a scarf on their hair. And they walk the streets at night like zombies. They're lookin' on the ground trying to find something. Cocaine.

Whore, coke whore. They are slick too. They set you up. They'll do anything to get with that dope. A blast. The cocaine turns them into instant ho's. Say, for instance, somebody might get 'em high. It might be a girlfriend or a boyfriend. And I guess it's so good a feeling to 'em that, "How can we get some more? Do they sell this shit?" Some people go, "whew!" And a woman, she got a piece of it, they make a prostitute out of you. It's like presto! Bang! They want to know where can I get some more. Have you ever had anything that's so good to you? I guess that's how it makes 'em feel. It makes a woman an instant whore. Instant. Just like you put Quik in some milk. Chocolate Quik in some milk, and it's instant chocolate. Hit that shit, you a instant whore. It just take one time. One time, Eli.

I could show you some women—um um um. Do anything for a blast. A friend of mine, Tracy—you know him, Tracy, right— he like them tricks. He make 'em bark at the moon. Bark at the moon: turn them into a dog for a hit. And they do it. They'll do anything. Got people that kill people for that stuff. It was in the news. Boy killed his mother and father. He made money at the car wash all day, and she jumped on him to get his money. And it just take one time. The hooker [the person who gets them hooked] could be anybody they meet. "Hey, baby, you wanta get high? You wanta try this? It's cool." Then, if you ain't got sense enough to say, "Look, I ain't into that," and you say, "Oh, what the hell, I'll try it," then boom, you're gone. One time.

I've never seen nobody that hit that shit walk away from it. I've seen guys get off work with their whole check. I go around the spot with a bag of dope. I sit back and watch them to make sure they don't try something funny. I'm lookin' around. See, I come up in the streets. They come, go, and come; he may have his whole check. He spends $5, then he coming back and [say], "give me four caps"—that's twenty—come back, "Give me another four caps," "Give me another four caps," "Give me another"—and another. Then he come back. "Can I get four for fifteen?" He might come back, he spent all of $400, $500: "Can I get a cap?" I might go ahead and throw him a couple. Then he come back. "I got this watch to sell. How much you give me for this gold chain?" You know, I got so much jewelry at home. I got almost $4,000 in jewelry—I mean expensive stuff—for $5, $10 dollars. This jacket I'm wearing here cost in the store $250. I bought it for $10—two caps. A VCR goes on the street for $20, $25. They give it up. I know one dude, he got strung out so bad, he went opened the door to his whole house and said, "Come in and buy whatever you want." He sold his refrigerator, washing machine. I got so many jackets. Leather? I got a lot of leather jackets.

What made me stop, really, I was storing some dope. Cops came and I threw some out. The guy I was dealing with, he was fronting me [giving credit]. I had to pay my front tab up, and that's what really broke me. See, you make good money, but it goes so fast. It's not the kind of money that you're making when you working and you have a direct deposit, and you come home and you're tired. That ain't the kind of money that you make [dealing]. It's quick money—easy come, easy go. There are a lot of people out there who are blowing their whole check. Life is nothing like it used to be. I was brought up with a mother and a father; he wasn't the best, but he was all right. And the old heads, who would help raise guys. But that's gone, gone out to sea. That's done. But the other cats bring in the new recruits. They bring in the young boys, show them what to do. There's a new breed now. They're breedin' 'em.

There's no ending to this, Eli. This will be causing the ending of the world. There's no ending, Eli. This is something you can't come back from. I know some people that messed with it, and it turned their life around. They just said, "The hell with it." But there's no turning back from this, Eli. This is the cause of the ending of the world, 'cause anytime you got the doctors and lawyers doing it—you know what I mean? It's people you may know. It's like aliens. You talking to a robot. Only thing you can do is stick close to your loved ones, your family. In the outside world it is like a jungle.

And it's so wild. The world's gonna be at an end, man, I'm telling you. It's something that you cannot fuck with. No cops, no preacher. This is like—it's worse than AIDS. I'd rather catch AIDS, 'cause AIDS gonna destroy you physically. I don't wanta die mentally. Just watch yourself getting apart. I seen people with nice cars. Next thing you see, their car ain't running. Next thing you see, they ain't got no money. Next thing you know, they walking around selling that stuff, they lost their job. This is something that's not gonna change.

Back in your time when you were coming up, or probably a little later than your time, guys were shooting needles or hanging around and stuff like that. It wasn't addictive like it is now. This drug [crack] is very addictive. This goes straight to your mind. Anybody I seen doing it is still doing it, and that's no lie.

See, when you selling big, you the Godfather. They had me going for a while. Yeah. I was riding around in a red Bronco, leased me a Bronco, extra-large red Bronco, gold jewelry on, got my girl with me, got my daughter. I get out the truck, people run over there to me. "Yo, John, what's up? Can we wash your truck for you?" I got a Cadillac, too, '78 Caddy, Coupe de Ville. Girls saying, "Oh, he's so fine." Now see, they didn't notice me when I didn't have no drugs, but now I'm the finest thing that walks. I'm King John.

I'm playing myself out 'cause you know what they're [the police] gonna do eventually is watch me, follow me, then bust me. I don't need that, so I backed off. You know, I'm smart. Now people see me, "Hey, John, how come you ain't rollin' no more? What you hittin'?" Uh-uh. I'm cooling out. I see something that, you get busted for 'caine, you gonna get time. No, I had to be cool. 'Cause I got locked up in September. I got out September 19. My birthday was September 21. I had to pay $750. When they stopped me, they didn't search my truck. Girl had stole $250 worth of crack. I go around the crib knocking on the door—boom, boom. My truck parked in the middle of the street. This is my pickup, I got a pick, a red pickup, sittin' high with big fat tires like Big Foot. I brought that from Atlanta. I didn't buy that with drugs. That was mine. I paid for that. That's a '78. I got the real big tires on it, sittin' high up in the air, four-wheel drive. I'm sittin' out there in my truck. I'm banging on the door early in the morning. Get my shit, bitch. I'm pumping it now, you gotta realize, this ain't John. I'm king. Then she calls the cops because I was disturbing her. Now, I don't wanta tell the cops what I'm at her house for, that she got my shit [drugs]. She fiending [needs a fix]. After you get a hit and you ain't got no more, you fiending.

I don't mess with them no more. 'Cause you know I'm a leader, man, really from the heart. And I'm smart, too smart for that. A lot of people I love got killed, man. I don't wanta die off of that shit, you know. So they locked me. They didn't search my truck. If they'd searched my truck, they would have came up with $1,300 worth of caps I had up under the seat. I was ready to drop some shit off, and I had $800 in my pocket. They never searched my truck, and I had a thirty-eight pistol inside my truck. I'd be in jail now. Eli, I'm gonna tell you something. When I tell you I was selling, I regret it, but I had a lot of fun, man, went a lot of places, bought a lot of things. It feels good to take your girl to an expensive restaurant, take her to a jewelry store. Audrey—the one I'm gonna get married to—I bought her all kinds of gold earrings, you know, bought her a little car. I can make in two months what you've made all your life.

Hey, it's easy to walk away from selling drugs. But it's hard to get out of the trouble that they bring. That's why I got out. I took the easiest road to walk away from it. I did bad. I've been broke for three months, and now it's opening up. I should have never dealt with 'em in the first place. Guys see me, take my size. I don't like that. But John ain't scared of nothing. I ain't never been scared of anybody. See, coming up in the street, I was like the boss, gang leader. I'm not scared for me; I'm scared for the people that believe in me. I hate to get knocked up with all that you did to get me where I'm at. All that you did for me, my mother did for me, people that supported me when I fell down.

Where were all my friends when I was going to jail and I needed money for a lawyer? Where were all of them then?

When I was selling big drugs: "Oh, John, you the greatest. You got this, you got that." Then, when I fell, the only people—you, my mother—that loved me, that cared for me was there. Where was all my fan club? Where was all the boosters—"Hey, hey, keep it up." So if I was to get back into and fall again, how would my friends look at me? How would you feel—"Hey, Eli, you seen John? He doing five years for selling drugs." It would upset you. I'm not trying to upset nobody.

It would upset me if somebody told me, "John, Eli's hittin' the pipe." I'd break down in tears. See, you're well educated. You've got a good background. Me, I ain't got nothing but the street. See, my mother's sick, my cousin had cancer. I hustled like that to send a lot of money home. See, people don't know your true inner feelings, your true ideas. I helped my mother out. Now my mother out the hole. Man, she doing good. She got a new car. My—it's my cousin, but we was raised like sisters and brothers—she got cancer and they cut her chest off, she lost all her hair. I had to support them, man. I helped out a lot of people that needed to be helped.

If you ever doubt the things I do, I can always come to you and tell you the truth about things. And it help me feel better, man. When you lie to a person, right, you can't live with it. I told you the truth about my life, man, about the way the things was. And you didn't turn your back on me. That's all I needed was a chance. Like to set a goal or to do things. Like I felt real bad when they shot me down. And that guy that we were talking to, he didn't really care. He can't look in his heart and see there's a young brother man trying to get something out of life, you know, trying to turn his life around. Right then I would have helped.

In this account, John Turner described crack houses; lives destroyed by drugs; people selling everything, including food stamps for their children, to buy drugs; crack whores who spend their days prostituting themselves for a high; people ringing his doorbell at all hours of the day and night, desperate for crack; the large amount of money he made; the cars he bought; the valuable things people gave him for a five-dollar capsule of crack; the way he was the king of the neighborhood. At the same time he suggested that he was a humane dealer and in fact often helped the victims of addiction.

John was ambivalent about this life and seemed to care about improving his condition, yet he was stuck in his environment, so much so that he was somehow drawn back to it even when provided with the opportunity to escape. When I was first getting to know him, these glimmers of hope, of corrigibility, that he displayed now and then spurred me to want to help him out. I felt that if only he had a break, he could make it. But over time, as I got to know him better, much of that feeling began to dissipate, because he never seemed fully committed to improving himself. Having been given several opportunities, John was increasingly obligated to help himself; yet he did not respond to these opportunities. My interest in helping him dwindled; I became more and more disappointed in his behavior, although I retained some hope for him. These concerns were interconnected with my curiosity about John's world and my desire to understand it, which is one of the reasons I continued to be involved in his life.

## TRYING AGAIN

At any rate, as we were leaving the restaurant, John sheepishly asked if I could lend him five dollars. This was after telling me how much money he had made selling drugs, how much leather clothing people had given him, and how much jewelry he had acquired. So what did this mean? If he really had no money, maybe he really had quit. Something must have scared or intimidated or provoked him to the point where he decided he had to get out. I gave him the five dollars, but that was not all he wanted. He also wanted his old job back. He wanted me to go see Curtis and persuade him to give him another chance. I said I would do what I could, but I had no intention of appealing to Curtis again. I thought that since I had given him the five dollars, I wouldn't see him again for a long time.

Then, one weekend when I had been out of town, I returned on

Saturday night to hear from my wife that John Turner had come to our house with his girlfriend. He had been looking for me, presumably because he wanted to hear about his prospects for a job. She told him that I was in my office, though in reality I had not yet returned to the city. John called my office repeatedly. "Where are you, man? I need a job." As my wife was telling me this after I had returned home—it was about nine that evening—John called, and I answered. John needed a ride from South Philadelphia to Southwest Philadelphia to his sister's house, where he was then living. Over the protestations of my wife, I agreed to go and pick him up and drive him there because I had by now come to realize that I must sever my contact with him, and in order to do that I had to communicate with him.

I drove to the corner at which we had agreed to meet, and John was waiting for me, along with his latest girlfriend. They got in the car and I drove them home, stopping for gas on the way. Now John wanted ten dollars. I gave it to him, but with the even stronger conviction that I had to end the relationship. So I asked him if he had ever thought about joining the army. "Can you do that?" was his response. In his mind, I was some kind of magician; I could make the impossible happen. I told him I would meet him at ten o'clock on Monday morning and we would go to the army recruiter together. He agreed to that and then, before we got to his sister's house, asked me if I had an extra suit. This was a total surprise, and I inquired what he needed a suit for. He said, "Well, I want to go to church on Sunday," invoking once again the image of respectability and decency that was supposed to keep me interested in helping him.

I said, "No, I don't have a suit," and he did not pursue it. I dropped him off at his sister's house, located in a very poor and dangerous neighborhood. We said our goodbyes. The next day, a Sunday, I looked over the want ads in the paper and noticed that many restaurants were in need of kitchen staff. I became encouraged at the thought that even if the army did not work out, there were job prospects for John.

On Monday we met punctually at ten o'clock. It was a rainy morning, and we got into a taxi and went downtown to the army recruitment office in Center City Philadelphia. I introduced myself and

John to the black sergeant seated behind the desk. I was dressed in a tweed jacket, and I explained that this young man was interested in enlisting in the army. The first question from the officer to John was "Are you on probation?" I wondered about the question. Did it have to do with the fact that there is such a high probability that young black males are in trouble with the law? Do such males gravitate to the army recruitment offices for something of a second chance, as John and I were doing? John, of course, had to say yes, to which the army recruiter replied, "When you get that cleared up, we can talk. We can't talk until you deal with that. You could go to the judge, go to your probation officer, and try to work out a deal. If the judge says OK, then maybe we can do something. We do that. We let people go into the army to get their lives together."

John could only say OK to that, and we left with the feeling that we had struck out. But we were determined to do as the officer had suggested. We walked to the probation office, only a few doors away. We went up to the sixth floor and tried to find John's latest probation officer. She was nowhere to be found. Her desk mate told us that she was out at the bank on personal business. We awaited her return for quite a while; as the time passed, John began to grow impatient and I was becoming more anxious to resolve the whole matter. Finally, we left and switched to my plan B, which was to investigate the want ads I had found the preceding day. John was certainly amenable.

As we were walking down the street on our way to the first of the restaurants, John began to question my position. He asked rather pointedly if I thought "all that professor shit works."

"What do you think?" I answered.

He was not at all sure. "If you had been a white professor, do you think it would have worked?" he wanted to know. He thought that professors have influence with recruitment officers, and that if I had been a "real" professor I probably could have persuaded the sergeant to accept him. He finally said, "It don't work, man. I think you're naïve." This marked a major development in our relationship, for never before had we approached having words.

We talked about this until we reached the downtown restaurant district. All the while John argued with me about my failure to get him into the army, thus dashing his high hopes. He said, "You didn't do it. You couldn't do it." I finally got fed up with this and took him into the first restaurant we came to.

We walked in and asked for the manager. I explained that John was looking for a job, had restaurant experience, and was a good worker. The manager, after looking us up and down, sent us back to the kitchen to talk to Al, a black man who appeared to be head of the kitchen staff. Al asked some of the same questions the manager had asked, then excused himself to confer with the manager. When he returned, he looked at John and said, "When can you start?"

I was very happy, but John was ecstatic. He had a look of surprised anticipation on his face. He said, "Right now!" We didn't even discuss wages. This was a former drug dealer now willing to work at anything, in part because he really did want something other than the tough life of the drug dealer in the streets. At that point I left to go to my office, but I asked John to call me later.

## GRATITUDE

John didn't call, but at four o'clock in the afternoon he came by. He walked into my office and gave me a huge bear hug, and his first words were "I got it man, I got it! How'd you do that?" again as though I had done something magical by getting him this job. All I had really done was to talk with the manager sensibly. But my very presence and the way that I spoke may have been what he was looking for. It might have led him to trust the job application John had filled out. John and I then went out to a restaurant to discuss the events of the day. He related the following:

> See, Eli, you didn't give up on me, and I'm really thankful about that. You were saying, "Let's go try here. Let's do this. Let's try that." And I tried it. I said—in my inner self, I said, "Well, this man's not givin' up on me. Therefore I'm not gonna give up on my own self." Because truthfully in my heart, I'm gonna tell you, I've given up. I was ready to run. Not in my heart, though, not really. Walking in the rain. How many friends

you know that stick by you like that? I'll tell you, you're the greatest when it comes to bein' a friend, man. You're the greatest. And see, what helps me the most, I have been great to people in my lifetime, and they accepted it the wrong way. But it's to know that someone's bein' great to me and I'm accepting it, you know, as they give it, not takin' advantage of it. Look, right now I'm where I'm the happiest man in the world—I got a job! The boss man say I can work as long as I want. They want me to work seven to six. Seven in the morning to six. Monday through Friday. I don't have to work on the weekend. Five dollars a hour. That's all I need. I won't bother nobody, nobody bother me.

And it's somethin' I don't like doin', but until something comes better . . . But see, it's the thing that gettin' out here, man, doin' something for yourself. But like, say when we was down at the [army] recruiter. Now, that guy seen that walk. If I was the recruitin' officer, I'd sit back and you gotta analyze it. I'm lookin' at it and say, "Well, this guy comin' down here, with a professor speakin' for him, this guy must be trying to turn his life around." So therefore I would have got on top of the case. I wouldn't let me walk out without my name. Notice, he didn't care if he took my name or care if he tried to help me. You notice I said, "Well, the probation office is right next door. Maybe you could take time and walk over there with us and say something. . . ."

You can always get a job selling drugs. But I'm glad I got this one. It's hard to get jobs, man. You can get 'em if you look like the way we looked. We looked respectable, and we just happened to pop in at the right time. When I seen him come down the stairs, I said to myself, "Watch me get this job." He had confidence in me. Then, after he hired me and he seen the way I work, he said, "We needed a guy like you." He said, "I'm glad you stopped by. You're full-time, Monday through Friday." Full-time. Every Friday I get paid. He said, "Saturday—if you wanta come in and get extra money, we'll pay you for that." I'm a worker. I will work every day, Eli. I'll get up every morning and go to work and whistle on the way to work.

Now, that recruiter oughta be thinking, "I see a young black man—not only a young black man; a young white man, a young yellow man, or whatever—trying to do something for themselves. Right now his past is not, you know, too good, but maybe we can make it better by helping him." But he didn't even care. That's why they won't talk to me no more, 'cause I can pick up on stuff real quick. He's through the system hisself. He say, "If you don't have this, you don't have that, I can't help you." Here it is, man. That's why we're not moving as a race, all right. Now say, for instance, if all the young black guys go up to another black guy on the street, "Oh, I need some money." And there's this package in his hand, you know. "And you can clock for me, and you turn in your money to so-and-so by that time, and you're cool."

It is so hard for me to get a job, but it's so easy for me sell drugs. A lot of guys see me who I knew comin' up. "I know this spot, John. I could fit you in there, man. They clock about $1,500." You walk away with $300, $400, $500 a day. You say, "No, man, I need a job. Something I can have for years to come and my daughter can be proud of me about." You hear what I'm saying?

But if you go—the average job you go to, they see a young black guy trying to get somewhere in life, it's no go, and I really felt bad hearing the recruiting officer—and I'm coming in with a professor, you know? And that's wild, that's deep. And come in here with a college professor. Eli, let me ask you something. Let me ask you a question. If it was—if I came in with a white professor, would it be different? Did that appear on your mind [occur to you]? See, when you say professor—right?—they don't believe it. 'Cause you don't look old enough to be a professor, you know. If I had come in with a guy with a big beard, with a evil look, with a not too nice attitude—the way professors look, like that guy that plays for Smith Barney—what do you think? Do you think [the recruiting officer] would have jumped a little more? 'Cause you gotta think. 'Cause if I was a recruiting officer, I would sit back and analyze: he appears to be a well-built, nice young man. He comes in with a professor that's speaking highly of him, not only jeopardizing his education, his thing—he's speaking up for another man. When a man speaks for another man, he must be a man of your qualification. He must have much respect for you. You understand? And I introduce you to my friends. I say, "This is my friend, and I'm proud to say you my friend." 'Cause I don't have too many friends who are professors. See, it really hurts to see people like that, man. I would never turn down a man that wants something in life. All right, so what, this man told me the truth, [that] he had a record and everything, but he's trying to turn his life around. Maybe if I get with the professor and join a team to help this man get something out of life . . .

But what about probation? But you know what? There's waivers for that, right? He could know somebody to help me get in there. Work as a team. You notice I said—as a team. Who's on first, what's on second, you know. We're a team. Now, I could look at it and say, "Well, this man's not his family member, so he's the first member of the team. If I join this team to help this black man get in the service . . ." Isn't that the better way to do it?

## JOHN'S ACCOUNT OF QUITTING HIS JOB

I then asked John to tell me what had led him to quit his job at the hospital, because I had not heard his side of the story. John said,

> See, Curtis is from the old school. The old school is where you shuffle. Where you got me a job, he got me in. He spoke to me more like a child. He always said I worked good and everything like that, but he give me the dirty stuff that nobody would do 'cause I was that type of guy—"Send John to do it." Like, the dishes. I would get all the dishes. I would get all the stripping of floors. The guy who worked with me wouldn't do that. They had that union thing—I'm in the union. Whereas I'm a man. If I'm working a job and there are certain things that

you have to do, I'm gonna do it. Regardless of whether I'm in the union to back me up or not—this is a job, right? The guy said, "I'm not putting my head into that," and he walked off. I said, "I'm a man." I rolled my sleeves up and washed my hands, you know. Whereas there are a lot of guys that's been on the job that's getting lazy. I'll be working here doing my job, they come get me. "Come on, I want you to go with this crew and do that." Now, if you've got a horse that's gonna work good, why dog him? They were dogging me. I came in there with the old-time attitude, like, "Hey, I work." See, a lot of the guys were old-timers. Twenty-five, thirty, thirty-five, forty, forty-three years old. And they were bucking the system.

And another thing, Curtis put my business in the street. See, he put it out how many kids I had. He would tell things like that. Then, when I was going back and forth to jail, he would tell everybody. That wasn't fair. I'd be standing around there— "You'd better get your work done. Them prison people [guard] don't play, they don't play." All the time, "Them prison people don't play." He was always talking about the guards. He called me "the halfway man." Just because daytime I'm working and nighttime I'm in jail. Then he said, "You're so busy riding on all them girls." Every day a different girl come pick me up to prison, you know. "What time you gotta be back in?" All that stuff. He was for me, but he was all in my business. I didn't really like it. And one day a bunch of us were checking out some girls, and he singled me out and said, "Keep that thing in your damn pants." I'd be talking to a girl on the job—and I could be on my lunchtime or I could be off—and he'd walk up. "There you go again. There you go again. There you go again. You need to keep that thing in your pants." And one time this girl I liked, he told her, "You already got seven kids. How many damn kids you need?" She was like, "Who's that, your father?" It kind of hurt her. I wanted to punch him in the head. And once everyone knew, it became a conversation. He told everybody my business. Everybody knew my business. I would go to a different part of the hospital—"That's the guy that got all them kids. I ain't touching him, he might get me pregnant." [Laughs] And the guys were jealous of me, man. I always been a very smart man. I can't help if I'm a well-built man. I'm not conceited. I didn't ever lift a weight in my life, but I got a nice chest, nice thighs, nice build, nice grade of hair. You know, ladies like that. I can't help it. That's just the way it was. I always been popular with the ladies. Different girls be flocking around me. Guys get jealous. I can't help it. See, I like the ladies. Natalia would drive me to work, kiss me, and she would pick me up late at work, you know? She was built. I bought a burgundy Regal. I was riding around in my Regal, spoke tires and everything. Then Wanda would come down and see me sometime on the job, on my lunchtime. I'd tell her, "Come have lunch with me." That doesn't mean I had to be seeing them or sleeping with them. A lot of guys were jealous. And I got tired of it.

See, I was young still in my heart, Eli. And I missed my mother, man. You know, I was away from home. I got out of jail. I was up here working. I just got tired of the ribbin'. See, I got a very bad temper, and I hope you will never see it. They kept agitating. You might know somebody that knows me, like Tracy Biggs. They can tell you, I got a real bad temper. But I'm the most nicest person you can meet. But what they was doing— what caused me not to rip on [fight] 'em [was] 'cause of you. I know you got me [the job] down there and you spoke highly of me, and I'm not the one that will embarrass somebody for the next man. So I had to keep my cool. I was a damn good worker. I was a great stripper [of floors], and they loved my work. I worked on a impact crew. They would call me in on different buildings. See, I couldn't sit down and go anywhere I wanted to go.

Started thinking about my mom and my family that we have. My brother and me used to play in the house. It got lonely for me. And too, my mom was sick. She wasn't making it too good. My mother was sick. You know, she phoned me, said she missed me. I missed her. Even though I come from a broken home, my mother and us always shared together. When we was cold, we'd all sleep in the same room, cuddle up. I miss it, man. I miss her now, but I'm a little older now. I was running around watching people—like when the holidays come, everybody go to Fourth of July over with their families. Christmas—I spent it in my room by myself this year. Right. Thanksgiving—what family was I gonna have Thanksgiving with? I don't have no family. I'm here by myself. I had to go, man. My heart was empty. I was working, making good money, but I walked around moping. I cried a lot. Sometimes I could just be sitting down, man, and crying, you know. I was lonely. 'Cause it's lonely being without a family. And I'm here all by myself. Being that we was so close— we didn't have much; we were very poor—but we was rich in love. After a while, watching my friends go home, watching what they got for Christmas, their families would lend them some money when they was broke, on the holidays, all the family would get together—and then I would go to my friends' house for their holiday, New Year's and stuff, and I would sit in the corner and watch how happy they are to see each other. . . . I gave Curtis notice and everything. I didn't like the way he talked to me. Talked to me like I was a little boy or something. I'm a grown man.

## CHILD SUPPORT

Yeah, my children. I'm not the type of guy to leave my kids. They're mine—and I'm gonna stand by and take care of 'em every day. I'm gonna do my part. None of my kids are on welfare. I may not have much, but everything I have, I give. Now that I'm back working, I can give more. What I missed, now I can fulfill, and I'll be more than happy to fulfill them. I mean, I'm the type of man, I want to give for my kids. Every Friday I would bring money up [from down South]. I'd give John Jr. twenty-five dollars, his mother twenty-five dollars, Salona fifty-five dollars. But really I've only got four kids. Phyliss wanted to take me to court. I made an agreement with her. She says she just wanted to be with me to have kids. She liked the way I was built. She thought I was a nice-status young man, she just wanted to have a kid by me. She never loved me. And some women will do that to you. Guys don't realize that, but some women just want to have kids by you. I want you to know she had two kids. She named them Scott after her. She said, "Well, you don't have to take care of them, and I don't want to see you around them." And I just went the last step. It's cold-blooded, but I go my way and let her go her way. She's making some money, good money. I don't go telling her how to raise them.

She's a much older woman than I am. When I met her, I had Little John and Jimmy. She knew I had kids. Why she go with me and have two more? See, she comes from a wealthy family, and they gets the best of everything. But if she wants to raise them to hate me, well, that's on her. See, I haven't seen Buddy, my son, in two years. Last time I seen him he was—what?—two years old. I can barely remember what he looks like. She had a little baby named Shevalle—she played with my mother a lot. I wanta go see 'em, but, you know, I don't wanta go up there 'cause I don't wanta go up there and argue. 'Cause, you know, she'll go, "What you doing up here?" "Come here to see these kids." "I thought we agreed for you never to see them again." They have nothing of mine, not my name. I have only my four kids.

John explained that the men at the hospital were always on his case, that they would tease him about his girlfriends and his children and also about his position as a halfway man, since during part of his time there he was still spending his nights in jail but was allowed out to work during the day. He talked about how the men embarrassed him in front of the girlfriends who came to see him, and he also cited the other workers who had not known his background. He claimed that they spread word of his reputation as a stud around the entire organization and that their talk was for the most part motivated by jealousy of his success with women.

He also brought me up to date on his women and children. He told me that one girlfriend had used him to get pregnant twice and then forbade him to see her or the children. He explained how lonely he had been after his mother left, how difficult Thanksgiving had been without her, how he had enjoyed being down South with her. But he had had to come back because of the terms of his probation and because of his children, whom he did not want to walk out on. He reiterated his disgust at what drugs have done to the black community in general as well as to various individual people in his life.

After telling me all this, John again asked me for money—$150 this time. Upon reflection and with a little resistance, I gave it to him, fully expecting never to see it again but also expecting never to see him again. His code of honor would forbid him to contact me again without paying me back, and my experience with him had taught me that he was unlikely ever to have the money. This was how I was finally able to sever our relationship. I had continued to help John even after it had become apparent that he was using me, because I wanted to see how he responded to various situations. At this point, however, I felt I had developed a rather complete picture of him; furthermore, I was beginning to feel uneasy about our association.

I have indeed not seen John since, but I have heard of him. The street life he found so compelling seems to have brought him to a corner in Baltimore. There he had an altercation with somebody over something, perhaps a misunderstood drug deal, and he wound up being shot in the gut. On the streets it is said that as a result of that shooting, he is "carrying around a bag" and will be for the rest of his life. He is now about twenty-seven.

## STREET LIFE VERSUS THE CULTURE OF DECENCY

An important lesson to be learned from John's story is that of the basic tension between the street and the decent, more conventional world of legitimate jobs and stable families. In John's case, when the two worlds collided, the street prevailed, in part because John lacked the personal resources to negotiate the occupational structure available to him. At the point when the wider system became receptive to him in the form of a well-paying job, it was too late. The draw of the street was too powerful, and he was overcome by its force.

When I met him, John—like so many young black men caught up in similar circumstances—appeared to be adrift between the street and the wider, more conventional society. But given the way he had been raised—learning at an early age to survive by the code of the street—the street had a profound advantage in the contest for his heart and mind. Moreover, the various pieces of human capital he had accumulated over the years were more easily negotiable on the street. The street proved much more receptive to John than did the wider, more legitimate society, so he was encouraged to invest his personal resources in the oppositional culture.

John rejected the means of achieving status sanctioned by the wider society; at the same time he accepted that society's goals of material success—money, gold, clothes, sneakers, cars.[6] Too often the wider system of legitimate employment is closed off to young men like John Turner: by prejudice, by lack of preparation, or by the absence of real job opportunities.[7] But they observe others—usually whites—enjoying the fruits of the system, and through this experience they often become deeply alienated. They develop contempt for a society they perceive as having contempt for them. The reality of racism looms large in their minds. Feeling that their opportunities for conventional advancement are blocked, young men like John are drawn to an alternative means of gaining the things they see that others have.[8] Here they are easily drawn into the street culture, where cunning intelligence mixed with street wisdom and physical prowess are highly valued. With these resources, they negotiate and compete fiercely for very scarce coin: respect and wealth.

This street-oriented subculture is often violent. A primary value is physicality and a willingness to resolve disputes through violence. Authority is asserted through conflict, and shouts, bites, punches, knife cuts, and gunshots are traded. It is very important to be bad, to be mean, because to be mean is also to be cool and highly regarded. It is essential *not* to be square or to emulate the wider society through behavior or sympathy.

The predatory influence of the street culture is an enormous problem for the rest of the inner-city population. It puts the entire community on guard and encourages a defensive posture in many otherwise ordinary situations. In particular, young people who are not strongly anchored in the conventional world are at risk of being preyed upon or of falling victim to the philosophy of the street. Given the drugs, poverty, unemployment, lack of opportunity, and other social problems besetting the community, well-meaning parents find it difficult to root their children in conventional values.

In fact, in underclass communities, conventionality and the street culture wage a constant battle for the hearts and minds of the younger residents, and this dichotomy has become an organizing principle. As was noted in Chapter 1, the residents generally divide their neighbors into those who are decent and those whom they associate with the street. The culture of decency is characterized by close extended families, low incomes but financial stability, deep religious values, a work ethic and desire to get ahead, the value of treating people right, and a strong disapproval of drug use, violence, and teenage pregnancy. The street represents hipness, status based on one's appearance, and contempt for conventional values and behavior, which are easily discredited because of their association with whites. These behaviors can include doing well in school, being civil to others, and speaking Standard English.

This oppositional culture is a product of alienation. It is alluring in large part because the conventional culture is viewed by many blacks in the inner cities as profoundly unreceptive. Young people observe the would-be legitimate role models around them and find them to be severely wanting and unworthy of emulation. Legal hard work seems not to have paid off for the old, and the relatively few hardworking people in the impoverished neighborhood seem to be struggling to survive. Some appear to be doing well, but their methods seem at best vague or out of range for the young people. Moreover, from their elders and peers they hear repeated tales of racist treatment, and by now most have experienced prejudice and discrimination firsthand. At the same time through street-oriented role models, a thriving underground economy beckons to them, promising enormous sums of money along with a certain thrill of getting over in a system that denies them respect. These activities offer them a certain power and prestige as well. Streetwise and impoverished young men are easily encouraged to find places in this underground economy.

In the past, manufacturing jobs provided opportunities for young men like John and at the same time supported the values of decency and conventionality by rewarding them. The loss of these jobs has damaged the financial health of the inner city and undermined the quality of available role models. One important casualty has been the relationship between old heads and young boys. The old head was a man (or a woman) of stable means whose acknowledged role in the community was to teach and support boys (a woman would support young women) and young men in their late teens and early twenties—in effect to socialize them to meet their responsibilities regarding work, family life, the law, and common decency. But since meaningful employment has become increasingly scarce and the expanding drug culture offers opportunities for quick money, the old head has been losing prestige and authority.

In his place, a new role model is emerging. The embodiment of the street, he is young, often the product of a street gang, and at best indifferent to the law and traditional values. If he works at the low-paying jobs available to him, he may do so grudgingly. More likely, he is involved, part-time or full-time, in the drug trade or some other area of the underground economy. Furthermore, he often derides conventional family life: he tends to have a string of women but feels little obligation toward them and the children he has fathered. His displays of self-aggrandizement through fancy clothes and impressive cars have an effect on young men like John, who may try to emulate him.

By enforcing conformity to such external displays of manhood, the oppositional culture ravages the individuality of those who fall victim to it, often eroding their sense of personal responsibility as well. In John's case, his very identity was derived from the oppositional culture, and ultimately it immobilized him in the face of conventional opportunity.

The story of John Turner sheds light on the social situation of the young black inner-city male. The progressive nature of the impact of the street points to a need both for very early intervention—

through programs such as Head Start—before the oppositional culture has had a chance even to begin developing in the child, and for continuing intervention with preadolescents and adolescents. It is extremely important, in particular, to give maturing boys (and girls) job training and education in the practicalities of operating in the world of work. This training must then be rewarded with real job opportunities. The system must be more receptive to the John Turners of the world—at an earlier stage of their development. Not to provide this sort of receptivity simply promotes alienation and fuels the oppositional culture. On the other hand, the creditable promise of opportunity nurtures in young people a more positive outlook and a hopeful sense of the future, while at the same time building a social framework for civility, law-abidingness, social peace, and a positive outlook.

The question of outlook is key here. John envisioned a good life but was unable to accept the changes in behavior necessary to achieve it. In fact, the street life competed quite effectively with his vision of the good life. My experience with John suggests that simply providing opportunities is not enough. Young people must also be encouraged to adopt an outlook that allows them to invest their considerable personal resources in available opportunities. In such more positive circumstances, they can be expected to leave behind the attitudes, values, and behavior that work to block their advancement into the mainstream. At present, it is clear, many of these young men and their female counterparts are being written off by mainstream society, a truth they know full well. And the world is poorer for their loss.

# The Conversion of a Role Model: Looking for Mr. Johnson

T EN years ago, at age seventeen, Robert was arrested and sentenced for the aggravated assault of a rival drug dealer. Having been convicted as a juvenile, he has now served his time. When he returned to the old neighborhood from prison, many people who had known him before his conviction believed that he would settle some old scores and revive his old drug gang, that things would get hot in the 'hood. Some of his old friends approached him with gifts, welcoming him back into the fold. Among these offerings was a pistol, ostensibly for his protection, which Robert flatly refused. He had decided in prison that he did not want to go that route again. He simply wanted some space, to catch up on "the haps" and to spend time with his girlfriend, Thomasina. He wished to find a way to earn money legitimately. Nevertheless, from the moment he set foot on his old turf, the people there expected to see some action.

When Robert was arrested, charged, and convicted, he had already developed a strong name on the street. Many considered him a big-time drug dealer, and he was one of the most feared people on the streets of the community. It was assumed that he would "get" anyone who crossed him. This reputation allowed him to go about the neighborhood unmolested. To be sure, people sometimes tested him, but this only made Robert stronger, for he took great delight in meeting the tests people set for him. He was a man, and in this environment nothing was more important than his manhood. Nevertheless, when he was incarcerated, his status and identity underwent a fundamental change. On the street his status remained high, but in prison in rural Pennsylvania he encountered white prison guards who treated him very badly. They called him "nigger" on an almost daily basis, planned Ku Klux Klan meetings in his presence, assigned him to "shit" work, and in other ways rode and harassed him all the while, hoping he "would strike out at one of them so they could extend [his] time." Robert says, "I was smart enough to avoid their traps, but many other black guys fell for it."

For the most part, he maintains, prison was "good for me. It made me think and reassess my life." In prison he became aware of his inability to read and the deficiencies of his vocabulary and decided he had an opportunity to rectify these problems. He had his friends and relatives send him books. He read and studied the dictionary, the Koran, the Bible, and other works, all from cover to cover. By the time he was released, he had gained a new attitude. He could see that a "game was being run" on the community. In prison most of the inmates were black or Hispanic, while most of the guards were white men from the surrounding rural areas. He felt that the guards and prison staff were being supported, if not subsidized, by "people like me." The streets in his neighborhood fueled the prison engine by providing young men who actively played their roles in a grand scheme. He knew he had to change himself and his community, and he committed himself to this end.

Since his release from prison Robert has shunned his previous materialism and become a somewhat ascetic individual—more calm, more thoughtful. Many of his former friends looked at him strangely, because they do not see the Ruck (his street name) they knew. He was always intelligent and motivated—this is what made him an upcoming leader in the drug trade—but now he was applying these traits not to living out the code of the street but to making the transition to a life of decency. This confused his old friends, because prison usually enhances one's prestige on the street, particularly in terms of code values like toughness, nerve, and willingness to retaliate for transgressions.

Yet Robert returned from prison to put his old street way of being behind him. Over the past months he has joined with three other young men—David, Tyrone, and Marvin, all desiring to change—to do what they can to support one another in turning their lives around. The young men grew up together in the local neighborhood, where they had their share of fights and run-ins with the law. Each of them has his own history, but there are common threads. They have all survived grinding urban poverty. They have endured the gamut of problems—welfare, single-parent households, emotionally and physically abusive fathers—and, like Robert, gravitated initially to the street, which provided them with family of a sort. On the street and in the gangs, they experienced a certain cohesion, bravado, and coming of age. Obtaining a high level of street knowledge from all of this, they understood the code very well. Nevertheless, something was missing from their lives. Their awareness of this prompted them to raise searching questions about their futures—where they would be in five, ten, or fifteen years. Would they be simply more casualties of the street? Could they really attain the "good life"? What were the impediments to such a goal? Whenever they would get together, they would discuss such issues. Robert was usually the main catalyst for this kind of talk.

After a few months of sitting around on one another's stoops discussing and critiquing the system and their roles in it, they decided to begin to take some concrete steps toward change. In this regard they summoned the decency from within themselves. They worked to move away from the lives of petty criminal activity, including hustling and drug dealing. They wanted to see themselves one day as solid pillars in their community. But how could they get on the road to that end? They decided to approach a well-known community activist named Herman Wrice.

For many years Herman has been a very active old head in the impoverished inner-city community. He has worked hard to close down crack houses and to frustrate drug dealers. Having lived in this community for so long, he is deeply invested in cleaning it up.

He feels strongly that the drug trade and the lack of jobs are the bane of the community's existence. Herman is highly visible in the community and has gone the extra mile in fighting drug dealing, to such an extent that from time to time his life has been threatened. But he has great courage, which is highly respected on the street, and strong motivation. In his crusade Herman organizes decent people in the community, including old heads, grandmothers, grandfathers, law-abiding youths, and their parents, to participate in antidrug vigils and marches in the community.

Often they select specific drug corners or drug houses and draw attention to them by demonstrating outside in the street. At their marches the police are usually present. Together they have closed down many drug corners and crack houses, not only in ghetto areas of Philadelphia but throughout the nation as well. Herman has become something of a media figure as a result of the television coverage of his activities. Indeed, he is the nemesis of hustlers and drug dealers. He has known many of the neighborhood's young men for years. He knows many of their mothers and fathers and other family members well. So Robert and the other young men viewed Herman as approachable; they reasoned, correctly, that he would lend them a sympathetic ear.

On a Tuesday afternoon in July 1997, the four of them went to Herman with their plan for turning their lives around. They simply requested some time to talk. Herman listened. They told him, essentially, "We'd like to change. Can you to help us?" Their approach was so unusual that Herman was at first incredulous and somewhat suspicious. After so many years of working with young people in the community, of harassing drug dealers and closing them down, was he now seeing some real success for his efforts? He speculated that the drug trade was becoming increasingly dangerous and competitive and that this was why these young men wanted out. Yet he remained uncertain and perplexed. The young men's request "blew my mind," he says. Were they on the level?

"If you're serious about wanting to improve the neighborhood, you can start by cleaning up this lot," he said, pointing to an overgrown and trash-filled vacant lot. His command was a test, and the young men may have known this, but they agreed to clean up the lot. The task required a couple of days' work, but the boys accomplished what they started. Herman was impressed, though still not totally convinced that they were serious. He therefore showed them another, bigger lot to clean up as well. This task took them even longer, but they did finish it.

Again they returned to Herman, who was more impressed though still not fully convinced. He knew they had been drug dealers, whom he sees as businessmen "but with a terrible product," and wondered whether they might become entrepreneurs. Could they sell fruit on a local street corner instead of drugs? Could this then grow into a larger market, contributing eventually to revitalizing the community? If so, Robert and the others might be visible role models of hard work, an example to younger people.

With this in mind he said to them, "OK, meet me down at the [food distribution] docks at five tomorrow morning." He was testing and probing, for he did not want to be taken in. His knowledge and understanding were that committed drug dealers don't just get up at five in the morning and present themselves for honest work. But these young men surprised him; they appeared promptly at five, and Herman presented his plan for them to become fruit sellers, pointing out how this effort, while small, could grow into something much larger. The boys listened intently. Herman can be a very persuasive person. They hung on his words. They appeared hungry for an opportunity to go legitimate, to make a difference in their own community.

Once Herman decided to help them, he gave them about $800 for materials and lumber to construct a fruit stand, which had to be built in compliance with the Philadelphia Licenses and Inspections (L&I) codes. Given the young men's inexperience, their first attempt was not very successful; in fact, the stand blew over in the wind. But Herman took them to the Italian Market, an open-air market full of wooden stands, and had them get the advice of people who knew about building stands. Robert and the other young men then went back and built another stand and painted it white as mandated by L&I. L&I also required them to bring the whole thing downtown for inspection. Herman intervened again and arranged through the district police captain to have the inspector come to them.

At first the young men purchased fruit from the docks, took it back to their community, and set up shop on a busy thoroughfare. People did begin purchasing fruit and vegetables from them. The boys were heartened by how easy it seemed to start up something legitimate. But Herman also told them about other important requirements of becoming small businessmen: issues like licenses and inspections, bookkeeping, and taxes. The young men were undaunted and attempted to rise to the occasion. At this point Herman approached various professors at the University of Pennsylvania, including myself. One professor at the Wharton School invited the young men to attend one of his seminars, making them the focus of a class on small-time entrepreneurship.

The class involved the nuts and bolts of starting up a small business. In the classroom Robert and the others encountered young white and black students of the Wharton School, not to mention a professor who was interested in them and their future. They were all ears, listening attentively and taking copious notes. The students and the professor provided them with much needed advice, but they also gave them accounting and tax books. The young men took it all in and left the class with their minds brimming with ideas about business. In addition, they occasionally attended my class on urban sociology, learning from, but also contributing to, the discourse. It seemed as though their dreams were being realized, if as yet only in a small way; they were gaining positive reinforcement for making constructive changes in their lives, and they were also learning something worthwhile.

Ever since the young men have had the stand up and operating, Robert has been the most consistent worker. He is serious and focused, the one who gets the fruit every day, stocks the shelves, and sells it in all kinds of weather. Having also acquired an aluminum hot dog stand that he began operating across the street, he literally runs back and forth between the two stands. In addition, he is what people in the community would call "free-hearted," sometimes giving away food when people ask for it, telling them to pay him when they get the money. His generosity cuts down on profits, but he still clears one to two hundred dollars a day. Now just a shadow of his former large-living, materialistic self, Robert is resigned to making do with relatively little. At the stand he calls passersby over and enjoins them to buy something or, if they can't do that, simply to contribute something "to the cause." And people do.

Robert's popularity and reputation in the community account in part for the group's success. His neighbors, friends, and relatives generally want to see him succeed. But the group has its detractors, most often among old friends who are still involved in the drug trade. When these people see Robert standing on the corner selling fruit, they mock him and the others. At times they flash their considerable wads of cash, or "cheese," as they call it, and laugh, putting Robert and his partners down as "little Hermans." While a term of derision in the minds of street toughs and hoodlums, "little Hermans" is a complimentary term in the minds of many upstanding men of the community, men who are now old heads "raised" by Herman and who remember with pride when they were little Hermans. Many of these men today work to follow the lead of Herman, in trying to revitalize their community and to rid it of drugs, violence, and other social scourges. When labeled little Hermans by their street peers, Robert and the others pretend to be unfazed, but they are in fact challenged and encouraged to settle on their new identity, trying out the role of "upstanding young men" of their community and, in fits and starts, learning to appreciate the positive connotations of the term "little Hermans." But serious as they are about turning their lives around and serving the community and its children as positive role models, the boys are beginning to confront the truth that this is not an easy or simple process.

For instance, as Robert and the boys experience success, they face the problem of how to make the transition from underground hustling activities to legal entrepreneurship—or, as Robert puts it, from "underground ghetto-nomics to above-ground economics"—and attain a semblance of organization. While Robert takes his role very seriously and usually does exactly what is required, he cannot always motivate the others to be as consistent in doing their parts. Still, he rarely complains. The group seldom engages in casting blame ortrading recriminations. One major operating principle the group has developed is that people do "what they are strong at." Robert knows he is strong at selling and at public relations. The others have their strengths as well. Two are still in high school. It may on the surface look as though the others are simply using Robert—getting over on him—but he does not see things this way. He contends that they are all working together toward the common goal of improving their lives and, by extension, their community.

From time to time minor conflicts and arguments over strategy arise, but they tend not to become very serious. The young men have a high threshold for physicality; they might raise their voices at one another, but then it stops. When explaining why they never get physical, they say, "We grew up together, and we're like brothers." Of course, their old ideology of alienation from mainstream society is a complicating factor in their transition. To be sure, many decent people may work two or three jobs to make ends meet or pick up some kind of more or less legal hustle, join forces with their relatives, or barter and trade favors and services with their neighbors and friends. People associated with the criminal element, on the other hand, tend to justify their criminal behavior by reference to racism, which they and their friends and neighbors face daily. Some of them remember the racism they have endured from whites and from the black "system operators," who are seen as standing in and acting as proxies for the white power structure.

Accordingly, many of those who remain part of the underground economy are quite embittered, if not profoundly alienated from the wider system, believing that this system is absolutely unfair to black people. Rather than feeling connected to the wider society and emulating it, they suspect and distrust anyone associated with mainstream institutions. They often demand that other blacks show solidarity with them. This orientation can—and does to some extent for Robert—inhibit a full conversion to participation in the world of L&I, Wharton, and legitimate, visible forms of entrepreneurship.

Robert's ambivalence became apparent one afternoon in early January 1998, while I was standing with him at his hot dog stand, watching him sell hot dogs. A customer approached once every ten or fifteen minutes. In between customers Robert was also manning-the fruit stand across the street and engaging in conversation with friends who happened by there as well. Because of his status on the street, younger and older fellows alike would often come by for advice.

Suddenly, a city L&I truck pulled up. Out hopped a black man of about fifty in the company of a forty-five-year-old black woman. They demanded to see Robert's license for the hot dog stand. Now, Robert had acquired the 1998 license, but had neglected to carry it on his person. In fact, he had misplaced the paperwork for the 1998 license and only had the sticker for 1997, which was displayed on his stand. He pointed out the sticker to the man, but the inspector insisted, "I need the current license."

When Robert could not produce the license, the inspector, clearly not inclined to give him a break, became gruff. Robert tried to explain that he had been there for a while and that he did in fact have his license but had lost it. The man was unmoved; he simply said, "This will be a lesson to you to get your license." I tried to intervene, explaining the situation, and asked if he could not just give Robert a warning. "This *is* a warning," he snapped, and I said nothing more. After a little more tense conversation between the two, Robert turned to me and said, "See how hard it is to fit into this system?" Then he muttered under his breath, "System operator," referring to the black man. The inspector overheard the comment, and the tension escalated.

Robert next invoked the name of the district police captain, who had been quite supportive of him and is a strong advocate of community policing. But this apparently carried no weight with the inspector, who proceeded to lecture Robert some more on the need for paperwork. Finally, he filled out a report form, which he wanted Robert to sign immediately. "Here, sign this," he said. "I got to read it first," said Robert. After a few seconds, the inspector became impatient, and said, "All right, all right," taking the clipboard and form and writing at the bottom where Robert's signature was to go, "Refused to sign." Robert then became outright angry, complaining about not having had enough time to read the form. People passing by looked over at what appeared to be the beginning of a commotion. A crowd was beginning to form. The inspector would not discuss the matter further, telling Robert he would have to go downtown now to deal with the matter. In the meantime, the inspector said, "You must cease operations right now, and if I see you operating, I'll confiscate it [the stand]. I've got a hook on this truck," he added, pointing to the back of his truck.

Robert stood fuming and frustrated. Clearly, he saw the inspector as picking on him—a young black man trying to abide by the system, trying to go straight, but getting no support from people he thought should be helping him the most: other black people who should know all about the racism of the system and so should collude with him against it. He could not understand why this man would not give him a break.

This alienation from "the system" and the belief that blacks have to mobilize against it helps to legitimate—for its participants—the code of the street, settling scores personally, going for oneself. The inspector sees himself as just doing his job. But Robert has his doubts. He feels that, because of politics and racism, the inspector would never go to the Italian Market and "pick on them, because he'd lose his job in two seconds. You don't see him coming after the Koreans either. He just gon' pick on another black man." Robert wants the inspector to be what is often called a "race man," but the inspector wants to see himself as a "professional." So he goes by the book and demands that Robert obey the rules and hold to the notion "that race doesn't enter into it." Robert views it very differently, though; he thinks the inspector is betraying his race.

Most people like Robert who are trying to make the transition from street to decent, to negotiate the wider system, eventually run up against this problem. Robert wants the system to be racially particularistic, to recognize him as an individual with his own problems and needs for special treatment and collusion against the system, but the system does not always cooperate.

On the street, in his old life as a drug dealer, a person like Robert could, and did, demand that others "make way" for him. In his street world he had a particular reputation, or name, and a history of resorting to violence to make sure that they did. He carried a gun. In giving all that up, he has stepped into a world where he has no particular status—where L&I doesn't fear him or want to please him. And because he carries no gun, his old friends on the street do not need to make way for him either. He has thus entered a kind of limbo with regard to his status and the rules that govern the management and outcome of conflicts involving him.

An illustration of his loss of power on the street came up recently when Robert was putting away his hot dog stand for the evening, locking it up in a fenced lot. While he was doing this, his backpack, which contained his licenses and other paperwork, was lying on the ground. While his back was turned, someone took the backpack. When he finished, Robert noticed the theft and became livid. Nobody would rob a drug dealer, he felt, for fear of being shot in retaliation, but "they" robbed him. In Robert's analysis, the people who took the bag knew they had a guardian angel in Herman because "they knew Herman would talk Robert out of doing something foolish to retaliate."

As Robert told me the story, I pointed out that the thief could simply have been a crack addict who made no such calculations. Robert admitted that he didn't know, but he said, "Even crack addicts have sense [know how far they can go with whom]. It makes you wonder, Is it better to be loved or feared?" In this comment Robert seemed to question his new orientation.

Yet his analysis is revealing in that it shows his awareness that as he makes his transition to a decent life he is losing something very important on the street—credibility, props (deference), and, ultimately, protection. The whole point of the street posture is to let people know, "If you mess with me, there will be consequences. Don't count on the law. Don't count on the cops. It's me and you." That's the essence of the street code. Robert's experience can be held up and studied as an example in microcosm of the difficulty of making the transition from the street to the decent world of law-abiding people who commit themselves to what might be seen as a code apart from the code of the street, a code of civility.

The problem for Robert is that as he leaves his old life and moves toward his new life, he is also entering what Victor Turner has called a "liminal status," becoming somewhat marginal to both groups. In this sense he also becomes weakened as a player in the neighborhood. Furthermore, the fact that Robert is now on parole means there are certain rules he absolutely must follow. If he engages in any form of violence, he risks returning to jail. He knows this, and the others know it as well. To survive in this community, one must be able to wield the credible threat of violence. It is not that the person must always engage in violent acts; rather, he must be able to threaten violence at some point to keep the "knuckle-heads" in line. Clearly, Robert cannot credibly threaten violence without jeopardizing his own freedom. Assuming this, some of the young men will try and test Robert, probing to see just what they can get away with in their dealings with him.

Over the months since his release from jail, Robert has been tested a number of times, from both sides of the fence. A probation officer recently placed him in handcuffs, only to let him go and apologize. Robert was provoked and very disturbed, for he could see no reason for such treatment, and later the officer could not give a good reason for it either. But the incident allowed Robert to see just how vulnerable he now was to the whims of individuals charged with upholding the system.

More recently, Robert has been forced to confront the tension between the street and the decent world even more directly. He has accepted a business proposition from a woman in the neighborhood, Ms. Newbill. For many years Ms. Newbill has been operating a carryout restaurant on the corner across from Robert's fruit stand. Lately, however, drug dealers have taken to hanging around, inter-cepting Ms. Newbill's customers. Part of what makes the carryout attractive for the drug dealers is that people hang out there: it is busy with traffic, and the dealers can blend in with the young people who are simply standing on the corner, and even sell drugs to some of them.

While Ms. Newbill was there alone, this is what they did. Police driving by couldn't always distinguish between the drug dealers and the kids just hanging out. In fact, adapting to the code, otherwise law-abiding and decent youths at times develop an interest in being confused with those who are hard-core street, because such a pos-ture makes them feel strong and affords them an aura of protection, even allowing them to "go for bad"—or pretend they too are tough.

Because of the presence of drug dealers, Ms. Newbill's business-declined, since few people wanted to run an obstacle course to buy sodas and hamburgers. When she complained about this to the dealers, their response was to rob her store at gunpoint. They also vandalized her automobile, which she parked outside the store. Wanting no further trouble, she had an inspiration. She offered to lease the deli section of the business to Robert for $800 per month in the hope that his presence, as a person with respect and props, could deter the drug dealers. Robert has accepted the challenge. He feels it's a good deal, just the opportunity he's been looking for to become a legitimate businessman and not just a street vendor. On his first day he made $91. If he can maintain that level of profit, he thinks, he can make a go of the business.

This involvement has given Robert an even bigger stake in the corner the store occupies, across the street from the fruit stand. He, Ms. Newbill, and the drug dealers all know this. One of the many ironies here is that in his previous life Robert established himself as a drug dealer on this very corner and, to this day, feels he can claim some "ownership" rights to it. In fact, he introduced to the drug trade the young dealers with whom he is now competing for the corner. And, invoking his "rights," he has told them that they must take their drugs off his corner, because they harm his legitimate business, that by continuing to sell, they are disrespecting him, or dissing him. Yet they still want to sell drugs on the corner and say they are entitled to do so because "this is where [they] grew up." Robert answers that they must be responsible young men and not defile their neighborhood. He also points out to them that such "defilement" hurts his own business, and thus must cease.

Before Robert was incarcerated, his was a big name in the neighborhood. He was an enforcer for a drug-dealing gang. This role gave him great props on the streets, indicating that he was not to be messed with. But now, as was pointed out above, he can be only a shadow of his former self, because such displays of violent behavior could get him arrested and reincarcerated. Having publicly come out as a little Herman, and a legitimate businessperson, he finds himself in a dilemma: Does he revert to his street self in pursuit of decent goals?

It's a predicament that Robert must confront on his own. He knows it, and his antagonists know it. They all know that the police are not the main players here, the ones to "get cool" with; rather, the "beef" is between Robert and the drug dealers. These are the people with whom he must now achieve a new understanding. They are testing his mettle, probing for weakness, to see if he is the same old Ruck. Much suggests to them that he is not. Above all, he is now on parole and thus must watch his step in dealing with people the way he would have dealt with them "back in the day," or the old days; moreover, his close association with Herman is something of a liability on the street.

Robert has been going through a gradual transformation, shedding his "old skin" and identity of Ruck and taking on his new identity of Robert, or Rob. His former street cronies constantly address him by his street name of Ruck, while the decent people of the community, people he is getting to know better, address him more consistently as Robert.

If Rob resolves the current tension and passes the test, he will be much stronger than he was before, garnering juice, or respect, and credibility from others he meets on the street. Bear in mind, Rob already has credibility and respect from many of the decent people who know him and what he has been up against; many are cheering for him, the celebrity of the neighborhood. It is the street element, specifically the local drug gang, that he must now impress. For his part, Herman understands that he must not fight this battle for Rob, that Rob must fight it for himself. After all, he will not always be with Rob. Choc is Rob's main opponent in the contest for the corner in front of Ms. Newbill's. He grew up and has been living in the area for a long time, and, as was indicated earlier, Rob helped raise him and introduce him to the drug trade. Choc's mother still lives in the area, just a few doors away from Rob's store.

Soon after taking control of the store, Rob confronted Choc about his drug-dealing activities. He said, "Listen, Choc, this has to stop. If you want to sell drugs, go somewhere else. You not gon' do it here. Go sit on your mother's step and sell. Don't sell in front of my business." Choc responded, "Why you want to do that [keep us from selling drugs here]? You know how it is. I got to eat. I got to make a living, too. Why you want to be so hard?" Rob answered that he also had to make a living and that the drug dealers were hurting his business. They could sell somewhere else; they did not have to sell on his corner. Choc responded that this is where his mother lives: "I grew up here, so I can do what I want. I'll die for this [corner], 'cause I got to eat. And ain't nobody gon' stop me from eating." Rob asked, "Is that how you feel?" Choc bellowed, "Yeah!" "All right, I'm gon' talk to your mama about it and see if she feel the same way."

Many people in the neighborhood are aware of the present tension around the corner by Ms. Newbill's. A beef has been created and infused with a certain social significance. People want to know what is going to happen next. Will Rob back down? Or will the boys back down? Either way, the result carries implications for the community and the local status order. Core elements of the code of the street are heavily in play: Can I take care of myself without going to the authorities? Do I have enough juice or personal power to do what I want? The metaphor of a chess game is not lost, as both Rob and Choc consider their next moves, with everyone anxiously looking on. Ostensibly, it is between them and nobody else. In fact, it is over who is going to rule the community in the long run—the decent folks or the street element. The struggle over the corner may be viewed as simply one battle in a war.

In trying out strategies for winning, Rob offered a scenario of what he might do in regard to Choc. He said, "I'm gon' go tell his mother, that if I crack him in his head he won't be selling drugs there. Now, there are three corners that he can't sell on: where I got the fruit stand, where Ms. Newbill's place is, and in front of the library or gym. He can go over to the vacant lot where the gas station used to be. I'll tell him, 'You can sell over there because my customers don't come that way,' but he knows that place is in the open, and Captain Perez [leader of local district] will get him if he do that. 'You can't sell on any other corner. But since you are gonna sell anyway, go over and sell on the vacant gas station lot.'" Rob knew that setting up business there would put Choc in the open so the captain could see him, and everyone knew that the captain was not to be trifled with.

Choc then sent five others of the local community to warn Rob, as a way both of getting the message back to Rob and of obtaining feedback on the situation and drumming up support: "Rob is gonna find himself with some problems" was a common sentiment. These five people, one by one, came back to Rob his first day on the job at Ms. Newbill's and told him what Choc had said—"that he will find himself in some problems." And they would inquire of Rob, "What's going on?" or "You closing down drug corners, now?" or "Choc feels some type o' way about all this [he's mad]."

Herman and I were at Ms. Newbill's on Rob's first day as the proprietor of his new business there. Rob made us cheesesteaks and then came and sat with us. It was clear that he was not himself. He was somewhat agitated, and his street antennae were on high alert, as he glanced back and forth at the front door, studying everyone who entered. Suddenly he said, "Did you see that? Did you see that?" Herman asked, "What?" "She nodded her head, gave a signal to somebody," replied Rob. We looked up and saw an older woman standing in line to pay for some soap. She was facing the street. We noticed nothing out of the ordinary. But Rob was very concerned. He seems to have thought the woman might be alerting someone outside that we were here: if they wanted us, here we were. This turned out to be nothing.

People entered and left. One person after another warmly greeted Herman, including a man who planted a kiss on the side of his face, with obvious affection and appreciation. Herman answered politely, indicating what we were up to that day: "We're having a Little League practice this evening at six. You got any equipment, a ball, a bat, anything?" The man answered affirmatively: "Yeah, I got something for you. How long you gon' be here?" "Until you get back," answered Herman. The man then left the store and in about ten minutes returned with a baseball bat and a ball. We were very pleased, for the youngsters with whom we were to practice this evening needed this equipment to start up their games.

Soon we received our food and soft drinks. People continued to enter and leave. It was clear that our presence was the support Rob needed. He relaxed, and we had easy talk for the next hour and a half, at which point we left. Every minute we were there, we were putting the word out that drug dealing would not be tolerated on this corner. Herman felt strongly that the young men who were coming and going were letting others know that we were there and that we were committed to being there. And that was what Rob needed on his first day at Ms. Newbill's.

After one man left, Herman said of him confidently, "Yeah, he know Rob will hurt that boy [Choc], so why mess up Rob's future by sending Rob back to jail for killing this nut. He's putting Rob's word out, that Rob is here to stay." The man was a crack addict named Johnny Brown, a mechanic—"the best there is when he can stay off that stuff." Brown is like a neighborhood courier who knows the latest about the neighborhood: "He know everything, including the shooting last night." He will also get the word to the neighborhood that another day has passed and that Rob has not been chased out. Everyone is watching, expectantly, taking in the drama. The atmosphere is something like that of *High Noon*, in part because there were shootouts on this busy, lucrative corner in the past. The stakes, financial and social, are high.

Moments later Maurice's brother Tip (a crack addict) comes in, approaches Rob, and asks, "Do you want me to get rid of him, ol' head? I know you, ol' head." In conversation the use of the term "ol' head" is most often an address of respect, but may also be slightly derisive, depending on the social context. Although the address does not always go by age, anyone over forty years old is considered to be past his prime and generally not as tough as the younger men. Reverent younger men may gently put such people in their place by calling them "ol' head." Rob says of Tip, "I didn't need his help. 'Cause then Tip would have been on the corner. In other words, you can't 'ask a devil to get rid of a devil, because then all you get is another devil.' "

The code of the street says, in certain circumstances, that each person will test the next person, probing to take his measure, in order to know how to behave toward that person. The people who survive respond by showing their tough sides. If they can do that, they deserve to be left alone. Herman comments, "Rob is like a test tube baby. He is an ongoing experiment, and we got to save this one." Herman's role, as it has been all along, is to help Rob through the obstacle course toward civility and decency. Herman can often be heard from the sidelines, coaching, "Now, don't go and bust the man in his face. There is always a better way [than violence]"—this is his constant message.

Because of his relationship with Herman—and Herman's relationship with the police—Rob now and then converses with the local police, who recognize him when they see him on the streets. On one recent afternoon Rob encountered a policeman, who said, "How you doing, Rob?" The local drug dealers see this, too, and their reaction might be "Aw, he's rattin' to the cops." This relationship with the police brings Rob respect and derision at the same time. His goal is to be completely on his own, to establish himself as a decent person in the community with the props of such a person, along with the props of the street life: toughness and decency, which are not easy to manage and to combine. But Rob must do so if he is to exist in the community with the status he would like. Without his knowledge of the code of the street, he would be in more peril. Possessing it is knowing to some degree what to do in what circumstances, and what not to do.

At this point Rob has figured out his next move with the drug dealers, but he does not know how it will work out. He is reluctant to bring Captain Perez into it, for doing so would hurt his long-term status and reputation on the street. Perez might come in with too much police power and authority, and that would lead the others on the street to say, "Aw, he had to bring in the police. Aw, he's just a pussy, he went and got them to help him." Not to involve the police will give Rob more "heart" on the corner, on the street, where standoffs like this must be settled "man to man."

According to the code, the man goes for himself, takes up for himself, and calls on no one else to fight his battles. Whether he is successful or not in dealing with the situation man to man, the outcome will become known around the neighborhood, and his status on the street will be affected. To have to resort to the cops or anyone else is to be judged a chump, to have lost heart. He loses "stripes," or respect, because he cannot deal with the threat by the street code. Practically speaking, the police cannot be present all the time. Hence real and enduring protection depends on having a name, a reputation, and credibility for being able to defend what is rightfully one's own, even to the point of engaging in physicality; in a word, the person must get with the challenger, get in his face, and deal with him.

What Rob did was to go see Choc's mother and threaten Choc through her. Standing at the Little League field that evening, he explained to me that he told her that her son's drug dealing in front of the store was hurting his business and that if it did not stop, he would be forced to "handle his business." "So I'm just lettin' you know." "Don't worry about [it], Ruck, I'm gon' talk to him," responded Choc's mother, Mrs. Harmon. "I'm just lettin' you know," Rob repeated, " 'cause I been knowin' y'all for a long time. And I didn't want to just move out like that, without talking to you first. He said he's 'willing to die for the corner.' " Unlike some other mothers, Mrs. Harmon did not deny her son's involvement in the drug trade. She owned up to his dealing drugs in front of the store, expressed her own exasperation with it, and indicated she would handle it.

Telling Choc's mother has turned out to be a deft move on Rob's part because it increases the number of people who can work to defuse the situation. Choc's mother has strong emotional reasons to prevail on her son. It also gives Choc an excuse for capitulating, for, even though he may feel manly and able enough to overcome Rob, he knows he is disturbing his mother. Now he can give in but still save face by telling his boys, "I did it for my mother." For the time being, Rob's strategy seems to have worked. The boys have stopped selling drugs on Ms. Newbill's and Rob's corner. Things have cooled down.

To reiterate, Rob was seen by the boys on the street to be in a weak position both because he was on parole and so had to watch his step and because he had affiliated himself with Herman, whom they view as square, as an informer, as a policeman—"And they can't do anything about it," says Herman. As Rob undergoes his tests, trials, and tribulations, a chorus of old heads cheers him on. For although the old heads do not condone selling drugs, they do observe the code of the street: to be worthy of respect, to be convincing, to be credible on the street, is to display heart, nerve, and manhood at once. Correspondingly, through his actions and words Rob let the dealers know in no uncertain terms that he is ready to do what it takes to be his own man, to put his own physical self in the gap, and to go back to jail if he must for standing his ground. On these issues the local old heads and Rob converge; they all understand that in this environment such an orientation is the mark of a "real" man, and here they refer back to the decent daddy in the person of Mr. Johnson, who is for them the embodiment of decency and manhood.

Rob still confronts major challenges. The test he went through is only one among many he will face in the future. He resides and operates in a community in which most of the residents are decent or trying to be. But there is also a street element that is less decent, poorly educated, alienated, and to some extent angry; finally, there is a criminal element that is not only street-oriented but often also in the business of street hustling and drug-related crime.

Rob has to navigate this environment, not simply as an ordinary person, not as a drug dealer, but as a legitimate businessman operating a carryout. That means that from time to time he has to meet with all kinds of people, some of whom are involved in scams, trying to shoplift, to sell him stolen goods. Every day will bring another test. He'll be tried by drug dealers because his corner is so valuable; it represents capital. As an issue of urban turf, somebody must run that corner: either the police or the drug dealers. In this case, for the time being, Rob is running it. But a new drug gang could come to town, make dibs on this corner, and challenge him. And this time he may not know the man's mother.

Thus far Rob is surviving, and his capital has grown. His business is expanding. Word has gotten around that he's serving food at a decent price and declaring that he's not putting up with the drug activity on the corner. The neighborhood has breathed a sigh of relief, and now people visit the store in large numbers. One man likened the situation to "sunshine after the rain, and now that the sun is out, the people have returned." Rob likens it to there being "a new sheriff in town," and his presence signals a new day for the "Stop and Go." Before the standoff between Rob and the drug dealers, many community residents, particularly the decent people,

stayed away. But since he has won—at least for the time being—
they have returned. The whole situation is public. Rob has in effect
retaken the corner, and his accomplishment affects not just that
corner but the whole neighborhood as well. For several blocks
around, a sphere of influence has been created that Rob controls
and the drug dealers are keeping out of. If the community could
take back more such corners, perhaps some real progress could be
made in shifting the balance of power from the street-oriented people to the decent people.

The task is difficult because Rob is navigating an environment of
so many alienated people, some of them without hope, some of
them ready to try to pull him down—for as he rises, they may feel
a sharp drop in their own self-esteem. As he gains more legitimate
clout, however, his influence spreads through the neighborhood and
he becomes a role model for those who lack direction or have fallen
into the street life: he has visibly pulled himself up and thus offers
them a profoundly different way out of the street. His example,
shows this way can work.

Yet it is a fine understanding of the code of the street that enables
Rob to survive the many physical standoffs that characterize ghetto
street life. It is by deftly interpreting and abiding by the rules of the
code that he is able to get through his days and nights, to manage
the respect necessary to keep the drug dealers, scam artists and others at bay, or in line. At the same time he must function in the
decent world as well, in the world of legitimate business practice—
licences, tax laws, and the like. The inner-city success story
therefore requires the ability to code-switch, to play by the code of
the street with the street element and by the code of decency with
others. Rob can do that, and in the process he works at setting an
example for other young people. In addition, he is helping organize
a Little League team and has plans for a Cub Scout den, the kinds
of groups that build up the community's institutions. Rob has thus
become an old head for today, a present-day young Mr. Johnson—
both creating opportunity and getting people to see the opportunity
and taking responsibility for helping themselves.

Rob's environment is one of persistent, concentrated urban poverty. Other such areas in the city include the neighborhoods of

Chelten and Germantown Avenues, Nicetown, Eighth and Butler, Thirteenth and Fitzwater, and Southwest—communities that thirty years ago were poor but safe, well maintained, and committed to standards of behavior fundamentally similar to those prevalent in more prosperous neighborhoods. People who remember those days, notably the old heads, are particularly alive to the tragically changed situation of today, which they characterize as a lost sense of security. Such people often stand around on corners or meet in one another's homes and talk about how it used to be: how young people would respect their elders, how houses and yards were kept up, how it was safe to walk the streets, how men worked and families stayed together so that most children lived in two-parent households, how many children looked forward to going to college, how drugs were far away.

The solution, as they see it, is to create more of the Mr. Johnsons of the past. Mr. Johnson, who most easily mimicked the decent daddy of the wider society, believed in a man's responsibility to take care of his family and his community. Mr. Johnson, say the old heads of today, would know what to do in the current situation. He would know how to protect the mothers and daughters and grandmothers. Of course, there is a certain sexism in this orientation, which harks back to gender relations of generations past.

Generally, the old heads have a particularly hard time understanding the profound alienation from which the oppositional culture has emerged. In that culture what is good in the community is that which opposes conventional society. For the old heads such a standard flies in the face of everything they know to be good and decent. And they fail to credit the structural aspects of the community's problem; they fervently believe that to approach troublemakers with such an explanation would simply encourage them, offering a rationalization or even just an excuse for the troubled young people to continue in their errant and irresponsible ways. Furthermore, they often deemphasize the reality of ghettoized second-class citizenship that so many inner-city residents are saddled with.

The decent people seldom form anything like a critical mass in the impoverished pockets of the city; more often, such places are replete with single-headed households of mothers and children, typically on welfare. In an environment where such people are present en masse and where the structural factors buffet the community, producing the drug dealers followed by stickup boys and other violent people, it is hard for the decent people to survive with their decency totally intact. Like Rob, and others profiled in this book, they must often wield the credible threat of violence in order to maintain their own dignity, at times putting their own lives on the line over little things that in their communities can so easily become contentious social issues. The quality of life that people may take for granted in other communities is not there for them. Hence, in the name of survival, they may find themselves at times acting, and even encouraging their children to act, in rather indecent ways, resulting in a generalized "streeting down" of the community. Such scenarios tend to occur, as we saw in Rob's case, in the most impoverished areas of the city, areas of profound social isolation; away from such areas there is likely to be a greater degree of civility, as the ratio of decent people to street-oriented people improves.

It must be stated again that the attitudes and actions of the wider society are deeply implicated in the code of the street. Most people residing in inner-city communities are not totally invested in the code; it is the significant minority of hard-core street youths who maintain the code in order to establish reputations that are integral to the extant social order. Because of the grinding poverty of the communities these people inhabit, many have—or feel they have—few other options for expressing themselves. For them the standards and rules of the street code are the only game in town.

And as was indicated above, the decent people may find themselves caught up in problematic situations simply by being at the wrong place at the wrong time, which is why a primary survival strategy of residents here is to "see but don't see." The extent to which some children—particularly those who through upbringing have become most alienated and those who lack strong and conventional social support—experience, feel, and internalize racist rejection and contempt from mainstream society may strongly encourage them to express contempt for that society in turn. In dealing with this contempt and rejection, some youngsters consciously invest themselves and their considerable mental resources in what amounts to an oppositional culture, a part of which is the code of the street. They do so to preserve themselves and their own self-respect. Once they do, any respect they might be able to garner in the wider system pales in comparison with the respect available in the local system; thus they often lose interest in even attempting to negotiate the mainstream system.

At the same time, as has been stressed throughout this volume, many less alienated young people have assumed a street-oriented demeanor as way of expressing their blackness while really embracing a much more moderate way of life; they, too, want a nonviolent setting in which to live and one day possibly raise a family. These decent people are trying hard to be part of the mainstream culture, but the racism, real and perceived, that they encounter helps legitimate the oppositional culture and, by extension, the code of the street. On occasion they adopt street behavior; in fact, depending on the demands of the situation, many people attempt to code-switch, moving back and forth between decent and street behavior.

Rob is caught up in a subculture that is a function of alienation and the social isolation that results from it—a culture rife with bad schooling, racism, poverty, and the devastations of drugs and violence. Crime is rampant there, but the police tolerate a good deal of it out of concern for their own safety. Captain Perez is more engaged, but most officers basically try to maintain order without hurting themselves. In addition, the community is composed of working-class and very poor people since those with the means to move away have done so, and there has also been a proliferation of single-parent households in which increasing numbers of kids are being raised on welfare. The result of all this is that the inner-city community has become a kind of urban village, apart from the wider society and limited in terms of resources and human capital. Young people growing up here often receive only the truncated version of mainstream society that comes from television and the perceptions of their peers.

In this kind of world Rob survives by the code of the street. It is the code that he has grown up with and that has given him his philosophy, his orientation, and his notions of right and wrong, racial particularism, and white society. According to the code, the white man is a mysterious entity, a part of an enormous monolithic mass of arbitrary power, in whose view black people are insignificant. In this system and in the local social context, the black man has very little clout; to salvage something of value, he must outwit, deceive, oppose, and ultimately "end-run" the system.

Moreover, he cannot rely on this system to protect him; the responsibility is his, and he is on his own. If someone rolls on him, he has to put his body, and often his life, on the line. The physicality of manhood thus becomes extremely important. And urban brinksmanship is observed and learned as a matter of course. This general situation has provided a training ground for Rob and many others like him. And this presuppositional framework is what he brings to bear on his aspiration to become a legitimate businessman. He reasons that what is valid for a gang-banger or a drug dealer on the street is to an extent also valid for a ghetto businessman operating out of Ms. Newbill's store. Other black ghetto proprietors often feel similarly. That is why Rob cannot call the cops to handle the drug dealers on his corner. The police will arrive and quickly leave, whereas he must live there for the long haul. He thus becomes invested in the local people's law and in its corresponding street justice, a response to the dysfunctional wider system.

These urban areas have experienced profound structural economic changes, as deindustrialization—the movement from manufacturing to service and high-tech—and the growth of the global economy have created new economic conditions. Job opportunities increasingly go abroad to Singapore, Taiwan, India, and Mexico, and to nonmetropolitan America, to satellite cities like King of Prussia, Pennsylvania. Over the last fifteen years, for example, Philadelphia has lost 102,500 jobs, and its manufacturing employment has declined by 53 percent. Large numbers of inner-city people, in particular, are not adjusting effectively to the new economic reality. Whereas low-wage jobs—especially unskilled and low-skill factory jobs—used to exist simultaneously with poverty and there was hope for the future, now jobs simply do not exist, the present economic boom notwithstanding. These dislocations have left many inner-city people unable to earn a decent living. More must be done by both government and business to connect inner-city people with jobs.

The condition of these communities was produced not by moral turpitude but by economic forces that have undermined black, urban, working-class life and by a neglect of their consequences on the part of the public. Although it is true that persistent welfare dependency, teenage pregnancy, drug abuse, drug dealing, violence, and crime reinforce economic marginality, many of these behavioral problems originated in frustration and the inability to thrive under conditions of economic dislocation. This in turn leads to a weakening of social and family structure, so children are increasingly not being socialized into mainstream values and behavior. In this context, people develop profound alienation and may not know what to do about an opportunity even when it presents itself. In other words, the social ills that the companies moving out of these neighborhoods today sometimes use to justify their exodus are the same ones that their corporate predecessors, by leaving, helped to create.

Any effort to place the blame solely on individuals in urban ghettos is seriously misguided. The focus should be on the socioeconomic structure, because it was structural change that caused jobs to decline and joblessness to increase in many of these communities. But the focus also belongs on the public policy that has radically threatened the well-being of many citizens. Moreover, residents of these communities lack good education, job training, and job networks, or connections with those who could help them get jobs. They need enlightened employers able to understand their predicament and willing to give them a chance. Government, which should be assisting people to adjust to the changed economy, is instead cutting what little help it does provide.

While moving people from welfare to work is an important goal that holds promise, in the short term, without enough positions, it merely creates more dislocation and the alienation that goes with that. Field research at various Philadelphia housing projects, particularly Martin Luther King Plaza, at Thirteenth and Fitzwater, and Passyunk Homes, makes it clear that most residents approach "the end of welfare" with tremendous fear and trepidation. They understand full well how scarce jobs are, and how difficult it is for them to qualify for the ones that *are* available. Residents of such places speak of the "impending doom" that will come with the end of welfare. They say their communities will be unlivable, that angry and alienated people will rob and steal from those who "have something." And while this may be true to some degree, what is really needed is a comprehensive plan that will allow no one to fall through the cracks.

People need to be seriously trained for positions that are available, and when they cannot acquire job training off-site, they should be provided with on-the-job training. At the same time the communities from which so many of the welfare recipients come are bereft of human and social capital. And this must be developed if the move from welfare to work is to succeed. Here the social infrastructure will need to be rebuilt. In order to accomplish this, the old heads of the community will have to be empowered and activated. In Rob's community the old heads are activated; they organize block cleanups, Little League, Boy Scouts, Cub Scouts, Campfire Girls, and other enterprises that promise to rebuild their communities. What these highly motivated people often lack is a helping hand from the local municipal and other authorities; they would be pleased to obtain even modest support for their activities. There should be a coordinated effort to assist such grassroots workers, for not to do so is a terrible human waste.

The emergence of an underclass isolated in urban ghettos with high rates of joblessness can be traced to the interaction of race prejudice, discrimination, and the effects of the global economy. These factors have contributed to the profound social isolation and impoverishment of broad segments of the inner-city black population. Even though the wider society and economy have been experiencing accelerated prosperity for almost a decade, the fruits of it often miss the truly disadvantaged isolated in urban poverty pockets.

In their social isolation an oppositional culture, a subset of which is the code of the street, has been allowed to emerge, grow, and develop. This culture is essentially one of accommodation with the wider society, but different from past efforts to accommodate the system. A larger segment of people are now not simply isolated but ever more profoundly alienated from the wider society and its institutions. For instance, in conducting the fieldwork for this book, I visited numerous inner-city schools, including elementary, middle, and high schools, located in areas of concentrated poverty. In every one, the so-called oppositional culture was well entrenched. In one elementary school, I learned from interviewing kindergarten, first-grade, second-grade, and fourth-grade teachers that through the first grade, about a fifth of the students were invested in the code of the street; the rest are interested in the subject matter and eager to take instruction from the teachers—in effect, well disciplined. By the fourth grade, though, about three-quarters of the students have bought into the code of the street or the oppositional culture.

As I have indicated throughout this work, the code emerges from the school's impoverished neighborhood, including overwhelming numbers of single-parent homes, where the fathers, uncles, and older brothers are frequently incarcerated—so frequently, in fact, that the word "incarcerated" is a prominent part of the young child's spoken vocabulary. In such communities there is not only a high rate of crime but also a generalized diminution of respect for law. As the residents go about meeting the exigencies of public life, a kind of people's law results, as was graphically illustrated in the case of Rob. Typically, the local streets are, as we saw, tough and dangerous places where people often feel very much on their own, where they themselves must be personally responsible for their own security, and where in order to be safe and to travel the public spaces unmolested, they must be able to show others that they are familiar with the code—that physical transgressions will be met in kind.

In these circumstances the dominant legal codes are not the first thing on one's mind; rather, personal security for self, family, and loved ones is. Adults, dividing themselves into categories of street and decent, often encourage their children in this adaptation to their situation, but at what price to the children and at what price to wider values of civility and decency? As the fortunes of the inner city continue to decline, the situation becomes ever more dismal and intractable. What are some of the chief consequences of persistent and concentrated poverty and social isolation in inner-city Philadelphia?

The inner-city ghetto economy is delicately balanced between (a) low-income jobs, (b) welfare payments, and (c) the underground economy of drug dealing, prostitution, and street crime. When the regular economy fails or contracts, the other elements tend to pick up the slack, and when these fail, residents become ever more desperate, giving rise to the local irregular economy. The irregular economy may be characterized as a barter system, which works by an exchange of favors. For example, an individual will repair a neighbor's car on the weekend, or help paint someone's steps, or perform a plumbing job, or style someone's hair, but take no money for it; rather, the person will wait to be paid back with a favor in the future.

Another consequence of concentrated poverty is the increasing alienation of so many people, particularly the young, who see all around them—on TV and elsewhere—opportunities and material things that they want but cannot obtain. Frustrated by their deprivations, they may turn to occupations that will satisfy their needs. Since the underground economy promises to do so, there is a close connection between poverty, alienation, and the underground economy.

When alienation becomes so entrenched, an oppositional culture can develop and flourish. This culture, especially among the young, gains strength and legitimacy by opposing the dominant society and its agents. But such opposition produces ever more alienation, and lines become hardened, polarities develop. And people, particularly young black males, become demonized. Those who experience contempt from society often cannot enjoy self-respect without dishing out contempt in return. Though certainly not espoused by all, this attitude gains sanction in inner-city communities among residents who can identify with the alienated, often angry street element, even while trying to keep it at arm's length.

But such distancing behavior becomes all the more complex when the whole community is victimized. In this context the community may get a bad name, while residents themselves, notably black males, are demonized. The resulting stereotypes are then so broadly applied that anyone from the community who dresses that way, who looks that way, is thereby placed at odds with conventional society. This underscores the huge communication gap between different urban neighborhoods, as well as between such neighborhoods and the broader society. The stereotyped person is often caught in a horrendous bind, because, though completely decent, he or she may take up this way of dressing, this way of looking, this way of acting, in order not only to preserve a measure of self-respect but to survive the street. But by such accommodation the person becomes further alienated from society, which has sought distance precisely in order to protect itself from people who, it assumes, are out to violate its norms, values, rules, and conventions. Such assessments exacerbate the unemployability of these young people. Moreover, employers sometimes discriminate against entire census tracts or zip codes because they cannot or will not distinguish the decent people from those neighborhoods. For too many who reside outside the ghetto, employers among them, the decent people outwardly resemble the indecent people; there is an easy confusion and no great need to worry about making distinctions. Many outsiders simply wish to avoid the ghetto and its inhabitants altogether.

Persistent poverty and joblessness also profoundly weaken the inner-city family unit. The existence of welfare has encouraged dependency, to be sure, but without jobs and income what other alternative exists? In these circumstances a culture of dependency has emerged and developed, in which young people are born and reared with the expectation that welfare, or "aid" (as community residents put it), will be there for them. This expectation has encouraged too many inner-city girls and boys to approach sexual activity carelessly. An underlying cause of teenage pregnancy is a lack of a sense of future. A baby becomes an extension of a young woman, of her family, and she often has as role models her sisters, her mother, and sometimes even her grandmothers, as well as neighbors and close friends—women who in her view are "doing all right." When the baby arrives, the ready welfare check has allowed young men to abdicate their responsibilities and to define "making babies" as a virtue. This is made all the easier when joblessness awaits the young men. Here, the decent daddy of old, the Mr. Johnson of community folklore, becomes a hard act to follow. In order to be an upstanding family head, a man must have a decent job. Without decent jobs, and the ready availability of welfare, the man in the role of provider can be and often is rendered irrelevant. With the availability of decent jobs, men and women can more easily form viable families, and their young people can more readily learn to value the future—and the profound alienation so widespread in many urban ghettos becomes less common.

When a critical mass of jobless people are concentrated in the inner-city community, various factors come together and conspire to produce an almost intractable result. In these circumstances alienation thrives, and little that is conventional retains legitimacy. The most desperate people, particularly the young and aimless, become mired in a kind of outlaw culture, one that nonetheless becomes legitimate to its adherents because the wider system, which seems at every turn to display its contempt for them and their community, has little legitimacy. And here dependency comes full circle. Welfare—or anything else of value offered by the wider society—is simply something to exploit, and one can gain status points for having done so. In this perspective even crime, especially when committed against people representing the wider society—and those who "have something" become worthy targets—can be considered not simply challenging and feasible but legitimate. As a result, sanctions are all the more profoundly undermined, and many residents feel under siege.

Amid so much deprivation street crime is a daily occurrence. A working assumption in the community is that criminals and "stickup boys" pick their people. Thus, it becomes important to avoid being picked as a victim of crime, and one does that by a kind of public vigilance, keeping an eye on everyone and anyone who "bears watching," who could perpetrate a crime. But equally important—and this is the central theme of this book—street life in the impoverished inner-city neighborhood is often dangerous and highly stressful for its residents, at times imperceptibly so. It is sometimes not until a person moves or travels away from such a place that he or she comes to appreciate the level of relaxation missed in the inner-city neighborhood. A key aspect of this is the social experience of constantly having to watch one's back and to deal in other ways with the ever-present violence.

In the community the police are often on the streets, but they are not always considered to have the community's best interests at heart. A great many residents have little trust in the police. Many assume that the police hold the black community in low repute and sometimes will abuse its members. As a result, residents are alienated from the police and police authority. With this attitude many people are afraid to report obvious drug dealing or other crimes to the police, for fear that the police might reveal their names and addresses to the criminals. It is thus better, many say, "to see but don't see." One is better off if one can simply avoid the problem; only in a dire emergency should one involve the police. Residents sometimes fail to call the police because they believe that the police are unlikely to come or, if they do come, may even harass the very people who called them. This is an experience unfamiliar to most middle-class people.

In the inner-city community there is a generalized belief that the police simply do not care about black people, that when a crime is committed in the black community, little notice will be taken. If a black man shoots another black man, the incident will not be thoroughly investigated. A double standard of justice is thought to exist: one for black people, and one for whites. This distrust is fueled by the lawlessness that is observed on the local streets of the community, most notably in the presence of open-air drug dealing and the prevalence of functional crack houses.[1] Residents often note that such people and places would not be allowed to operate in the white community, but they thrive in the black community. Such observations reinforce people's belief that they are on their own, and this attitude has crucial implications for the code of the street, as I have argued in this work. The following account of a thirty-five-year-old black male residing in an impoverished inner-city neighborhood is germane:

> The thing about it is [this]: I was in a situation when someone pull a gun on me. [Afterward] I went directly to the [local] police station, tried to do the right thing. The rules is this: you gotta have a address of the person. I tell them I know the vicinity they live in, I know their nickname. They don't even [want to] talk to you. You can check it out with the Philadelphia law—they don't even talk to you. See, that's a for instance. So now, what am I supposed to do now? If you go down there and you don't have the name and the address of the person . . . I know 'cause

I saw the person—that don't count. Now, I gotta protect myself. I worry about that. I be paranoid. I live here. I can't move away from this thing. I got kids and stuff like that. So what am I gonna do now? You tell me. . . .

When the cops come, they don't even wanta take a report half the time. You can tell they not gonna do nothin'. You know they not gonna do nothin'. You get stuck up, they don't even look. And people [the law-abiding and the criminals] know. So that's why people takin' things they don't have. That's why everybody got a gun on and all that stuff.

What's the bottom line significance? Who is the system constructed to protect? Tell me. Is it to protect the ones that live around the corner here in these grass roots? . . . I'm just lookin' at the weeds. Would you have that in your neighborhood? There's like three lots back there. . . . They found bodies in these lots within the last year or so. The police came around here. The newspeople came around here. Da-da-da. We seen a lot of lights. The next year after that I seen the same grass right there again. We got abandoned houses. We got babies dying on Similac. We got, what, welfare programs gettin' cut. We got mothers runnin' around. What?

Get worse now. How's it gonna get any worse?

The sound of sirens pierces the air, as police cars speed by. The man continues,

So what? We live with that every day. Here come the cops—so what? What they gonna do? They gonna run up here, they gonna say a few words, and then what? The technicalities of how a officer can get himself involved—look, if a cop's up on that corner and somebody get his ass beat on this corner, if the cop don't see it, he can't do nothin'. That's what they tellin' us. I can get my butt beat around the corner, run to the police, tell him, "He did it!," and he still tell me he can't do nothin'. See, *this* is where we live at.

"Abandoned is what you are," chimes in another ghetto resident who has just walked up. The first man continues,

> He [the policeman] could be sittin' right there on the corner having his lunch. I could be getting my brains kicked out around the corner. I run to the police, I tell him, and he say, "I can't do nothin' unless you file a report." By the time that happens, what am I supposed to do? Am I supposed to let this joker [the assailant] keep contending on me, beatin' me when he see me?

## IN CONCLUSION

In a sea of destitution there are increasing numbers of street kids who are out scavenging. At the extreme are those who are living on the street, sleeping in cars and abandoned houses. But there are also kids who have families but little adult supervision; they get raised mainly by the street. Their home lives are often severely compromised by joblessness and drugs. These children—they can be as young as ten—are often out on the streets at ten and eleven o'clock at night, sometimes mugging people for money.

All these social consequences of persistent urban poverty and joblessness coalesce into acute alienation from mainstream society and its institutions, especially among the young. What has formed as a result is a kind of institutionalized oppositional culture, a reaction to a history of prejudice and discrimination that now finds its way into schools and other institutions; it makes meaningful participation in institutions dominated by those closely associated with the wider society problematic, if not impossible, for many. The most public manifestation of this alienation is the code of the street, a kind of adaptation to a lost sense of security of the local inner-city neighborhood and, by extension, a profound lack of faith in the police and the judicial system.

In dealing with these problems, society needs to take a number of initiatives—above all, the development of jobs that pay a living wage.

We also need political leadership that articulates the problem and presses hard to build coalitions that invest themselves in efforts to secure full inner-city enfranchisement.

It is understandable that the traditional old heads and other decent people of the community should focus on the idea of individual responsibility. These people believe that whatever success they have achieved in their own lives has been the result of personal determination, and thus they are inclined to blame those who have not been successful for not having made enough of an effort. Not to blame the victim would be to make it too easy for those victims of inner-city problems. And it would give the decent people no way of distinguishing themselves from the street people. Therefore, even though the old heads are aware of the existence of discrimination and joblessness, their solution is to build up the grit of the community through the return of the decent daddy and the support of the grandmother.

Despite their working conceptions of the world, the old heads are the saving grace of the community. Because the well-paying manufacturing jobs are unlikely to return, their orientation of making do with what one has is in some ways the height of responsibility. By telling people to be responsible, they are affirming that something can be done, that there is hope for the future. For that they are to be admired. In fact, they, as well as the other "decent" people in this book, can be considered the heroes of this story. The wider society, however, sees too little of them. The old heads are present in the community, but they no longer form the critical mass they once did. In order to survive in today's inner-city environment, they are forced at times to act in indecent ways, to be ready to deal forcibly with those who would violate them and their loved ones. This is most clearly seen at the core of the ghetto—at ground zero, so to speak. As one moves out of that profound social isolation, the ratio of decent to street-oriented people improves.

Neighbors in the inner city are encouraged to choose between an abstract code of justice and a practical code geared toward survival in the public spaces of their community. Increasingly, inner-city residents are opting for the code of the streets, either as a conscious decision to protect themselves and their self-esteem or as a gut reaction to a suddenly dangerous situation. Children growing up in these circumstances learn early in life that this is the way things are, and the lessons of those who might teach them otherwise become less and less relevant. Surrounded by violence and what many view as municipal indifference to innocent victims of drug dealers and users as well as common street criminals, the decent people are finding it increasingly difficult to maintain a sense of community.

A vicious cycle has thus been formed. The hopelessness many young inner-city black men and women feel, largely as a result of endemic joblessness and alienation, fuels the violence they engage in. This violence then serves to confirm the negative feelings many whites and some middle-class blacks harbor toward the ghetto poor, further legitimating the oppositional culture and the code of the street for many alienated young blacks. But when jobs disappear and people are left poor, highly concentrated, and hopeless, the way is paved for the underground economy to become a way of life, an unforgiving way of life organized around a code of violence and predatory activity. Only by reestablishing a viable mainstream economy in the inner city, particularly one that provides access to jobs for young inner-city men and women, can we encourage a positive sense of the future. Unless serious efforts are made to address this problem and the cycle is broken, attitudes on both sides will become increasingly hardened, and alienation and violence, which claim victims black and white, poor and affluent, will likely worsen.

# Notes

PREFACE

[1]The ethnographic approach is to be distinguished from other, equally valid approaches, most notably the social psychological. A sensitive and compelling social psychological analysis of the phenomenon of murder is in Jack Katz, *Seduction of Crime: Moral and Sensual Attractions in Doing Evil* (New York: Basic Books, 1988). Katz's purpose is to make sense of the senseless; he explains how criminal violence that cannot be justified on material grounds or through a cost/benefit analysis becomes compelling to offenders. The analysis offered here is not an effort to explain the offender's motivation. I focus on the distinctive collective reality that patterns of criminal violence create in inner-city neighborhoods. The "code of the street" is not the goal or product of any individual's actions but is the fabric of everyday life, a vivid and pressing milieu within which all local residents must shape their personal routines, income strategies, and orientations to schooling, as well as their mating, parenting, and neighbor relations.

[2]See Howard S. Becker, "Problems of Inference and Proof in Participant Observation," *American Sociological Review* 23 (1958): 652–50, and his *Sociological Work*. See also Clifford Geertz, *Local Knowledge: Further Essays in Interpretive Anthropology* (New York: Basic Books, 1983).

INTRODUCTION

[1]This is to be distinguished from the position of Marvin E. Wolfgang and F. Ferracuti, *The Subculture of Violence* (London: Tavistock, 1967), which identified and delineated more explicitly a subculture of violence. Wolfgang and Ferracuti postulated norms that undergirded or even defined the culture of the entire community, whereas the code of the street applies predomi-

nantly to public *behavior* and is normative for only a segment of the community. For important ethnographic analyses of street-group codes, see Martín Sanchez Jankowski, *Islands in the Street: Gangs and American Urban Society* (Berkeley: University of California Press, 1991); J. Hagedorn, *Gangs, Crime, and the Underclass in a Rustbelt City* (Chicago, Lakeview Press, 1988); Ruth Horowitz, *Honor and the American Dream: Culture and Identity in a Chicano Community* (New Brunswick, N.J.: Rutgers University Press, 1983); Frederic Thrasher, *The Gang: A Study of 1313 Gangs in Chicago* (Chicago: University of Chicago Press, 1928); W. F. Whyte, *Street Corner Society* (Chicago: University of Chicago Press, 1943); Mercer Sullivan, *Getting Paid: Youth Crime and Work in the Inner City* (Ithaca: Cornell University Press, 1989).

[2]This pattern is often described in police computer maps showing progressively deeper shades of red as the risk of violent crime increases. The staging areas of highly dense pedestrian activity are also described in computer maps of crime "hot spots." See Lawrence W. Sherman, Patrick R. Gantin, and Michael E. Buergers, "Hot Spots of Predatory Crime: Routine Activities and the Criminology of Place," *Criminology* 27 (February 1989): 27–55.

[3]See Douglas S. Massey and N. Denton, *American Apartheid: Segregation and the Making of the Underclass* (Cambridge: Harvard University Press, 1993).

[4]For a plausible description tracing the tradition and evolution of this code, with its implications for violence on the streets of urban America, see Fox Butterfield, *All God's Children* (New York: Knopf, 1995).

CHAPTER 1

[1]For comparisons in the ethnographic literature, see St. Clair Drake and Horace R. Cayton, *Black Metropolis: A Study of Negro Life in a Northern City* (New York: Harper & Row, 1962). For a discussion of "regulars," "wineheads," and "hoodlums," see Elijah Anderson, *A Place on the Corner* (Chicago: University of Chicago Press, 1978). See also Elijah Anderson, "Neighborhood Effects on Teenage Pregnancy," in *The Urban Underclass*, ed. Christopher Jencks and Paul E. Peterson (Washington, D.C.: Brookings Institution, 1991), 375–98.

[2]See Elijah Anderson, *Streetwise: Race, Class, and Change in an Urban Community* (Chicago: University of Chicago Press, 1990).

CHAPTER 2

[1]See Barney Glaser and Anselm Strauss, *Status Passage* (Chicago: Aldine Publishing Co., 1971).

[2]See Lee Rainwater, *Behind Ghetto Walls: Black Families in a Federal Slum* (Chicago: Aldine, 1970).

[3]For a distinction between "animal" and "cool" ways of being a "badass," see Jack Katz, *Seductions of Crime* (New York: Basic Books, 1988), 97–99.

[4]For an insightful historical analysis of materialism among inner-city youth, see Carl H. Nightingale, *On The Edge* (New York: Basic Books, 1993).

[5]See Lawrence W. Sherman, Patrick R. Gantin, and Michael E. Buergers, "Hot Spots of Predatory Crime: Routine Activities and the Criminology of Place," *Criminology* 27 (February 1989): 27–55.

[6]For an intriguing analysis of the social and historical roots of what I call the code, see Fox Butterfield, *All God's Children* (New York: Knopf, 1995), and Nicholas Lemann, *The Promised Land: The Great Black Migration and How It Changed America* (New York; Knopf, 1991).

[7]See Butterfield, *All God's Children*.

[8]See Elliot Liebow, *Tally's Corner: A Study of Negro Streetcorner Men* (Boston: Little, Brown, 1967); Elijah Anderson, *A Place on the Corner* (Chicago: University of Chicago Press, 1978); and Martín Sánchez Jankowski, *Islands in the Street: Gangs and American Urban Society* (Berkeley: University of California Press, 1991).

[9]For a comparison, see Sara Lawrence Lightfoot, *The Good High School: Portraits of Character and Culture* (New York: Basic Books, 1983).

[10]See Anderson, *A Place on the Corner*.

CHAPTER 3

[1]See Loic J. D. Wacquant and William Julius Wilson, "The Cost of Racial and Class Exclusion in the Inner City," in *The Ghetto Underclass*, ed. William Julius Wilson (Newbury Park, Calif.: Sage, 1989), 8–25; and William Julius Wilson, *The Truly Disadvantaged: The Inner City, the Underclass, and Public Policy* (Chicago: University of Chicago Press, 1987).

[2]See Michael B. Katz, *The Undeserving Poor: From the War on Poverty to the War on Welfare* (New York: Pantheon, 1989); and Fred Block et al., *The Mean Season: The Attack on the Welfare State* (New York: Pantheon, 1987).

[3]See Elijah Anderson, *Streetwise: Race, Class, and Change in an Urban Community* (Chicago: University of Chicago Press, 1990).

[4]See Charles Valentine, *Culture and Poverty: Critique and Counter-proposals* (Chicago: University of Chicago Press, 1968); Barry Bluestone and Bennett Harrison, *The Deindustrialization of America: Plant Closings, Community Abandonment, and the Dismantling of Basic Industry* (New York: Basic Books, 1982); and Wilson, *Truly Disadvantaged*.

[5]Judith Goode and Jo Anne Schneider, *Reshaping Ethnic and Social Relations in Philadelphia* (Philadelphia: Temple University Press, 1994).

[6]See Joleen Kirschenman and Kathryn Neckerman, "We'd Like to Hire Them, But . . . ," in *The Urban Underclass*, ed. Christopher Jencks and Paul E. Petersen (Washington, D.C.: Brookings Institution, 1991), 203–32.

[7]See Elijah Anderson, "Some Observations on Black Youth Employment," in *Youth Employment and Public Policy*, ed. B. Anderson and Isabel Sawhill (Englewood Cliffs, N.J.: Prentice-Hall, 1980), 64–87.

[8]This issue, strongly related to ethnic competition in the workplace, has deep roots in Philadelphia's history. See Roger Lane, *Roots of Violence in Black Philadelphia, 1860–1900* (Cambridge: Harvard University Press, 1986).

[9]Personal interview.

[10]See Anderson, *Streetwise*.

[11]Terry Williams, *The Cocaine Kids: The Inside Story of a Teenage Drug Ring* (Reading, Mass.: Addison-Wesley, 1989).

[12]For the definitive ethnography of the crack culture, see Terry Williams, *Crackhouse* (New York: Addison-Wesley Publishing Company, 1992). See also Jeffrey Fagan and Ko-Lin Chin, "Social processes on initiation into crack cocaine," *Journal of Drug Issues* 21: 313–31.

[13]For an analysis of the interaction contingencies and strategies in "doing stickup," see Jack Katz, *Seductions of Crime* (New York: Basic Books, 1988), Chapter 5.

[14]For valuable insights into these phenomena, see Darnell Hawkins, *Homocide among Black Americans* (Lanham, Md.: University Press of America, 1966).

CHAPTER 5

[1]Fox Butterfield, *All God's Children* (New York: Knopf, 1995).

[2]St. Clair Drake and Horace R. Cayton, *Black Metropolis: A Study of Negro Life in a Northern City* (New York: Harper & Row, 1962).

[3]For sociological literature attesting to the significance of the inner-city father, see Frank Furstenberg, Jr., "Fathering in the Inner City: Paternal Participation and Public Policy," in William Marsiglio, ed., *Fatherhood: Contemporary Theory and Social Policy* (Thousand Oaks, Calif.: Sage Publications, 1995); also Terry Williams and William Kornblum, *Growing Up Poor* (Lexington, Mass.: Lexington Books, 1985).

[4]See Marian Wright Edelman, *Families in Peril: An Agenda for Social Change* (Cambridge: Harvard University Press, 1987), and Christopher Jencks and Paul E. Peterson, eds., *The Urban Underclass* (Washington, D.C.: Brookings Institution, 1991).

CHAPTER 6

[1]Faustine C. Jones, "The Lofty Role of the Black Grandmother,"*The Crisis* 80, no. 1 (1973): 41–56; Herbert Gutman, *The Black Family in Slavery and Freedom* (New York: Vintage Books, 1976).

[2] E. Franklin Frazier, *The Negro Family in the United States* (Chicago: University of Chicago Press, 1939), 150.

[3]See Gutman, *Black Family*; Kenneth M. Stampp, *The Peculiar Institution: Slavery in the Ante-bellum South* (1956; reprint, New York: Vintage Books, 1989); John Blassingame, *The Slave Community* (New York: Oxford University Press, 1971); Frank F. Furstenberg Jr., Theodore Hershberg, and John Modell, "The Origins of the Femaled-Headed Black Family: The Impact of the Urban Experience," in *Philadelphia: Work, Space, Family, and Group Experience in the 19th Century*, ed. Theodore Hershberg (New York: Oxford University Press, 1981), 435–54; Nicholas Lemann, *The Promised Land: The Great Black Migration and How It Changed America* (New York: Knopf, 1991).

[4]Frazier, *Negro Family*; William Julius Wilson, *The Truly Disadvantaged: The Inner City, the Underclass, and Public Policy* (Chicago: University of Chicago Press, 1987); Gerald David Jaynes, *Branches without Roots: Genesis of the Black Working Class in the American South* (New York: Oxford University Press, 1986).

[5]Jones, "Lofty Role"; Jaquelyne J. Jackson, "Aged Blacks: A Potpourri in the Direction of the Reduction of Inequities," *Phylon* 32 (1971): 260–80.

[6]Wilson, *Truly Disadvantaged*; William Julius Wilson, *When Work Disappears: The World of the New Urban Poor* (New York: Knopf, 1996); Theodore Hershberg, "Free Blacks in Antebellum Philadelphia," in *The Peoples of Philadelphia: A History of Ethnic Groups and Lower-Class Life, 1970–1940*, ed. Allen F. Davis and Mark H. Haller (Philadelphia: Temple University Press, 1973), 111–33; Elijah Anderson, *Streetwise: Race, Class, and Change in an Urban Community* (Chicago: University of Chicago Press, 1990).

[7]Jaquelyne J. Jackson, "The Blacklands of Gerontology," *Aging and Human Development* 2 (1971): 156–71; Jasper C. Register and Jim Mitchell, "Black-White Differences in Attitudes toward the Elderly," *Journal of Minority Aging* 7, nos. 3–4 (1982): 34–36.

[8]Linda M. Burton and Vern L. Bengtson, "Black Grandmothers: Issues of Timing and Continuity of Roles," in *Grandparenthood*, ed. Vern L. Bengtson and Joan F. Robertson (Beverly Hills: Sage Publications, 1985), 61–77; Vern L. Bengtson, "Diversity and Symbolism in Grandparental Roles," ibid., 11–85; Jackson, "Aged Blacks."

[9]Bengtson, "Diversity"; Andrew J. Cherlin and Frank F. Furstenberg, Jr., *The New American Grandparent* (New York: Basic Books, 1986); Lillian E. Troll, "The Family of Later Life: A Decade Review," *Journal of Marriage and the Family* 33 (1971): 263–90.

[10]Arthur Kornhaber and Kenneth L. Woodward, *Grandparents, Grandchildren: The Vital Connection* (Garden City, N.Y.: Doubleday/Anchor Books, 1981).

[11]St. Clair Drake and Horace R. Cayton, *Black Metropolis: A Study of Negro Life in a Northern City* (New York: Harper & Row, 1962); William C. Hays and Charles H. Mindel, "Extended Kinship Relations in Black and White Families," *Journal of Marriage and the Family* 35 (1973): 51–57; Carol Stack,

*All Our Kin* (New York: Harper & Row, 1974); Jerold Heiss, *The Case of the Black Family* (New York: Columbia University Press, 1975).

[12]Doris Y. Wilkinson, "Play Objects as Tools of Propaganda: Characterizations of the African American Male," *The Journal of Black Psychology* 7, no. 2 (August 1980): 1–16.

[13]Patricia J. Dunston et al., "Black Adolescent Mothers and Their Families: Extending Services," in *The Black Adolescent Parent*, ed. Stanley F. Battle (New York: Haworth Press, 1987); Harriet B. Presser, "Sally's Corner: Coping with Unmarried Motherhood," *Journal of Social Issues* 36 (1980): 107–29.

[14]Constance W. Williams, *Black Teenage Mothers: Pregnancy and Child Rearing from Their Perspective* (Lexington, Mass.: Lexington Books/D. C. Heath, 1991).

[15]Annette U. Rickel, *Teen Pregnancy and Parenting* (New York: Hemisphere Publishing, 1989).

[16]See Doris Y. Wilkinson, "Traditional Medicine in American Families: Reliance on the Wisdom of Elders," *Marriage and Family Review* 11, nos. 3–4 (1987).

[17]See Doris Y. Wilkinson, "Afro-American Women and Their Families" in *Women and the Family: Two Decades of Change*, Beth B. Hess and Marvin B. Sussman, eds. (New York: Haworth Press, 1984).

[18]For an insightful analysis of the crack initiation process, see Fagin and Chin, "Social Processes of Initiation into Crack Cocaine," *Journal of Drug Issues* 21: 313–31.

[19]Carolyn C. Perrucci et al., *Plant Closings: International Context and Social Costs* (New York: Aldine de Gruyter, 1988); Barry Bluestone and Bennett Harrison, *The Deindustrialization of America: Plant Closings, Community Abandonment, and the Dismantling of Basic Industry* (New York: Basic Books, 1982).

[20]Wilson, *Declining Significance* and *Truly Disadvantaged*.

[21]Edelman, *Families;* Jencks and Peterson, *Urban Underclass;* Doris Y. Wilkinson, "Afro-American Women and Their Families," in *Women and the Family: Two Decades of Change*, Beth B. Hess and Marvin B. Sussman, eds. (New York: Haworth Press, 1984).

CHAPTER 7

[1]For a discussion of gangs, see James F. Short Jr. and Fred L. Strodtbeck, *Group Process and Gang Delinquency* (Chicago: University of Chicago Press, 1965); James F. Short Jr., "Why Gangs Fight," in *Gang Delinquency and Delinquent Subcultures*, ed. James F. Short Jr. (New York: Harper & Row, 1968), 246–56; and Gerald D. Suttles, *The Social Construction of Communities* (Chicago: University of Chicago Press, 1972).

[2]For a discussion of territoriality, see Elijah Anderson, *Streetwise: Race, Class, and Change in an Urban Community* (Chicago: University of Chicago Press, 1990) and "Neighborhood Effects on Teenage Pregnancy," in *The Urban Underclass*, ed. Christopher Jencks and Paul E. Peterson (Washington, D.C.: Brookings Institution, 1991), 375–98.

[3]The social stigma of public defenders may amount to a legal disadvantage. See Erving Goffman, *Stigma: Notes on the Management of Spoiled Identity* (New York: Simon & Schuster/Touchstone Books, 1963).

[4]See Joleen Kirschenman and Kathy Neckerman, "We'd Like to Hire Them, But . . . ," in *Urban Underclass*, ed. Jencks and Petersen, 203–32.

[5]See Elijah Anderson, "Some Observations on Black Youth Employment," in *Youth Employment and Public Policy*, ed. B. Anderson and Isabel Sawhill (Englewood Cliffs, N.J.: Prentice-Hall, 1980), 64–87.

[6]See Signthia Fordham and John Ogbu, "Black Students' School Success: Coping with the Burden of 'Acting White,' " *Urban Review* 18, no. 2 (1986): 187ff.; and also Robert Merton, *Deviance*.

[7]See William Julius Wilson, *The Truly Disadvantaged: The Inner City, the Underclass, and Public Policy* (Chicago: University of Chicago Press, 1987); Kirschenman and Neckerman, "We'd Like to Hire Them"; Anderson, "Some Observations."

[8]See Richard A. Cloward and Lloyd Ohlin, *Delinquency and Opportunity: A Theory of Delinquent Gangs* (Glencoe, Ill.: Free Press, 1960); Robert Merton, "Social Structure and Anomie," in *Social Theory and Social Structure* (New York: Macmillan, 1968).

CONCLUSION

[1]See Terry Williams, *Crackhouse* (New York: Addison-Wesley Publishing Company, Inc., 1992).

# Bibliography

Anderson, Elijah. 1978. *A Place on the Corner*. Chicago: University of Chicago Press.

———. 1980. "Some Observations on Black Youth Employment." In *Youth Employment and Public Policy*, ed. B. Anderson and Isabel Sawhill, 64–87. Englewood Cliffs, N.J.: Prentice-Hall.

———. 1989. "Sex Codes and Family Life among Poor Inner-City Youths." *Annals of the American Academy of Political and Social Science* 501:59–78.

———. 1990. *Streetwise: Race, Class, and Change in an Urban Community*. Chicago: University of Chicago Press.

———. 1991. "Neighborhood Effects on Teenage Pregnancy." In *The Urban Underclass*, ed. Christopher Jencks and Paul E. Peterson, 375–98. Washington, D.C.: Brookings Institution.

———. 1994. The Code of the Streets. *Atlantic Monthly* (May).

———. 1997. "Violence and the Inner City Street Code." In *Violence and Childhood in the Inner City*, ed. Joan McCord, 1–30. New York: Cambridge University Press.

Anyon, Jean. 1997. *Ghetto Schooling: A Political Economy of Urban Educational Reform*. New York: Teachers College Press.

Becker, Howard S. 1958. "Problems of Inference and Proof in Participant Observation." *American Sociological Review* 23: 652–60.

———. 1966. Introduction to *The Jack-Roller: A Delinquent Boy's Own Story*, by Clifford R. Shaw. Chicago: University of Chicago Press.

———. 1970. *Sociological Work*. Chicago: Aldine.

———. 1973. *Outsiders: Studies in the Sociology of Deviance*. New York: Free Press.

Bengtson, Vern L. 1985. "Diversity and Symbolism in Grandparental Roles." In *Grandparenthood*, ed. Vern L. Bengtson and Joan F. Robertson, 11–25. Beverly Hills, Calif.: Sage Publications.

Blassingame, John. 1972. *The Slave Community*. New York: Oxford University Press.

Block, Fred, et al. 1987. *The Mean Season: The Attack on the Welfare State*. New York: Pantheon.

Bluestone, Barry, and Bennett Harrison. 1982. *The Deindustrialization of America: Plant Closings, Community Abandonment, and the Dismantling of Basic Industry*. New York: Basic Books.

Blumstein, A., D. P. Farrington, and S. Moitra. 1985. "Delinquency Careers: Innocents, Desisters, and Persisters," In *Crime and Justice: An Annual Review of Research*, ed. N. Morris and M. Tonry, 187–219. Chicago: University of Chicago Press.

Bourgois, Philippe. 1995. *In Search of Respect: Selling Crack in El Barrio*. Cambridge: Cambridge University Press.

Burton, Linda M., and Vern L. Bengtson. 1985. "Black Grandmothers: Issues of Timing and Continuity of Roles." In *Grandparenthood*, ed. Vern L. Bengtson and Joan F. Robertson, 61–77. Beverly Hills, Calif.: Sage Publications.

Butterfield, Fox. 1995. *All God's Children*. New York: Knopf.

Campbell, Anne. 1991. *The Girls in the Gang*. Cambridge: Basil Blackwell.

Cherlin, Andrew J., and Frank F. Furstenberg Jr. 1986. *The New American Grandparent*. New York: Basic Books.

Cloward, Richard A., and Lloyd Ohlin. 1960. *Delinquency and Opportunity: A Theory of Delinquent Gangs*. Glencoe, Ia.: Free Press.

Cohen, Albert K. 1955. *Delinquent Boys*. New York: Free Press.

Coleman, James. 1988. "Social Capital in the Creation of Human Capital." *American Journal of Sociology* 94: S95–S120.

Davis, Allen F., and Mark H. Haller, eds. 1998. *The Peoples of Philadelphia: A History of Ethnic Groups and Lower-Class Life, 1790–1940*. Philadelphia: University of Pennsylvania Press.

Dembo, Richard. 1988. "Delinquency among Black Male Youth." In *Young, Black, and Male in America*, ed. Jewelle Taylor Gibbs, 129–65. Dover, Mass.: Auburn House.

Dollard, John. 1932. *Criteria for the Life History*. New Haven: Yale University Press.

Drake, St. Clair, and Horace R. Cayton. 1962. *Black Metropolis: A Study of Negro Life in a Northern City*. New York: Harper & Row.

Du Bois, W. E. B. 1899 [1996]. *The Philadelphia Negro*. Philadelphia: University of Pennsylvania Press.

Duneir, Mitchell. 1992. *Slim's Table: Race, Respectability, and Masculinity*. Chicago: University of Chicago Press.

Dunston, Patricia J., et al. 1987. "Black Adolescent Mothers and Their Families: Extending Services." In *The Black Adolescent Parent*, ed. Stanley F. Battle, 95–110. New York: Haworth Press.

Edelman, Marian Wright. 1987. *Families in Peril: An Agenda for Social Change*. Cambridge: Harvard University Press.

Edin, Kathy, and Laura Leine. 1997. *Making Ends Meet: How Single Mothers Survive Welfare and Low-Wage Work*. New York: Russell Sage Foundation.

Ellwood, David. 1998. *Poor Support*. New York: Basic Books.

Emerson, Robert M. 1969. *Judging Delinquents: Context and Process in Juvenile Court*. Chicago: Aldine.

Fagan, J. A. "Intoxication and Aggression." 1990. In *Crime and Justice: A Review of Research*, ed. N. Morris and M. Tonry, 241–320. Chicago: University of Chicago Press.

Fagan, J. A., and K. L. Chin. "Social Processes of Initiation into Crack Cocaine." *Journal of Drug Issues* 21: 313–31

Fine, Michelle. 1991. *Framing Dropouts*. Albany: State University of New York Press.

Fordham, Signthia, and John Ogbu. 1986. "Black Students' School Success: Coping with the Burden of 'Acting White.'" *Urban Review* 18, no. 2: 177ff.

Frazier, E. Franklin. 1939. *The Negro Family in the United States*. Chicago: University of Chicago Press.

Furstenberg, Frank F., Jr. "Paternal Participation and Public Policy." 1995. In *Fatherhood: Contemporary Theory and Social Policy*, ed. William Marsiglio. Thousand Oaks, Calif: Sage Publications.

Furstenberg, Frank F., Jr., Theodore Hershberg, and John Modell. 1981. "The Origins of the Female-Headed Black Family: The Impact of the Urban Experience." In *Philadelphia: Work, Space, Family, and Group Experience in the 19th Century*, ed. Theodore Hershberg, 435–54. Oxford: Oxford University Press.

Gans, Herbert. 1995. *The War against the Poor*. New York: Basic Books.

Geertz, Clifford. 1983. *Local Knowledge: Further Essays in Interpretive Anthropology*. New York: Basic Books.

Gibbs, Jewelle Taylor, ed. 1988. *Young, Black, and Male in America: An Endangered Species*. Dover, Mass.: Auburn House.

Glaser, Barney G., and Anselm L. Strauss. 1972. *Status Passage*. Chicago: Aldine.

Glasgow, Douglas G. 1980. *The Black Underclass: Poverty, Unemployment, and Entrapment of Ghetto Youth*. New York: Jossey-Bass Publishers.

Goffman, Erving. 1959. *The Presentation of Self in Everyday Life*. New York: Doubleday/Anchor Books.

———. 1963. *Stigma: Notes on the Management of Spoiled Identity*. New York: Simon and Schuster/Touchstone Books.

Goode, Judith and Jo Anne Schneider. 1994. *Reshaping Ethnic and Social Relations in Philadelphia*. Philadelphia: Temple University Press.

Gurr, Ted Robert, ed. 1989. *Violence in America*. Vol. 1 of *The History of Crime*. Newbury Park, Calif.: Sage Publications.

Gutman, Herbert. 1976. *The Black Family in Slavery and Freedom*. New York: Vintage Books.

Hagedorn, J. 1988. *Gangs, Crime, and the Underclass in a Rustbelt City*. Chicago: Lakeview Press.

Hawkins, Darnell. 1986. *Homocide among Black Americans*. Lanham, Md.: University Press of America.

Hays, William C., and Charles H. Mindel. 1973. "Extended Kinship Relations in Black and White Families." *Journal of Marriage and the Family* 35: 51–57.

Heiss, Jerold. 1975. *The Case of the Black Family*. New York: Columbia University Press.

Hershberg, Theodore. 1973. "Free Blacks in Antebellum Philadelphia." In *The Peoples of Philadelphia: A History of Ethnic Groups and Lower-Class Life, 1790–1940*, ed. Allen F. Davis and Mark H. Haller, 111–33. Philadelphia: Temple University Press. Reprint; Philadelphia: University of Pennsylvania Press, 1998.

Hirschi, Travis. 1969. *Causes of Delinquency*. Berkeley: University of California Press.

Holzer, Harry. 1987. "Informal Job Search and Black Youth Unemployment." *American Economic Review* 77, no. 3: 446–52.

Horowitz, Ruth. 1983. *Honor and the American Dream: Culture and Identity in a Chicano Community*. New Brunswick, N.J.: Rutgers University Press.

Hughs, Mark Alan. 1991. "Employment Decentralization and Accessibility: A Strategy for Stimulating Regional Mobility." *Journal of the American Planning Association* 57, no. 3: 288–98.

Hunter, Albert. 1975. *Symbolic Communities*. Chicago: University of Chicago Press.

Jackson, Jacquelyne J. 1971a. "The Blacklands of Gerontology." *Aging and Human Development* 2: 156–71.

———. 1971b. "Aged Blacks: A Potpourri in the Direction of the Reduction of Inequities." *Phylon* 32: 260–80.

Jankowsky, Martín Sanchez. 1991. *Islands in the Street*. Berkeley: University of California Press.

Jaynes, Gerald David. 1986. *Branches without Roots: Genesis of the Black Working Class in the American South, 1862–1882*. New York: Oxford University Press.

Jencks, Christopher, and Paul E. Peterson, eds. 1991. *The Urban Underclass*. Washington, D.C.: Brookings Institution.

Jones, Faustine C. 1973. "The Lofty Role of the Black Grandmother." *The Crisis* 80, no. 1: 41–56.

Kasarda, John D. 1995. "Industrial Restructuring and the Changing Location of Jobs." In *State of the Union, America in the 1990s*. Vol. 1, *Economic Trends*, ed. Reynolds Farley, 215–67. New York: Russell Sage Foundation.

Kasinitz, Philip, and Jan Rosenberg. 1989. "Missing the Connection: Social Isolation and Employment on the Brooklyn Waterfront." *Social Problems* 43, no. 2 (May): 180–96.

Katz, Jack. 1988. *Seductions of Crime: Moral and Sensual Attractions in Doing Evil*. New York: Basic Books.

Katz, Michael B. 1989. *The Undeserving Poor: From the War on Poverty to the War on Welfare*. New York: Pantheon.

Kelly, Delos H., ed. 1990. *Criminal Behavior: Text and Readings in Criminology*, 2nd ed. New York: St. Martin's Press.

Kirschenman, Joleen, and Kathy Neckerman. 1991. "We'd Like to Hire Them, But . . ." In *The Urban Underclass*, ed. Christopher Jencks and Paul Peterson, 203–32. Washington, D.C.: Brookings Institution.

Klerman, Jacob Alex, and Lynn A. Karoly. 1994. "Young Men and the Transition to Stable Employment." *Monthly Labor Review* (August): 31–48.

Kotlowitz, Alex. 1991. *There Are No Children Here: The Story of Two Boys Growing Up in the Other America*. New York: Doubleday.

Kozol, Jonathan. 1991. *Savage Inequalities*. New York: Harper Perennial.

Ladner, Joyce A. [1971]. 1995. *Tomorrow's Tomorrow: The Black Woman*. Lincoln: University of Nebraska Press.

Lane, Roger. 1986. *Roots of Violence in Black Philadelphia, 1860–1900*. Cambridge: Harvard University Press.

Leidner, Robin. 1990. *Fast Food, Fast Talk: Service Work and the Routinization of Everyday Life*. Berkeley: University of California Press.

Lemann, Nicholas. 1991. *The Promised Land: The Great Black Migration and How It Changed America*. New York: Knopf.

Lightfoot, Sara Lawrence. 1978. *Worlds Apart: Relationships Between Families and Schools*. New York: Harper-Colophon Books.

———. 1983. *The Good High School: Portraits of Character and Culture*. New York: Basic Books.

Massey, Douglas, and Nancy Denton. 1993. *American Apartheid: Segregation and the Making of the Underclass*. Cambridge: Harvard University Press.

Matza, David. 1964. *Delinquency and Drift*. New York: John Wiley.

Merton, Robert. 1957. "Social Structure and Anomie." In *Social Theory and Social Structure*. Glencoe Ill.: Free Press. Also, "The Self-Fulfilling Prophecy," in the same volume.

Miller, Walter B. 1990. "Lower Class Culture as a Generating Milieu of Gang Delinquency." In *Criminal Behavior*, 2nd ed., ed. Delos H. Kelly, 213–26. New York: St. Martin's Press.

Nightingale, Carl Husemoller. 1993. *On The Edge: A History of Poor Black Children and Their American Dreams*. New York: Basic Books.

Orfield, Gary, and Susan E. Eaton. 1995. *Dismantling Desegregation: The Quiet Reversal of Brown v. Board of Education*. New York: New Press.

Osterman, Paul. 1980. *Getting Started: The Youth Labor Market*. Cambridge: MIT Press.

———. 1995. "The Youth Labor Market Problem." In *Poverty, Inequality, and the Future of Social Policy*, ed. Katherine McFate et al., 387–414. New York: Russell Sage Foundation.

Park, Robert. 1925. *The City*. Chicago: University of Chicago Press.

Perrucci, Carolyn C., et al. 1988. *Plant Closings: International Context and Social Costs*. New York: Aldine de Gruyter.

Portes, Alejandro, and Saskia Sassen-Koob. 1987. "Making It Underground: Comparative Material on the Informal Sector in Western Market Economics." *American Journal of Sociology* 93, no. 1 (July): 30–61.

Presser, Harriet B. 1980. "Sally's Corner: Coping with Unmarried Motherhood." *Journal of Social Issues* 36, no. 1: 107–29.

Rainwater, Lee. 1970. *Behind Ghetto Walls: Black Families in a Federal Slum*. Chicago: Aldine.

Register, Jasper C., and Jim Mitchell. 1982. "Black-White Differences in Attitudes toward the Elderly." *Journal of Minority Aging* 7, nos. 3–4: 34–46.

Regoli, Robert M., and John D. Hewitt. 1991. *Delinquency in Society: A Child-Centered Approach*. New York: McGraw-Hill.

Reinarman, Craig, and Harry G. Leaven, eds. 1997. *Crack in America: Demon Drugs and Social Justice*. Berkeley: University of California Press.

Rickel, Annette U. 1989. *Teen Pregnancy and Parenting*. New York: Hemisphere Publishing.

Sampson, Robert J. 1987. "Urban Black Violence: The Effect of Male Joblessness and Family Disruption." *The American Journal of Sociology*, 93, no. 2: (348–82).

Scheff, Thomas J. 1984. *Being Mentally Ill: A Sociological Theory*, 2nd ed. New York: Aldine.

Shaw, Clifford R. [1930] 1966. *The Jack-Roller: A Delinquent Boy's Own Story*. Chicago: University of Chicago Press.

Sherman, Lawrence W., Patrick R. Gantin, and Michael E. Buergers. 1989. "Hot Spots of Predatory Crime: Routine Activities and the Criminology of Place." *Criminology* 27 (February): 27–55.

Short, James F. 1990. *Delinquency and Society*. Englewood-Cliffs, N.J.: Prentice-Hall.

Short, James F., Jr., and Fred L. Strodtbeck. 1965. *Group Process and Gang Delinquency*. Chicago: University of Chicago Press.

———. 1968. "Why Gangs Fight." In *Gang Delinquency and Delinquent Subcultures*, ed. James F. Short, Jr., 246–56. New York: Harper & Row.

Simmel, Georg. 1971. *George Simmel on Individuality and Social Forms*, ed. Donald N. Levine. Chicago: University of Chicago Press.

Smith, E. W. 1975. "The Role of the Grandmother in Adolescent Pregnancy and Parenthood." *Journal of School Health* 45, no. 5: 278–83.

Spergel, Irving. 1964. *Racquetville, Slumtown, and Haulburg.* Chicago: University of Chicago Press.

Stack, Carol. 1974. *All Our Kin.* New York: Harper & Row.

Stampp, Kenneth, M. [1956] 1989. *The Peculiar Institution: Slavery in the Ante-bellum South.* New York: Vintage Books.

Sugrue, Thomas J. 1996. *The Origins of the Urban Crisis: Race and Inequality in Postwar Detroit.* Princeton: Princeton University Press.

Sullivan, Mercer. 1989. *"Getting Paid": Youth Crime and Work in the Inner City.* Ithaca: Cornell University Press.

Suttles, Gerald D. 1972. *The Social Construction of Communities.* Chicago: University of Chicago Press.

Sykes, Gresham M., and David Matza. 1990. "Techniques of Neutralization: A Theory of Delinquency." In *Criminal Behavior,* 2nd ed., ed. Delos H. Kelly, 207–12. New York: St. Martin's Press.

Thrasher, Frederic M. [1927] 1963. *The Gang.* Chicago: University of Chicago Press.

Troll, Lillian E. 1971. "The Family of Later Life: A Decade Review." *Journal of Marriage and the Family* 33: 263–90.

Valentine, Charles. 1968. *Culture and Poverty: Critique and Counter-Proposals.* Chicago: University of Chicago Press.

Wacquant, Loic J. D., and William Julius Wilson. "The Cost of Racial and Class Exclusion in the Inner City." In *The Ghetto Underclass,* ed. William Julius Wilson. Special edition of *The Annals of the American Academy of Political and Social Science* 501: 8–25.

Walker, Alice. 1982. *The Color Purple.* New York: Pocket Books.

Wilkinson, Doris Y. 1984. "Afro-American Women and Their Families." In *Women and the Family: Two Decades of Change,* ed. Beth B. Hess and Marvin B. Sussman. New York: Haworth Press, 1984.

———. 1980. "Play Objects as Tools of Propaganda: Characterizations of the African American Male." *The Journal of Black Psychology* 7, no. 1 (August): 1–16.

———. 1987. "Traditional Medicine in American Families: Reliance on the Wisdom of the Elders" *Marriage and Family Review* 11, nos. 3–4.

Williams, Constance W. 1991. *Black Teenage Mothers: Pregnancy and Child Rearing from Their Perspective*. Lexington, Mass.: Lexington Books/D.C. Heath.

Williams, Terry. 1989. *The Cocaine Kids: The Inside Story of a Teenage Drug Ring*. Reading, Mass.: Addison-Wesley.

———. 1992. *Crackhouse: Notes from the End of the Line*. Reading, Mass.: Addison-Wesley.

Williams, Terry N. and William Kornblum. 1985. *Growing Up Poor*. Lexington, Mass.: Lexington Books.

Wilson, William Julius. 1980. *The Declining Significance of Race*. 2nd ed. Chicago: University of Chicago Press.

———. 1987. *The Truly Disadvantaged: The Inner City, the Underclass, and Public Policy*. Chicago: University of Chicago.

———. 1989. "The Underclass: Issues, Perspectives, and Public Policy." In *The Ghetto Underclass*, ed. William Julius Wilson. Special edition of *The Annals of the American Academy of Political and Social Science* 501: 183–92.

———. 1996. *When Work Disappears: The World of the New Urban Poor*. New York: Knopf.

Wolfgang, Marvin E., and F. Ferracuti. 1967. *The Subculture of Violence*. London: Tavistock.

Wolfgang, Marvin E., Leonard Savitz, and Norman Johnston. 1970. *The Sociology of Crime and Delinquency*, 2nd ed. New York: John Wiley.

# Index